Beyond the
Smoke and Mirrors

Beyond
the Smoke
and Mirrors

TURMOIL IN THE PPM INDUSTRY

WILLIAM R. DEXHEIMER

Starrhill Press

Montgomery

Starrhill Press

P.O. Box 551

Montgomery, AL 36101

Copyright © 1999 by William R. Dexheimer.
All rights reserved under International and Pan-American Copyright
Conventions. Published in the United States by Starrhill Press, a division of
Black Belt Publishing, LLC, Montgomery, Alabama.

ISBN 1-57359-018-5

Design by Randall Williams
Printed in the United States of America

STARRHILL PRESS IS AN IMPRINT OF BLACK BELT PUBLISHING

The Black Belt, defined by its dark, rich soil, stretches across central
Alabama. It was the heart of the cotton belt. It was and is a place of great
beauty, of extreme wealth and grinding poverty, of pain and joy. Here
we take our stand, listening to the past, looking to the future.

To all who have contributed experiences that have given me the opportunity to write this book,

*and to John,
who taught me not to procrastinate about the things you want to accomplish in life.*

Contents

Acknowledgment

I EXPRESS my appreciation to Anita Smith for her help with this book. Without her organization, commitment, and intensity, the book would not have become a reality.

A Physician's Note

I FIRST met Bill Dexheimer six years ago when our neurology group was looking around for a physician practice management company with which to partner.

As physicians in this nation, we all remember that particular period of time all too well. It was during those early Clinton Administration days, when there was so much talk about healthcare reform, and when managed care was becoming such a big issue. Many of us felt that the only way to deal with managed care from a doctor's perspective was to become big enough, strong enough, that you couldn't be abused.

Actually, I think a lot of what drove the physician practice management, or PPM, industry to grow so fast was that doctors were afraid they were going to be left out, that managed care was going to bury them. I think they felt that if they didn't get going, if they didn't get into a PPM company, that their colleagues and their competition would.

By way of background on my partners and myself, we are a large group of neurologists. We're based in West Palm Beach, Florida, with access to a market that extends from Boca Raton to Port St. Lucie. During "The Season," that market represents a population of a little more than a million people.

We were novices when we embarked on the PPM quest that led us to meet Bill Dexheimer. As we looked around to see what various PPM companies had to offer, we met individuals from a number of different companies. We did not find anyone who particularly impressed us, who had what we thought was the "big picture." That changed when we met Bill Dexheimer.

It's not difficult to be impressed with Bill just by virtue of his

10

appearance. He's a big, imposing-looking guy. But the impression went far beyond that.

As we talked, it became clear that Bill had a much better understanding of and a much better approach to the market than the other PPM people with whom we had interacted. Bill had the "big picture."

This conversation marked the beginning of an extended professional relationship with Bill which in turn led to a personal friendship.

There are several things about Bill Dexheimer that stand out in my mind. One thing is that Bill is an idea person. I think a real key to PPM companies is that they must bring some value to a practice. I think the new company he has founded, Genus Aesthetic Medical & Dental Group Inc., has a lot of potential.

In this book Bill presents a very concise analysis of the development of the PPM business. His years of "hands-on" experience give him a unique insight into the real day-to-day issues that must be understood in order to have a successful relationship between the doc and business partner. His list of six questions to consider before a "deal" is signed should be must reading for any physician or dentist contemplating a PPM relationship. His analysis of the industry makes Genus an exciting "living laboratory" to study Bill's seasoned approach to the industry.

Additionally in this book Bill reveals a little more of himself and what brought him to the field of healthcare. His early football injury, the difficult and painful loss of his brother, the lessons he learned from a physician and from the administrator of a physicians' practice who both influenced him, all help us understand what makes Bill Dexheimer the complex and interesting guy that he is.

This book, *Beyond the Smoke and Mirrors,* will help all of us understand the intricacies of this new and developing PPM industry.

CARL H. SADOWSKY, M.D.
West Palm Beach, Florida

From the Author

MANY THINGS you learn in life come together somewhat like a puzzle. There's a piece here, and a piece there.

I think of pieces of a big "puzzle" when I reflect on my own 17 years of experiences dealing with physicians — first through hospitals and then through the rapidly developing physician practice management (PPM) industry.

This book deals with my views on some "pieces" of the young PPM industry — my views from several different "perches" where I have been standing along the way.

The PPM industry of which I write has brought value to many people in this nation since its beginnings in the late 1980s. Despite recent problems, I think the PPM industry will continue to bring value. True, there have been ups and downs and shakeouts, but I think ultimately the difficulties will produce positive fallout. More challenges and hurdles lie ahead. Also, innovations and improvements are on the horizon.

Via the pages of this book, I want to take you on my tour of some stops I have made "where the action is" in the early and current days of PPM companies, or PPMCs.

Stop Number One on this tour was not only an early stop for me professionally; it also was in my opinion the beginning point for the PPM industry in the United States. That first stop is inside what I consider to be the forerunner for the PPM industry, where it all began — the hospital-owned physician practices. As head of a primary-care physician network for a large hospital system in the 1980s and early 1990s, I was up to my eyeballs in this arena. It was there where I first came to relate to physicians in a major way in a practice management environment. It was there where I came to understand many crucial issues with which doctors were and are dealing. I will be reflecting on some "yesterdays" and crystal-ball gazing about the future of hospital-owned physician practices.

The next stop on the tour — the next piece in this puzzle — is what I call the "traditional" PPM industry, some early leaders in PPMCs. It seems a bit strange to use the term "traditional" in writing about an industry that had its beginnings a mere decade ago. Usually that term is reserved for describing early phases in a much older evolvement. However, there has been a lot of water over the dam with PPMCs in a relatively short period of time — enough to create several "eras" of development in a few years.

In this book, I speak to the early days of the PPMCs from my view as having been a member of the founding management team of what became the biggest, fastest-growing, and I dare say most-written-about and most-talked-about PPMC in the national history of this industry — MedPartners. As one who wrote much of the original business plan for MedPartners and became MedPartners' first chief operating officer, I reflect on the foundation of MedPartners. This includes looking at some differences in the core of MedPartners and PhyCor, the PPM pioneer that we considered our main competitor when we founded MedPartners in 1993.

From where I have stood, this book would not be a real book if I didn't give my readers a "tour stop" to analyze the 1998 failed MedPartners and PhyCor merger. That failed merger deserves and receives a long stop. For I firmly believe several key issues spotlighted in that aborted transaction will have long-term implications not only for MedPartners and PhyCor but also for the future of the overall PPM industry.

As another tour stop, I will glimpse into a phase of the PPM industry's future development as illustrated by "niche" companies that are cropping up. I'll take this look through the new niche that I know best — my own new PPM niche company which I opened for business in 1997, Genus Aesthetic Medical & Dental Group Inc.

And, before the tour comes to an end, I have a few little detours —

personal detours that I think give insight into why I view some things the way I do.

When you start writing a book — and this is my first — it's a bit uncanny the paths and turns it can take. The "detours" to which I refer came as a result of some of the unexpected paths and turns I encountered in this writing process.

For most of my 42 years, I've been a rather private person. Actually, to be totally candid, I admit I have been an intensely private person. When I began writing this book, it never occurred to me to write about anything personal. I was planning to stick strictly to the "business" pieces. I mean, why do anything else if you're writing a business book? However, the more I found myself expressing my strongly held opinions — why I like and can relate to doctors, what kinds of standards I think a company should have — I became increasingly aware that my professional views were driven not just by my "business pieces" but also by my "personal pieces."

It was a very personal event — something that happened to me when I was a teenager — that propelled me into the healthcare industry in the first place. What I learned from that experience influences me in my work every day, and I will discuss that on one of the "detours" in the tour.

Then there was the tragedy in my family. Every family experiences some type of tragedy. The biggest one I've experienced to date produced shock, grief and ongoing loss. It also produced some positive impressions concerning the high-standard product that's possible in healthcare. I take a look at this area on one of the "detours."

And, no doubt there are two individuals who account very much for my own high respect for doctors and also my high respect for office managers who manage doctors' offices. These individuals have been real drivers for me in my work in the PPM industry. Thus, the final stops on my tour are to meet these two people — a physician and an office manager. I think they serve as role models who have bits of wisdom for all of us.

As I take you on my tour through the pages of this book, I hope it will generate food for thought about this changing physician practice management industry for several groups of people. I hope there will be points of interests for those inside the PPM companies, those inside today's hospital-owned physician practice networks, and analysts and investors focusing on the PPM industry. I hope there will be points that connect with physicians and dentists and their staffs who already interact, or who in the future might interact, with a more traditional PPM company or with one of the spinoff niche companies. And, last but far from least, I hope this book will touch a few patients (or clients) along the way.

WILLIAM R. DEXHEIMER
Birmingham, Alabama

Beyond the
Smoke and Mirrors

PART ONE:

Some PPM Roots

1

A Long String Running Out:
The Hospitals' Reign
as the Nation's First PPMCs

IN 1992, I was sitting in my office worrying. I was CEO of a hospital primary-care physician network in Birmingham, Alabama. And I was thinking, "This is all going to come apart!"

There no doubt were men and women in similar positions across the nation who were thinking much the same thing.

I didn't believe the hospital-supported physician practice network I was running was going to come apart because it had failed to be successful. Quite the contrary.

For six years I had been running this network to recruit primary-care physicians for a large hospital. I had run the network successfully under two structures — first as an "inside-the-hospital" operation and then as an "outside-the-hospital" operation. It had been successful in terms of numbers and quality of primary-care physicians recruited to the hospital's "roster." It had been successful in both building new physician practices from scratch and in further developing already-existing practices.

However, despite its success, I thought the network we had so carefully carved was in danger of coming apart because of the strong opposition and threats that were coming its way.

I thought the network was in jeopardy of falling victim to the opposition of two powerful sets of critics — the federal government, and disgruntled physicians.

It occurred to me many times in the early 1990s that it's an unusual scenario for the federal government and physicians to agree on the same target for opposition. And, in being opposed to hospital-owned physician practices, the federal government and the physicians were taking aim at these kinds of physician networks for very different reasons.

Early 1990s Opposition from the Feds

From the federal government, this was not opposition that was aimed specifically at hospital-owned physician practices. It was instead opposition that was aimed at anything that could be interpreted as self-referral when it came to healthcare providers who were being reimbursed with federal funds for healthcare services.

Those of us who have been in health-related endeavors for a long time knew we needed to take notice as this issue of self-referral first came to the forefront in Washington several years ago and as it has escalated in years since. We have seen the issue hashed and rehashed; we've seen it subjected to numerous viewpoints and interpretations of just what indeed does constitute conflict of interest or self-referral.

The year 1992 was a real pivotal point in this because there was an awful lot of discussion about self-referral going on in Washington. This was the year when the far-reaching law known as "Stark I" entered our world. Bearing the name of its chief advocate, California Democrat U. S. Rep. Pete Stark, that law didn't mandate any kind of slowdown or halt to hospitals owning and managing physician practices. But it did indeed hint around the edges. It did, for example, deal with self-referral as it related to physician ownership of medical laboratories.

As I pondered the implications of "Stark I" in 1992, I viewed the legislation as a sign of more things to come related to hospitals being in the business of owning physician practices. I vividly recall sitting in my office trying to sort out in my mind where our own hospital-funded physician practice network stood in light of the issues being addressed in Washington.

Based on how things stood at the time, I believed the structures we were using were lawful. But I also thought if the tide kept turning, if similar legislation continued to be expanded, the physician network we were running would not continue to be viewed as legal in the eyes of federal overseers. What was bothering me was, given what already had come down the pike, what could lie just over the horizon? Was the string in danger of running out?

In short, I was envisioning that the day easily could come when, with a stroke of a pen, it would all be over. I sat there in my office reading what was coming out of Washington and I thought, "There's going to be a day sooner or later when someone just strokes the pen and legislates that, effective on such and such a date, it will no longer be lawful for hospitals to own and manage physicians' practices."

Early 1990s Opposition from the Physicians

The other point of attack I was seeing on hospital-owned physician practices in the early 1990s — one that was becoming increasingly bothersome — was the opposition from certain groups of physicians.

Unlike the federal government issue, the physician opposition was not something coming down from Washington that could simultaneously affect numerous hospitals all over the country. Instead, the physician opposition to hospital-owned practices was a phenomenon taking place within individual medical staffs in individual hospitals.

This physician opposition definitely was taking place inside the hospital with which I was dealing. However, we weren't in a situation by ourselves. The same kind of opposition was taking place within many medical staffs in many hospitals around the nation. Although this was a local issue, it was a widespread local issue.

I observed this physician opposition as being forged primarily by two factions of opposition from very different corners of the medical staff:

One faction of opposition consisted of those "outside the loop." These were members of the hospital medical staff whose practices had not been purchased by the hospital, who felt the hospital with which they were associated was giving preferential treatment to medical staff members whose practices the hospital had purchased. In the case of the hospital for which I ran a primary-care network, many of the specialists were opposed to the hospital investing money to support the primary-care physicians' practices. It was an issue of the hospital supporting one subset of the medical staff and not supporting the rest of the medical staff to the same degree.

Ironic as it might seem, the other faction of opposition came from physicians who were "inside the loop" — those whose practices had been purchased by hospitals. Some of the primary-care physicians whose practices were being purchased by the hospital weren't happy with their relationship with the hospital after they sold their practices to the hospital. These dissatisfied physicians felt that the hospital often was implementing changes in their practices that created an advantage to the hospital but didn't satisfy their needs as physicians. These physicians felt they were being pushed to do things which contributed to the hospital's bottom line while at the same time compromised their own income.

Both factions of physician opposition shared common threads. Each faction in its own way spoke to the issue of not having "aligned incentives" — the hospital's incentives not being aligned with the physicians. It was an issue I'll address later on in the book. In this same context, both factions of opposition related to the issue of "the three legs of the stool." The physician was one leg, the hospital was a leg, and the third-party payer was a leg. In the view of a physician disagreeing with how a hospital was handling hospital-owned physicians' practices in that period, the physician often felt his leg of the stool was missing.

The Same Forces Still Around

The same forces that were bothering me back in 1992 are still around today to haunt the hospital-owned physician practices. Rather than going away, they have become stronger — to the point I think now the hospital-owned physician practices are more vulnerable than ever.

I have seen those forces in action to some degree since I first started developing a hospital-based physician practice network. Those factors were the reasons I felt in the early 1990s that the road was getting rocky for hospital-based physician practice management. Those factors fed into the development of the industry we know as "physician practice management," or PPM — an industry in which I have been deeply involved. My own experience with these factors via a hospital-based physician practice network fed directly into the founding of what now is the nation's largest PPM company, MedPartners. And these forces feed strongly into some views I hold today about where trends are headed for hospital-based physician practice networks.

Getting into Hospital-Based Physician Practices in a Big Way

The journey that led me into the world of PPMCs, or physician practice management companies, really starts in the Spring of 1986. I was 29 years old. I was hired by a large, modern hospital in the Birmingham area to develop a primary-care physician network to serve that hospital.

The hospital that hired me to develop this network was AMI Brookwood Medical Center. By the time Brookwood hired me, I had become fairly adept at physician recruitment and development in the role as an assistant hospital administrator at Lloyd Noland Hospital, a 319-bed hospital six miles to the west of downtown Birmingham. As part of my responsibilities at Lloyd Noland, I was involved in outpatient development with family-care centers.

When I came on board at Brookwood, as senior vice president for development, Brookwood had been in existence just slightly more than a decade. It was the newest hospital in an area filled with hospitals. The Birmingham area had healthcare as a major industry and had forged a national reputation in healthcare development.

Brookwood had leapt onto the Birmingham healthcare scene as an "oddity" — as a for-profit hospital located in the midst of several long-established and very successful hospitals that were "not-for-profit." The "AMI" part of Brookwood's name stood for American Medical International, a national healthcare chain that had purchased the hospital several years after it opened its doors.

When Brookwood was founded in the 1970s, a great number of the initial investors were physicians in the Birmingham area — many of them specialty physicians. Brookwood's genesis and its early-day focus was as a specialty hospital, with limited representation by primary care.

Thus, when I came to specialty-oriented Brookwood to develop a primary-care organization, I was hired to head up a network that was an "oddity" in a hospital that in the Birmingham area already was an "oddity."

Primary-Care Physicians in the Role of "Gatekeepers"

I came to Brookwood at a time when the healthcare industry all across the nation all of a sudden was taking notice of the perceived changes in the "power" of the primary-care physicians. In Birmingham, people were just starting to talk about managed care as a new and powerful force in the management of both healthcare delivery and reimbursement.

The leaders in the healthcare payer arena nationwide were tossing around the term "gatekeepers." In this new world of managed care, the primary-care physicians were being set up as the "traffic cops" to decide if and when to refer patients for a wide variety of healthcare services, including specialty care. Translated, this meant that the managed-care programs were looking to the primary-care physicians to determine if and when third-party payers should approve reimbursement for various services.

Thus, the mid-1980s marked the beginning of the primary-care physician being newly knighted as the decision-maker, when historically the primary-care physician had been at the bottom of the healthcare hierarchy. And, in the case of specialty hospital Brookwood, this was an institution which in the mid-1980s was badly in need of an infusion of geographically dispersed primary-care physicians. Brookwood needed more primary-care physicians if the hospital was to become an effective contracting entity in a managed-care environment where the gatekeeper was becoming the entry and control point to the system.

Building a Primary-Care Network for a Hospital

My charge was to develop a multi-site, geographically dispersed primary-care group affiliation or association, an independent practice association (IPA).

The goal was to put primary-care physicians on the map in a wide range of communities in several counties in a growth corridor to the south of Birmingham, bounded by two interstates and one major highway.

As part of that goal, we also were trying to achieve a primary-care physician marketshare and prevent the development of any new competing hospital to the south of Brookwood.

We pursued the rather large task of building this network of high-quality primary-care physician services in those communities, so they could augment the hospital delivery system.

To accomplish our goal, we used a combination of approaches — acquisitions, management contracts, and new development.

In a typical acquisition, we would acquire an existing practice and grow it, by adding incremental physicians and/or services. Today I look around with pride at a number of clinics we acquired which are still going strong, utilizing some of the systems, support and manpower we facilitated.

In terms of new clinics to develop the network, we would build new clinics and recruit physicians. Some of the physicians we recruited came to us; in some cases, we pursued them.

I recall one physician practicing at a local hospital who wanted to start a new family practice in Vestavia, an affluent small city very near Brookwood. I helped him realize his dream, and his practice became part of the Brookwood network.

I did a similar thing with a young physician who wanted to get out of emergency medicine and set up his own family-care practice.

One of my key sources of pride among our new developments was a clinic that's now a successful internal medicine practice in a small community to the south of Brookwood. We started from scratch, recruiting the young physicians as they were finishing their residency training. Today, the physicians in this clinic are a mainstay in their community.

Stir among the Specialists

The physician network quickly attained high visibility within the Brookwood organization. Between 1986 and 1989 we built a primary-care organization that became real strong. Strategically the building of this strong primary-care network was good for Brookwood, for the organization as a whole.

However, not everyone was happy. Building a strong primary-care network was not popular with a lot of people. The perception by some of the specialty physicians at Brookwood was that it was threatening. Strengthening primary care by using the hospital's resources was threatening to people who didn't want to see primary care strengthened and their power base diluted.

The hospital's CEO was in a difficult position. Here was a primary-care organization that was part of the hospital strategy but was perceived by some specialists as benefiting a subset of the medical staff — namely the primary-care physicians. The bottom line was that, while the primary-care network was strategically beneficial to the hospital as a whole, it posed a politically difficult situation for administrative leaders in the hospital who populated their important committees with threatened people.

Let's look at this whole scenario from the point of view of the hospital administrator. Brookwood's hospital administrator was interacting with a large and growing medical staff. His hospital had in-house resources that were supporting one group of his physicians — the primary-care physicians — but not supporting the other physicians — the specialists.

So, in late 1988, the private discussions began on the subject of how to minimize the conflict. How could Brookwood continue to receive the strategic and economic benefits of its primary-care network but at the same time diffuse some of those physicians who were so opposed to it?

The Founding of Strategic Health Resources (SHR)

In April of 1989, a separate entity — separate from AMI Brookwood Medical Center — was created to contract with Brookwood for the development and management of primary-care physician services. This newly created separate entity was given the name Strategic Health Resources, or SHR. And I became its chief executive officer.

SHR was formed to create the perception of an arms-length relationship between the controversial primary-care network and the (Brookwood) hospital.

The strategy was to de-politicize the hospital-driven primary-care network development. This was to be accomplished by physically moving the network's offices from the hospital premises and deleting the network from the hospital's official organizational structure.

My role continued to be the same — I was in charge of the primary-care network. However, my employment relationship with the hospital changed, and the logistics changed. My office moved out of Brookwood into a nearby office building. I was no longer a senior vice president for development within the Brookwood organization. Instead, I was now the CEO of this new organization, Strategic Health Resources. And this new organization had only one client which provided its funding — AMI Brookwood Medical Center.

The Goals of SHR

As I reflect on it, it is as though we had three goals with Strategic Health Resources.

The Number One goal and the Number Two goal were the same as when I had been hired three years earlier to develop the primary-care network. Number One, we were proceeding to develop a set of services that could be entirely focused on the development and enhancement of primary-care physician practices, to strengthen Brookwood's primary-care support. Number Two, we were trying to prevent the establishment of a competing hospital to the south of us.

And then, in setting up Strategic Health Resources, there was a new third goal — to administer this network through a more independent structure which was separate and apart from the hospital.

I'll venture to say we did real well with the Number One and Number Two goals.

Number One, with enhancement of primary care, Strategic Health Resources indeed did develop some innovative value-added resources that could be drawn down by primary-care physician practices. Secondly, where blocking our competition was concerned, we definitely were successful. As of this writing, no hospital has been built in the Birmingham area to the south of Brookwood. I think that has greatly contributed to Brookwood's continued success and its ability to hold on to its marketshare.

Then there's Goal Number Three — operating Strategic Health Resources independently of the hospital. In giving a "score" to our success with this goal, I can't give unqualified high marks. Instead, I'll have to give the report like "On the one hand, and then on the other hand." On the one hand, all things considered, I'd say there's no doubt that Strategic Health Resources became an effective conduit to accomplish some things that could not be accomplished inside the political structure of the hospital. On the other hand, even though SHR was created as a separate entity from AMI Brookwood Medical Center, what we ended up with was more of a facade of independence than a reality. And you didn't have to dig past the funding to find that it was a facade. Even after Strategic Health Resources was created and our offices were relocated in an office building off the Brookwood campus, we never pursued non-Brookwood relationships. SHR never took on another client in addition to Brookwood, even through it could have been beneficial to do so. SHR gained a little edge of independence and so did the hospital.

From SHR's side, the organization had more of an identity after it became separate. It wasn't buried so much in hospital bureaucracy as before. We had more of a defined focus, and SHR's employees could have more of a commitment to a separate entity. From the hospital's side, the so-called "separation" probably helped considerably with internal operations when the top hospital executives were questioned about the financial support and push for primary-care. When that happened, the hospital administrator could point down the road to SHR's offices and take his detached position: "Hey, that organization — SHR — makes its own decisions. That organization lives its own life. The hospital doesn't control that organization."

However, when all was said and done, Strategic and Brookwood were still joined contractually with a lot of money flowing in one direction.

My Concerns: Limitations, Incentives and Motivation

As I looked around SHR particularly in 1992, I was having a hard time enjoying myself because my mind was so consumed with the organization's limitations, incentives and motivations.

Despite the fact that we did a great deal to help the physicians with whom we dealt, I was frustrated that our ties to the hospital often stood in the way of our going any further on the physicians' behalf. I plainly saw that the opportunities the physicians needed to achieve could not be accomplished through the hospital, because the hospital's incentives and the physicians' incentives simply were not aligned. It was an irrevocable fact that SHR's contractual and financial allegiance to the hospital often was an obstacle rather than a facilitator in addressing the physicians' needs. The truth was that no matter how much lip service was given or how pure the hospital's intentions, the hospital could not be totally dedicated to a physician's needs, because the hospital and the physicians had different incentives.

Also, the whole subject of hospital motivation in purchasing physician practices hung heavily over me. This bothered me more as every day went by, stretching back to 1991 and increasing in 1992. I thought about this issue of motivation in light of relevant discussions going on at the time in the halls of Congress and in federal agencies in Washington, D.C.

I was becoming increasingly aware of a fact staring me clearly in the face — that hospitals around the nation were purchasing physician practices for the wrong reasons. They had the wrong motivation.

The way I looked at the "wrong motivation" issue was this: The hospitals' main reasons for purchasing physician practices didn't have anything to do with helping physicians and patients. Instead, their main reasons had to do with taking defensive steps to respond to competitive threats that impacted utilization of hospitals. Translated, that meant the main motivation for a hospital to purchase a physician practice had to do with increasing utilization of the hospital and grabbing as much marketshare as possible. The way a hospital benefited was to solidify the referral patterns. That meant physicians split-admitting to various hospitals would shift business exclusively in the direction of the hospital that purchased their practice. Purchased physician practices were being used by hospitals to fill hospital beds and to increase utilization of ancillary services.

Now, if you're involved in activities to try to get additional referrals, and in Washington they're writing laws right and left with the intention of blocking self-referrals, it doesn't take a rocket scientist to see that maybe you should be taking a closer look at what you're doing.

In 1992, I was taking that closer look.

Exit SHR, Enter MedPartners

After Strategic Health Resources was created, I headed it for almost four years. We ran hard and stayed immersed in conflict with our single client, AMI Brookwood Medical Center.

In late 1992, SHR's contract with Brookwood ended. In January 1993, the assets of SHR were purchased by a newly formed physician practice management company, or PPMC, called MedPartners. (More about the founding of and the early concepts of MedPartners in Chapter 2.) I became a member of MedPartners' founding management team.

There is no doubt that one of the driving forces in creating MedPartners was the fear there might be a day when legislation could make it unlawful for hospitals to own and manage physicians' practices. I think this was one of the conditions that spawned not only MedPartners but a number of other PPMCs as well.

Some Predictions for the Future

I believe within the next five years hospitals in this nation will be out of the business of owning physician practices. I predict the PPM companies still will be there. Right now, hospitals owning physician practices is big nationwide, but I think the trend is already stalled and ultimately will go away.

As this unfolds, it is my feeling we'll be seeing large hospital groups divest themselves of their physician practices. I think we'll see them basically take their physician service components out of their portfolios and put them into other entities.

Molding these changes are the same conditions I was confronting back in the early 1990s: The pressure of intensifying legislation from the federal level in regard to self-referral, and the pressure hospitals are feeling inside their organizations from members of their medical staffs.

I think you'll see hospitals divest themselves of those relationships because either the legislation will get tougher or there will be, from hospitals' perspectives, some troublesome interpretations of legislation already on the books. Also, additional legislation is likely to be added.

In my opinion, hospitals are vulnerable for gray areas to be interpreted as black-and-white. I think you will see cases in which some not-for-profit hospitals will lose their tax-exempt status over hospital-owned physician practices and related issues.

Rather than risk the penalties of gray being turned into black and white to their disadvantage, I believe many hospitals will just decide to divest themselves of the ownership of physician practices.

Hospital leaders are keenly aware of the increasing scrutiny they face with hospital-owned and hospital-managed physician practices. Those calling the shots with these programs for years have tried to work out kinks in the programs' structural imperfections. They have used various approaches to keep these programs in line with something the federal government would continue to condone and also something the hospitals could manage more effectively while at the same time drawing less criticism. One approach has been to convert some of the hospital contracts with physicians to employment contracts. But none of the approaches have proven real effective. No approach has been unquestionably safe.

Today's Escalating Pressure from Federal Laws

The reason we refer to U.S. Rep. Pete Stark's first major self-referral legislation as "Stark I" is that we now also have "Stark II." The second Stark legislative wave, effective since 1995, continues to deal with the issue of self-referral in regard to Medicare and Medicaid patients. It bans physicians from having an ownership interest in various types of health-related services and facilities to which they refer Medicare and Medicaid patients.

This legislation does not say it's illegal for hospitals to own physician practices. However, the legislation has the core of its rationale firmly rooted in these troublesome areas of prohibition of payment for referrals and prohibition of ownership of services to which you control volume.

In my mind, and in the thinking of many others around this nation, the "stark" implication of Stark I and Stark II is just one example among a number of trends in place that puts this whole issue of hospital-owned physician practices in a big gray area. It's all part of this umbrella of federal scrutiny that has to do with federal anti-kickback statutes, increasingly being referred to as the fraud and abuse issue. It's all part of this federal scrutiny that examines healthcare providers for evidence they are purchasing Medicare and Medicaid referrals.

It's a scrutiny that's widespread. It's a scrutiny that's showing itself in many ways.

The biggest horror story, one which we've all followed with much interest, has been the federal investigation of the nation's largest healthcare chain, Nashville-based Columbia/HCA Healthcare Corp. In light of this endless fraud investigation Columbia has been forced to restructure. For months, federal enforcers have been probing Columbia's records looking for evidence of illegal physician self-referrals and Medicare billing. Among the more severely affected Columbia operations has been its home-care division. As a fallout of all this, Columbia has been unwinding its hospital-physician syndication arrangements, which allow physicians to hold an ownership interest in an individual hospital or in Columbia hospitals in a defined market.

In looking at this overall issue of increased federal-level scrutiny, I think the not-for-profit issue is worthy of note, too. In recent months, we have been seeing the Internal Revenue Service taking a close look at how it interprets joint ventures between for-profits and not-for-profits. As time goes by, it is possible this could impact on physician practices owned by for-profit and not-for-profit joint ventures.

Today's Escalating Pressure from Medical Staffs

As hospitals continue to experience controversy within their medical staffs over the issue of hospital-owned physician practices, there's no way this can be divorced from the increasing insecurities felt by many of today's physicians.

Today's physician practice patterns indeed figure strongly into this equation. Those patterns include increasing physician mobility and decreasing physician loyalty to hospitals. All this makes hospital-owned physician practices an even more politically charged issue with the physicians than it was a decade ago.

In terms of interacting with their medical staffs about hospital-owned physicians' practices, today's hospital administrators have tremendous burdens on their shoulders. Many hospital administrators are becoming increasingly weary of juggling the in-house ramifications of what they're trying to accomplish in a hospital-based physician practice system. These administrators face almost insurmountable internal problems in relating to members of their medical staffs on this issue.

Think about it. You're a hospital administrator. You have 150 active physicians on your medical staff. How can you politically subset a faction of your medical staff — say 50 of your medical staff members — and be a business partner with this 50-member subset of your medical staff but not include the other 100 members? It sets the stage for conflict.

Look at it from the point of view of Dr. John Jones, a hypothetical medical staff member. Dr. Jones is working hard, beating his head against the wall, going to the bank to borrow money to expand his office and to buy new equipment. Down the street from where Dr. Jones has his office, there's a new clinic opening its doors. The physician who will staff this clinic is a physician that Dr. Jones knew in medical school — Dr. Don Smith. Later this month, Dr. Jones will start seeing Dr. Smith at medical staff meetings at the hospital, because now Dr. Smith will be using the same hospital that Dr. Jones uses. The only thing is, Dr. Smith has an arrangement with the hospital that Dr. Jones does not have. The hospital is helping Dr. Smith to set up his clinic and will manage and support that clinic. The hospital is providing Dr. Smith with the latest technology. The hospital is on the line for Dr. Smith's lease. And, thanks to the hospital, Dr. Smith has a guaranteed salary in place not only for himself but also for the new associate fresh out of residency who is about to join him in practice.

Now, from the view of Dr. Jones, how is that a fair system in a very political environment called "The Hospital"? It's politically charged.

More Joint Ventures between Hospitals and PPM Companies

With the trends that are in the making now, I don't think it takes a lot of foresight to see where we're going.

In short, what we will see will be more evidence of hospitals linking with the PPM companies. I think some of the trends that will be unfolding with hospital-based physician practices will be sources of new business for many PPMCs. I believe some of these trends will be sources of relief for many hospitals.

It's already happening. We're already seeing hospitals outsource some of their physician practice management services to PPM companies. The PPMCs and the hospitals will be busy developing models to work out these joint ventures.

One of the biggest challenges the two entities will face in these joint ventures will be that there's still an underlying lack of a mechanism to manage and control these relationships. (I'll delve more into management information and control systems issues in the book's next section, in Chapter 5.) However, there are some bright people working on the problems with these systems, and with time the answers will come.

By virtue of experience, I'm personally very aware of some of these joint-venture issues. After my experience in hospital-based PPM networks parlayed into my co-founding MedPartners and serving as its first chief operating officer, I was deeply involved in trying to develop one of the early models for a PPMC/hospitals joint venture that I think will become popular. When I was with MedPartners, we tried very diligently to develop a model that would be a win-win-win situation. We discussed at length governance models and economic models and systems and all those criteria that would go into a joint venture. The goal here is to do something that meets with the hospital's interests, the physicians' interests, and the PPM companies' interests. It's the three-legged stool that we talked about at MedPartners.

The timing is much more appropriate today for these joint hospital-PPM company ventures than in my early years with MedPartners.

One reason is the mounting pressure on the hospitals — the expanding threat from the federal government and the even-more-vocal dissatisfaction on the part of hospital medical staffs.

Another reason, a positive one, is that hospitals and PPM companies are now communicating better than ever before.

Better Working Relations between Hospitals and PPMCs

In the early to mid-1990s, the rapport did not exist between hospitals and PPM companies. In fact, the opposite was the case. Paranoia was rampant.

I've seen this from inside the hospitals. I've seen it from inside the PPM companies. I watched the competition between hospitals and PPM companies rise to a fever pitch in the mid-1990s. The hospitals saw the PPMCs as the enemy, and vice versa. It was like both sides were consumed with the "I win, you lose," the "I'll control you" mentality. It was like both sides were consumed with the goals of subordinating one to the other, with the pronouncements that they were going to beat up on one another.

But times and relationships are changing. Attitudes are mellowing. I think many of the hospital leaders and PPM-company leaders have gotten over the concept that the PPMCs are out to do in the hospitals, or the hospitals are out to do in the PPMCs.

I believe that paranoia has played out. What has evolved in the place of the paranoia is that a number of major hospital companies have concluded that relationships with well-run PPMCs can indeed be structured in a way so that there's definitely room to coexist in a mutually beneficial environment.

The PPMCs now are out there with refined models that address the hospitals' needs as they are today. The better the PPMCs get, the better the hospital companies at the senior level will understand the opportunities. And I believe it's a matter of time until that mentality trickles down to hospital leaders at the local level — to the local hospitals owned by major chains.

So what accounts for this change in attitude?

One factor is the background and attitude of the "players" who are making these decisions about joint ventures between hospitals and PPMCs. What we're already seeing and will continue to see is that people representing both sides are business people who approach issues with a business mentality. They aren't letting history and emotion and personalities get involved in the discussions of mutually beneficial business relationships.

It's like bringing in attorneys to discuss transactions, because they don't bring any baggage to the table. Oh, there still are the "hard-liners." There still are some people out there in the hospitals and also in the PPMCs who are playing off the emotions of yesterdays. However, I predict we'll see even the hard-liners settle down. Even in places where onlookers never thought possible, some productive joint ventures will emerge between hospitals and PPM companies.

Another catalyst toward this diversification for hospitals is that they see they have much to gain with joint ventures with PPMCs. This has come about as more and more hospital leaders in recent years have come to feel that hospital-owned physician practices carry an increasing risk and burden. These hospital leaders are driven by the view that if hospitals can accomplish some high-quality objectives without the onus of having to own and manage these physician practices, why not enter into joint ventures with PPM companies?

Management is maturing. They're now realizing that you don't have to be all things to all people.

The Hospitals Laid the First Bricks

As I look back on the nationwide development of hospital-owned physician practices in light of what has transpired in the past five years or so, I think the hospitals should be credited with some real ground-breaking in the management and development of physician practices.

In fact, in my view there's no doubt the hospitals should be credited with laying the foundation for the industry we now know in this nation as PPM, or physician practice management.

Beginning in the late 1980s and picking up steam in the 1990s, one PPM company after another has sprung up across the nation — companies like PhyCor and MedPartners and many others.

Several years before any of these new companies took root, the hospitals were the first organizations acquiring physician practices. And I believe the hospitals provided enough valuable ideas for the PPM companies that they deserve to be known as the nation's first PPM operations.

Sure, we have never referred to the hospital-based physician practice management networks as "PPMCs." And both structurally and operationally, the hospital-driven physician practice programs have not been managed by structures and strategies used in today's PPM companies. They have functioned as operating units of hospitals, as hospital divisions, embedded in the hospital by design with really no intent to differentiate them on the P&L. Operationally and strategically, they have been fueled by hospital systems and not by practice management systems. They have not independently pursued contracts with payers for covered lives.

However, they were there first. They forged the way.

As one who has been involved in this physician practice management business first from the hospitals' side and then from the PPM company side, I am glad to see these two entities recognizing joint opportunity.

2

Making Big and Bold Tracks:
The Founding of MedPartners

DURING THAT same period in the early 1990s when I was becoming so concerned about the future of hospital-based physician practice management, I was having discussions with a healthcare executive by the name of Larry House.

I found Larry to be an incredibly bright guy — a visionary who could see ahead and who was willing to take risks. Larry also had a strong track record, including valuable experience as an executive on the ground floor of the development of HealthSouth Corporation, which had been founded by Richard Scrushy in 1984.

The subject of the conversations I was having with Larry was the whole concept of physician practice management. We both believed in it strongly. We felt it was a wave of the future. We knew that physicians around the nation were ready for and could benefit from someone providing a hand in management.

Larry and I also agreed that the hospital was not the ideal vehicle to deliver business management services to the physicians. We agreed that the ideal business partner for a physician instead was a business company that was set up to operate independently and to actually function as a partner to the physicians in areas of growth and development.

In his dealings with physicians through HealthSouth, Larry was interacting with physicians who were increasingly asking him to develop business services tailored just for them. And I was hearing the same need expressed as I dealt with physician practice management as CEO of Strategic Health Resources.

Since I had been heading an organization that was attempting to accomplish physician practice management on behalf of a hospital, I had become acutely aware — even painfully aware — that the hospital wasn't an appropriate organization to buy and manage physician practices. I had analyzed and reanalyzed this whole issue. No matter how hard I had tried to rationalize, to be optimistic, to have an open mind, I couldn't see the position of the nation's hospitals changing for the better in the physician practice management arena.

Just by the very nature of the way the business matters of physicians and hospitals are structured — including their third-party reimbursement — the physicians and the hospital often have incentives that are in conflict with one another. It's not the fault of hospital executives that they cannot meet physician needs and at the same time continue to meet the needs of their hospital. It's just a fact that the whole opportunity for aligned incentives does not exist for the hospitals and the physicians.

At the time Larry and I were having our pre-MedPartners conversations, there already had been a progressive new business "model" designed and put into operation for a business company that could reach out to the physicians with business assistance. The industry that would be known as the PPM industry had been born. Nashville-based PhyCor, with beginnings dating back to the late 1980s, was clearly the industry's big pioneer.

Larry and I talked about the PhyCor model at length. We felt that this basic premise — an independent business company set up to assist physicians with business matters — was an opportunity whose time had come. We both concluded that there was a huge universe out there for such a new industry — an industry that did not have any interest other than the interest of the physician as its focus.

It was obvious, too, that the size of the universe had room for another PPMC to be created. After all, there were some 650,000 practicing physicians around the nation. And many of them no doubt were at the point they wanted to "partner" with an entity that could help avoid

Hillary Rodham Clinton's legislated healthcare reform.

Larry and I made the decision that we would participate as members of the founding management team in the forming of a new PPM company. We would set up this company to support "the third leg of the stool." This would be a company that had resources committed to it that were totally designed to protect and further develop the interests of the physician.

Timing is everything in a business venture. And the timing was right to start MedPartners.

"Folding in" One Company into Another

Once we formulated our plan, things moved fast.

Larry became MedPartners' founding chief executive officer. I became MedPartners' founding chief operating officer. The new venture received support from HealthSouth founder and CEO Richard Scrushy. Although Richard would not take a role in the day-to-day operations of the company, he made initial funding assistance available.

Strategic Health Resources (SHR) was able to play a strong role in MedPartners' beginnings. Since MedPartners bought the assets of SHR, it was simple to fold it into MedPartners. The SHR people and experience and systems jump-started the MedPartners operation.

No time was lost. As soon as the official life of SHR came to an end, we were operating as MedPartners. We already had an office, people on board. Some of these same people who moved over from SHR to help start MedPartners in 1993 today are still MedPartners employees.

Looking back on my experience with SHR, it seems a natural that this company became an incubator for, a predecessor for, MedPartners. For several years, we had been deeply involved at SHR in the same types of basic physician services that we now started dealing with at MedPartners. This included reimbursement advice, coding, assistance with practice expansion, medical records, staffing, and billing and collection. What could have been a better "laboratory" for MedPartners?

And, since we were independent to think and plan and move without having to keep a hospital's needs uppermost in mind, MedPartners could add growth and development features that had not been possible in the Strategic Health Resources-AMI Brookwood structure.

An Opportunity to Use a Decade of Experience

From my viewpoint, it was an opportunity to take a top slot in a new company in a new industry called PPM. It was a logical use of what by this time had been a decade of experience for me in working with physicians.

I realize now even more than I did then that my early days at MedPartners were strengthened by the length of time I had been interacting with physicians.

Fortunately for me, I had the valuable opportunity to start working with physicians during the early 1980s, when challenges and opportunities of unprecedented magnitude were taking place in the way medicine was practiced in America.

I was a hospital assistant administrator when federally-inspired "diagnostic related groups" (or DRGs, as we called them) were rolled out. The DRGs would prove to be an early development in what would be a string of legislation dealing major change to third-party reimbursement and helping to plant the seeds for what we now know as managed care.

Even as I watched the physicians trying to adjust themselves to federally dealt changes such as DRGs in the 1980s, they also were balancing massive changes in the way they interacted with the key entities in their professional lives. Things were changing in the way they related to their patients, to the hospitals where they practiced medicine, and to one another. They were confronting changing patterns of patient loyalty to physicians, spurred by drastic changes in patients' insurance coverage, and also by looming issues such as malpractice suits. They were seeing breakdowns in physician loyalty to hospitals and in hospitals' loyalty to physicians, sometimes manifested by open hostilities. And, as healthcare competition raged virtually out of control, the physicians found hospital pitted against hospital and physicians often pitted against physicians.

At the same time I had a chance to see challenges confronting the physicians in the 1980s, I also saw opportunities begin to emerge. I saw the advent of new technologies and techniques that could dramatically expand physicians' abilities to practice medicine. I saw business structures evolve that could aid physicians in managing their practices more efficiently.

As we went forward with MedPartners in 1993, it was exhilarating to be in the trenches with the physicians via this exciting new business company structure called the PPMC.

Learning from a PPM Pioneer

When we were planning MedPartners in the months prior to the 1993 incorporation, I participated in drafting the original business plan. I wrote the "concept piece." Hal Knight, an Ernst & Young manager who had performed accounting services for HealthSouth and who became MedPartners' first chief financial officer, wrote the "numbers piece."

As I've previously noted, there's no doubt that the pioneer in this still-young PPM industry was Nashville-based PhyCor. In writing the concept piece of MedPartners' original business plan, I came to know PhyCor about as well as any outsider could know PhyCor. The reason is that I studied that company inside and out. As is true with anyone putting together a new company, you study the other plans that are out there.

In many respects, the MedPartners plan was a modified PhyCor plan. In other respects, the MedPartners plan was a departure from the PhyCor plan. Although we intended from the start for MedPartners to address the same basic mission as PhyCor, we also intended from the start that MedPartners' approach to developing its company would be far different from the PhyCor approach.

Two PPMCs with the Same Mission

From the time they were founded, down to their very roots, both PhyCor and MedPartners agreed on a central mission.

That mission was based on the view that the physician is the center of the universe in healthcare delivery.

With that concept in mind, both companies were intent on focusing on the physician. In the early days both companies focused on adding value to the physician, on facilitating access to capital for the physician, on bringing management services to the physician.

In the eyes of both companies, the physician really was (and is) the only one who could execute decision-making in the healthcare system. From that sense, both companies shared the business view that it was the physician and not the hospital or the payer that was the key to the healthcare delivery system.

If you were to put an interpretive "spin" on how strongly MedPartners and PhyCor did feel and do feel about the power of the hospital's role as compared to the power of the physician's role, it could go like this: A hospital is no more than a hotel without the support of the physicians who make up the hospital's medical staff.

Now keep in mind that these guys who started PhyCor were ex-Hospital Corporation of America guys. They were hospital guys. They understood why the physician was so important. In their experience, they likely in effect had said, "Hey, wait a minute. We've been living this. We have seen all this firsthand. Where we really need to focus is on the physician." Hospital people know that the physicians have a power via their medical license which makes them the integral piece of the healthcare delivery system.

Larry House and I also had been dealing with physicians for years. We also believed that if you had a company that could extend the abilities of a physician to practice medicine, then the physician could make maximum use of his powers to deal effectively with the obstacles being placed in his path.

Two PPMCs with Different Strategies

Although the core mission of PhyCor and the core mission of MedPartners were one and the same, the strategies these two pioneer PPMCs used in developing their companies were as different as daylight and dark.

If I were going to describe the PhyCor and MedPartners initial strategies in a nutshell, I'd say that PhyCor had a "buy strategy" and that MedPartners initially had a "build strategy."

In having a "buy strategy," PhyCor built its base mainly by purchasing and affiliating with existing well-established multi-specialty practices in second-tier markets. Many of these practices were clinics that had been in existence for 30 or 40 years. The idea was if these clinics were already established in a given market, the energy and focus would be on acquiring something already proven and working to make it continue to dominate. It was an astute approach, and a conservative one.

By contrast, in having a "build" strategy, MedPartners was building virtual multi-specialty delivery systems from scratch. We were building these systems from "pieces." Our first step would be to zero in on a geographical area and to attempt to affiliate with that area's best cardiology group, best orthopedic group, best urology group, etc. Once we had relationships with these physician groups, we would wrap a contracting vehicle around them so they could function as a single multi-specialty delivery system — thus enabling all parts of the delivery system to engage with the managed-care market from a common point.

As we built these multi-specialty delivery systems from pieces, we had to factor in geographic coverage — because you need the geographic coverage for access to managed care. In charting this geographic spread, we had our eye on addressing the metropolitan areas that were the target markets for MedPartners. Unlike PhyCor's second-tier market strategy, MedPartners had its sights on targets in 55 U.S. markets.

I remember vividly those days of attempting to create the multi-specialty delivery systems. What we were doing was difficult. However, it was challenging, exhilarating. We would hypothesize and say, "Okay, with a given population of X, how many internists do you need? And how many orthopedists? Etc., etc., etc." As we made our projections, we had several objectives. We were trying to predict utilization within a given population by specialty. We were executing a development plan that would produce new multi-specialty delivery systems with both the geographic coverage we needed and the appropriate mix of specialty and primary-care services.

We developed a name for our approach in putting together these multi-specialty delivery systems. We called it the "Cell Theory" — an analogy to the biological cell theory about the makeup of an overall biological organism. Just as we were taught in biology that the organism is the sum of the properties of autonomous cells put together, each multi-specialty delivery system we were developing took on characteristics that were the sum of the various physician groups that we were bringing together.

By the time we put together our MedPartners public offering documents, we even included in the documents a diagram of our "Cell Theory." If you put what we were doing on a graphic, you could see the analogy as it related to a nucleus, an atom, a cell.

The "Cell Theory" was a fascinating approach. And it helped create the foundation for MedPartners.

Who Had the Toughest Job?

There's no doubt in my mind that the PhyCor "buy-what-already-exists" strategy, of buying into existing practices, was a much easier transaction than the more complex MedPartners' "build-your own."

In the PhyCor approach, the company was dealing with practices that already had cohesive cultures and where most crucial governance issues had already been addressed by the physicians within their respective organizations.

By contrast, with our MedPartners' approach there was so much work to be done. We couldn't transform overnight from individual groups to a multi-specialty delivery system. These different specialty groups had their own agendas. This meant they had their own individual assets, they had their own real estate, they had their own accounts receivable, they had their own equipment, they had their own management. It was all so culturally diverse. In the process of putting together some of these multi-specialty transactions — transactions which brought good for many people involved — we saw many interesting aspects of human behavior.

As I look back on it, the way PhyCor did it and the way MedPartners attempted it could be compared like this: The MedPartners way was like the pioneers forging through a dense forest to build new cabins and a new town while the hostile Indians were doing war-dances all around. By contrast, PhyCor was going into already cleared and charted territory, where the cabins and the town had been in place for years, and where the "cavalry" had already arrived to create a peaceful environment.

Setting the Stage for the Future

I believe the "buy strategy" that formed the roots of PhyCor and the "build strategy" that formed the roots of MedPartners represent far more than just "Two Strategies."

In my way of thinking, these extremely different core strategies instead represent the beginning chapter of what I would term as "A Tale of Two Very Different Companies."

The same risk-taking, barnstorming style that drove MedPartners and the same conservative, methodical approach that drove PhyCor were ways of thinking that continued to carve out the destinies of the two companies. These contrasting styles fueled viewpoint after viewpoint, decision after decision, strategy after strategy, as the mid-1990s wore on. The contrasting styles played clear-cut roles in the success of each as MedPartners and PhyCor took their respective places as No. 1 and No. 2 in the nation's PPM industry.

As one who observed these different paths closely, I strongly feel the differences early on set the stage for some events that would take place in late 1997 and early 1998. Those events, what led up to them, and their aftermath would shake up the whole PPM industry.

PART TWO:

Spotlight on a
Failed PPM Merger

3

Standing at the Altar:

The 11th Hour Crash of a Merger Deal

FROM THE moment I heard the formal announcement on October 29, 1997, that the nation's two largest physician practice management companies were planning to merge in an $8 billion deal, I thought it was a fairy tale.

I never believed this merger between "No. 1" MedPartners and "No. 2" PhyCor would or should take place.

By the time the dust settled on this unlikely courtship — and the announcement was made January 7, 1998, that the impending marriage indeed was being called off — I felt somewhat like a caring but somewhat jaded former family member standing on the sidelines shaking my head.

For I had reason to understand much of the turmoil that led to the broken engagement.

I didn't have to possess psychic powers or make use of a magical crystal ball to come up with my predictions that MedPartners and PhyCor made for unlikely — perhaps even impossible — bedfellows in this still-young industry called physician practice management, or PPM.

My prediction came because, as the cliche goes, I had "been there and done that." I had been exposed to the inside of MedPartners from the very beginning, back to when the company was just a germ of an idea in the heads of a limited few — Larry House, Richard Scrushy, Hal Knight and myself. After MedPartners went into operation in 1993, I took a leading role in operations and in development out in the field as I functioned as this new PPM company's first chief operating officer. As the company became very big very quickly and acquired Mullikin Medical Enterprises and other holdings in the Western United States, I became chief operating officer-East. Then, after being totally enmeshed in MedPartners for four and a half years, I left in the Spring of 1997 — to set up and lead a new company.

But I would be less than candid not to admit that, even during the period when I was busy birthing a new company, I was still tuned in with peak interest to news about the much-touted MedPartners/PhyCor deal. I was interested in the details.

MedPartners was good to me, professionally and personally. It was good to me as a young company executive. It was good to me as a major stockholder. I predict that in the future this company will be good to others — other employees, other stockholders.

But along the way, in the next months and extending over the next few years, I predict a drastic shift in the PPM industry — a shift that will have to confront some of the harsh realities and looming problems that played roles in the failed merger between MedPartners and PhyCor. As we all know, that shift already is under way.

Factors Behind the Failed MedPartners/PhyCor Merger

I attribute the failed MedPartners/PhyCor merger to two factors.

The existence of either one of these factors alone could have caused problems big enough to call off a union.

However, put both factors together and you've got a situation that can cause a split at the altar even as the preacher is on the verge of announcing, "We are gathered here to join . . . "

The first factor that made the MedPartners/PhyCor planned marriage go sour was simply that these two parties were and are so different. Their corporate cultures were deeply, probably irrevocably, incompatible.

These two companies announcing an impending merger thought differently, acted differently, had different types of strategies and philosophies. Although they were in the same type of overall business, their backgrounds, their experiences, their goals were very different. And it wasn't a difference that could complement, broaden or strengthen one another. It was the kind of difference that could set the two at perpetual odds, causing them to limit or even destroy one another. It was like John and Mary deciding to get married, but having backgrounds, attitudes and thought processes so opposed that they are chronically appalled and frustrated with one another even as they pick out wedding invitations and place orders for flowers and champagne.

The second factor that made the MedPartners/PhyCor planned marriage go sour is that there's a major problem facing the entire PPM industry, and particularly those PPMCs that have gotten into the risk business. That factor is the lack of workable information systems — systems that can give the industry the data it needs to make sound predictions as to where it's headed financially in light of the challenges that growth demands.

This data from sound information systems becomes increasingly crucial in a healthcare-linked industry dealing with chronic reform, rigid third-party payer strategies, and a growing managed-care environment. This need for reliable information systems tugs especially hard at MedPartners, a company that has been a risk-taker by nature and which has ventured deeper and deeper into the risky, murky waters of managed care. When I speak of information systems, I'm talking about systems which can give you data on such key questions as: Who's eligible for insured coverage on a given day? What's the profile of the patients or clients eligible for services? How sick or how well are they now? How sick or how well are they likely to be in the future? How many healthcare services, and what types of healthcare services, are likely to be used by the insured group over a given period? What price tag should healthcare providers such as physicians place on individual health services? What price tag should be placed on beneficiaries' insurance or HMO premiums?

Lessons for Any Business Courtship

I firmly believe that these two factors — culture incompatibility and systems unavailability — can serve as a lesson not just to the PPM industry, but to any companies considering a merger.

If there is a pressing problem with either of these two factors between two companies considering a merger— if there's a major mismatch in the cultures of the two companies, if there's a lack of basic systems in the industry that would strain one company in absorbing the other — take a long, hard look before you "marry up." In short, "look before you leap."

Make sure, first of all, that you are being enough of a realist to spot these factors, that you aren't seeing your relationship through the eyes of just the investment bankers. And then, if you're willing to go forward with a union despite these factors, make sure you have a plan for dealing with the challenges.

If you face either of these two obstacles to a major degree — culture incompatibility or systems unavailability — know that you are taking on a burden.

It would be better for you to do as MedPartners and PhyCor did, and back away from the altar with a little egg on your face in front of all your friends that you invited to the wedding, than to go forward with a union that faces insurmountable obstacles.

Under the Microscope

In the next three chapters in this section, I want to examine culture incompatibility and systems unavailability. I want to look at these factors as they apply to MedPartners and PhyCor, but in many ways as they can apply to any business.

Also, I want to take a look at some of the trends I foresee down the road for the overall PPM industry. Some of these trends have come to light partially as a result of underlying issues becoming more prominent in the rather public dissection of the anatomy of the proposed MedPartners/PhyCor merger.

And, here again, even as the MedPartners/PhyCor proposed marriage has been writing some new chapters in the history of the PPM industry, it has also been producing some business wisdom for the overall business community, no matter what the nature of our business might be.

4

Apples and Oranges:
A Mismatch in Corporate Cultures

THERE ARE many people who like apples, and who would argue with you that the apple has preferable characteristics to oranges, pears, grapefruit or bananas. They relish every bite of a mellow, juicy red or yellow apple. They thrive on apple pies and apple tarts and apple dumplings.

There are other people who would invariably cast their vote for oranges. They'll take their oranges any way they can get them — in freshly-squeezed orange juice, in orange marmalade, or just sitting at the breakfast table eating the orange sections.

A valid case can be made for the merits of the apple. Likewise, a case can be made for the merits of the orange.

But one thing's for sure. You're not going to be able to walk into the grocery market and purchase a merged version of the apple/orange. Each one stands on its own. To try to merge them would be an attempted mixing of the unmixables. To try to merge them could only destroy the distinctive tastes that have made each a success in its own right.

I think there's an analogy to be made here with the MedPartners/PhyCor situation. In my mind, trying to merge these companies indeed was like trying to merge apples and oranges.

When does "Different" Become an Asset or a Liability?

Just because two businesses are different does not mean that they are like apples and oranges to the extent that they shouldn't merge.

In fact, often the case is quite to the contrary. I can think of many instances in which "different" is actually a plus — a recipe for bringing aboard new assets, for creating a value-added chemistry that can capitalize on the old "two heads are better than one" theory. Many mergers have worked exceptionally well because two merging corporations possessed culture differences that were deal-makers rather than deal-killers.

These "synergies" can occur when businesses come together to share welcomed differences and welcomed additions that extend their capabilities. Those synergies include additional marketshare, an additional body of knowledge, new ideas, and additional capital, technology, and human resources.

However, it's when the differences represent conflicts in crucial areas that a red flag should go up. This is when "different" could mean staring a formidable liability in the face. This is when "different" could mean significant conflicts in such core-culture issues as strategy, operating structure, goals and management styles.

Such was the case with MedPartners and PhyCor.

"Deal-killers"

I believe that MedPartners and PhyCor were embroiled in some "deal-killer" culture differences that raise red flags for any two entities thinking of a merger.

To address my definition of the type of basic culture difference that constitutes potential "deal-killer" level, let's go back to our hypothetical engaged couple, John and Mary, in Chapter 3, "Standing at the Altar."

The deal-killer type issues I'm going to address about MedPartners and PhyCor are the core kind that could compare to some fictional-yet-plausible differences standing between our young man, John, and his sweetheart, Mary:

John does not want to have any children, but Mary wants at least three.

John is Jewish and insists that Mary convert to his faith, while Mary is Catholic and insists that John convert to her faith.

John is a country boy and a loner who wants to buy a 40-acre farm and live close to nature, while Mary is a city girl and people-person who wants to live in a townhouse in the middle of a large city.

The presence of these traits doesn't make John or Mary a bad or a good person. But, like apples and oranges, these traits do make them different in very fundamental ways.

Four "Culture" Differences with MedPartners and PhyCor

I think there were four conflicting differences that added up to major corporate culture incompatibility between MedPartners and PhyCor and helped cause the proposed merger deal between these two companies to be aborted:

- Low-key personality and style versus flamboyant personality and style.
- Decentralization versus centralization.
- "Pure-play" strategy versus "tossed salad" strategy.
- Conservative mentality versus risk-taking mentality.

A Personal Note

When MedPartners went into operation in early 1993, I had just had my 36th birthday.

On one hand, I was fortunate at that young age to have more than a decade of healthcare-and-business education and experience under my belt.

I had an undergraduate college degree in healthcare management and a master's degree in business administration. I had worked in hospital administration as an evening administrator and assistant administrator. I had been a hospital senior vice president in the area of outpatient operations, physician recruitment, and development. I had created a company that recruited primary-care physicians and developed a primary-care network to supply a large hospital system, and that company had become a predecessor for MedPartners.

Yet, on the other hand, at age 36 I was not yet seasoned enough in my professional exposure and experience to have settled on my own viewpoints and preferences in regard to business culture and style.

I'm 42 now. The past six years have been packed with career-molding experiences. I've participated in one way or another, often in the "quarterback" slot, in some 120 physician/business company transactions. I've made more than 250 presentations to physicians. I've had several years out in the field and in the corporate offices of MedPartners, working with hundreds of physicians and business leaders. I've dealt with professional and private investors around the nation, raising millions of dollars in business funding. And, in recent months, I've had to do a great deal of soul-searching about vision, strategy and management style as I've made key decisions about my future.

Along the way in the past six years, I've been aware of the "settling-in-place" of some of my own key viewpoints and preferences about business culture and style.

I've come to know, for example, that my basic style and viewpoints are much more of a natural match for the conservative PhyCor approach than for the somewhat more liberal MedPartners.

I feel much more comfortable with the PhyCor decentralized style than with the MedPartners centralized approach.

Like PhyCor, I favor a "pure-play" strategy in which a business sticks to its stated business mission and focuses on a limited product menu, rather than venturing into the "tossed-salad" world of a widely diversified product line.

And, whereas PhyCor is not the heavy risk-taker and MedPartners has a history of having a healthy appetite for risk, I have opted for putting together business plans with limited risk.

In short, I guess it would be fair to say that, although I had a good ride with MedPartners, grew professionally, and came out well financially, some of the frustrations I felt with this company were no doubt some of the same frustrations that PhyCor felt in trying to reach a merger deal agreement.

Low-key Versus Flamboyant

Whether the leaders of companies realize it or not, their companies are just like people in that they develop a style. Companies are like people in that they take on a "look," a set of habits, a lifestyle.

It's like one woman who feels dowdy unless she has "big hair," and another who feels uncomfortable with anything except a casual, wind-blown look.

It's like one businessman who can't function at a meeting unless he's wearing a three-piece suit, while another does his best leading if he's dressed in jeans and Nikes.

It's like one CEO who doesn't care what kind of vehicle he drives as long as it gets him where he wants to go, while another selects a vehicle not only for its function but also for the statement he feels it makes about him and his company.

In the days and weeks after the announcement was made about the merger plans of MedPartners and PhyCor, I read many newspaper articles that described comparisons between the styles of the two companies.

Some of these articles dealt with the obvious major differences in the physician practice markets which had been addressed by the two companies. PhyCor had focused on large clinics, second-tier markets, self-contained organizations that had a dominant position in a given market. By contrast, MedPartners had focused on major urban markets (some 55 of them), and in some cases had dealt with huge, complex healthcare delivery systems. PhyCor had limited its ventures into the risk market and managed-care contracts, whereas MedPartners had created a wide-open structure that courted managed-care contracts and at times took full risk. Both strategies are sound, but PhyCor didn't have the transmission and appetite for the challenges that MedPartners sought in the markets it pursued.

In addition to news articles that dealt with the obvious strategic differences between MedPartners and PhyCor, there were other articles that dealt with the somewhat more subtle style differences. My attention was especially caught by the focus of news reporting during one particular several-day period when the proposed merger was pending. Writers of this group of articles turned their attention to some of the interesting day-to-day lifestyle differences in PhyCor and MedPartners. For example, these articles noted that when PhyCor executives traveled, they showed up at their destinations on commercial airlines and in rental cars, while traveling MedPartners execs showed up in corporate jets and limousines. I think that example gave more than minor insight into a comparative assessment of the style of these two companies. It's clear to me that PhyCor has by nature been low-key in style, while MedPartners has tended toward the more flashy, flamboyant style. And one would be taking too lighthearted a view of these style differences to think of them as petty and inconsequential. For these style differences are symbolic of what has made these two companies tick.

Decentralization Versus Centralization

Back in the 1980s, I became senior vice president and chief development officer for a Birmingham, Alabama-based hospital at that time owned by American Medical International (AMI), based in Beverly Hills, California. I went on to set up and serve as president and CEO of a primary-care physician network that was funded by AMI. So I had a relationship with AMI from the mid-1980s until the early 1990s.

In those capacities, functioning in AMI-linked entities located thousands of miles away from the corporate headquarters of AMI, I got a good taste of some of the issues that have to do with decentralization versus centralization.

I saw widely differing attitudes among AMI executives in Birmingham as to how they related to AMI. I saw differing attitudes on whether Birmingham-based AMI executives felt their first priority was to keep close tabs on what was going on "at home" or to constantly engage in courting and playing politics with AMI's corporate offices — the regional offices in Atlanta and the main headquarters in Beverly Hills. Some Birmingham-based AMI execs seemed to feel that the sun literally rose and set in what went on at AMI's corporate offices and chose to have contact with "corporate" whenever possible.

I know that my own attitudes about whether it was more important to keep my eye on Beverly Hills or Birmingham were heavily influenced by some of the physicians with whom I dealt to develop AMI-affiliated clinics. Those physicians placed a top priority on what was going on at home, there in the Birmingham area — with their patients, their staffs, their clinic buildings, their day-to-day operations, their plans for the future. Since it was my job to recruit these physicians into the AMI fold and to support them, the priorities of these physicians became my priorities. I came to understand the problems and needs faced by these physicians and the patients they served. I never felt I could focus on addressing these primary-care needs by making unnecessary trips to Atlanta or Beverly Hills. Thus, I stayed in Birmingham and dealt with the physicians, letting AMI directives funnel down to me in an orderly fashion and making very few trips to corporate offices.

Then one night something happened at an AMI board of directors meeting in California that validated and intensified my line of thinking. On that night, the AMI board members took actions to cut 80 percent of their corporate office support! They emptied entire office buildings in Beverly Hills!

Despite the extent of that major AMI corporate personnel cutback, from my perspective and from the perspective of many of my administrative and physician colleagues in Birmingham, the cutback really didn't have any impact on the operation of the AMI-hospital or AMI-clinics in Birmingham with which we were associated.

As I look back now, I know it was during the years I was associated with AMI when I started becoming a staunch advocate of the decentralized system of management.

When I saw that the AMI board members could make huge slashes in their centralized operations and AMI-owned hospital and clinic operations thousands of miles away didn't even notice, it made me start thinking seriously that a company really can remain decentralized. To have an efficient operation, a company doesn't have to build a mammoth infrastructure to facilitate extensive centralization. In fact, I think building a big complex infrastructure is where your problems can begin.

Another thing I saw during my AMI period was how much more efficiently — and more compassionately — a physician's problem or a patient's problem can often be resolved at a local level, rather than via a directive issued miles away by a corporate worker who has no firsthand knowledge of the problem. I saw the benefits that can be derived from the communication, the bonding, just the mere existence of trust produced by proximity — by physicians' offices dealing directly with their own patients.

Although I'm targeting my comments here specifically toward healthcare companies and physician practice management (PPM) companies, I think a vote for decentralization has valid applications in many arenas of business and industry.

In fact, I'll go further and say that the building of a mammoth infrastructure really can at times exist primarily for the benefit of individuals who hold jobs at the corporate level — not for the benefit of the company, not for the benefit of the shareholders, and, in the case of a health-related business, not for the benefits of the patients or for providers such as the physicians and the hospitals.

I have a very strong belief in placing as much control as possible at the site where the service is actually being rendered, where the product is actually being produced. When that's translated to the physician practice management (PPM) industry, it means I believe a PPM company should place as much control as possible on site at the offices of the physicians with whom the company is partnering and not at the site of the company's corporate offices.

To address this issue of decentralization versus centralization where it applies to MedPartners and PhyCor:

There is no doubt this is one of the big corporate culture "deal-killer" differences that figured into the failed merger for these companies.

PhyCor has a tradition of decentralization, with small corporate offices and most functions pushed out into the field.

MedPartners, on the other hand, has a tradition heavy with centralization. I, unfortunately, lived it. Some of the most heated arguments I had with MedPartners CEO Larry House were over management matters related to centralization versus decentralization. Larry and I had a major philosophical difference there.

I believed in a decentralized management system. There were a number of centralization-versus-decentralization issues where I fought Larry and some of my colleagues to push the management back into the field. I felt strongly that the goal of management should be to push the resources down where they can be used. My message was to get the management closer to the physicians and to the patients, where I believe it's more effective.

There was one albatross in particular — MedPartners' move toward centralized billing for physicians' offices. To put it in simple terms, Larry and I were polarized on that issue.

Even as MedPartners was implementing centralized billing, I was on many occasions MedPartners' highest-level representative out in the field dealing with physicians who were savvy about their business operations and who were telling me they were very reluctant to relinquish control of their billing and collections. And what these physicians were telling me was consistent with my own belief that you need to make sure you don't move decision-making and accountability away from the patient.

With patient billing and collection, it's in the physician's office where you're obtaining the initial information concerning the patient's condition and the patient's insurance. And it's in the physician's office where the patient is going to present information and questions about payment. Those communications are crucial. Control of these communications needs to be left "at home," there in the offices where the patients are known by the physicians and their staffs.

After spending millions on consultants, systems and people, MedPartners ultimately abandoned its centralized billing and spent huge amounts moving it back into the field.

"Pure-play" Strategy Versus "Tossed-salad" Strategy

It would be too narrow a strategy focus for Ford Motor Company if this big motor vehicle manufacturer were to decide to manufacture only pickup trucks, or only midsize cars, or only vans.

However, it likely would be a stretch of the company's resources and vision if Ford decided also to venture into the gasoline business and to start building highways.

Such is the analogy I see with the "pure-play" strategy as it applies to MedPartners and PhyCor.

PhyCor has remained focused on a "pure-play" business mission. The company was set up as a PPM company, to help manage physicians' practices. And it appears to stick to that mission.

By contrast, MedPartners started out adhering to that same mission and gradually diversified its product more and more to the point that it definitely, in my mind, became a tossed salad.

From the time MedPartners incorporated in January 1993, through its initial public offering in February 1995 and on until August 1995, the company stuck with a "pure-play" mission. We were doing transactions with physician practices to partner with them, with MedPartners' role being to bring value-added management support and infuse capital. I know the tenor of these transactions, because I personally negotiated many of them.

In August 1995, MedPartners took the first major detour from its original mission — with its $414 million deal to buy California-based Mullikin Medical Enterprises. On the one hand, the Mullikin deal provided MedPartners with an opportunity to grow quickly. On the other hand, it was that deal which plunged MedPartners very deeply into the risk business, the managed-care business that for years has been so prevalent on the West Coast. This whole world of managed care and risk cries out for information systems that can provide crucial data. Development of those systems is in its infancy; the needed information systems are spotty, incomplete, or in many cases either unreliable or just plain nonexistent. Also, the structure of what MedPartners bought on the West Coast was so different from its Eastern operations. After MedPartners bought Mullikin, MedPartners began in a sense to operate like two separate companies. The Mullikin West Coast holdings represented essentially big consolidated managed-care operations that were set up like a totally separate business from the diverse physician groups I was dealing with on the East Coast. The West and the East each represented a different environment, a different animal, with different cultures and different needs. The dynamics were totally different. It was like they were running a couple of huge Wal-Marts out West and we were running 110 or so physician specialty shops in the East.

Then, in February 1996, MedPartners embarked on what I consider its single most profound departure from its original "pure-play" mission of managing physician practices. This came when MedPartners bought Illinois-based Caremark International Inc. for $1.9 billion. The Caremark deal added 1,000 physicians. That part was consistent with the MedPartners' mission of dealing with physician practices. However, the Caremark deal also added a pharmacy benefits management service — a totally different-type business from the business of managing physician practices. All of a sudden, we had all these "pieces" to manage at MedPartners.

I think it was when MedPartners did the Caremark deal that it really stopped being fun for me. I never liked the Caremark deal. I never saw the fit. I felt the Caremark deal marked the beginning of when we became tossed salad. I felt our story changed. We always had positioned ourselves as a pure-play physician practice management company. Then we were in the pharmacy benefit management business and who knows what else. And, in getting into pharmacy benefit management via the Caremark deal, we were now also in the international business. We were trying to merge multiple cultures into one organization. To me, we had all kinds of businesses that no one understood completely. I felt that it became difficult to clearly articulate our strategy of the company, that it was hard to communicate in a credible way what we were doing. It became hard to answer people when they said, "You're not what you said you were. How does this fit?" Frankly, I didn't think we had good answers. I thought in doing the Caremark deal, MedPartners went from something that was easy to define to something that was really a tossed salad.

Since PhyCor had remained focused on its original business mission of physician practice management, I feel that this "tossed-salad" strategy issue likely became a real point of culture incompatibility with MedPartners when merger-talk time arrived.

Conservative Mentality Versus Risk-taking Mentality

If I were to choose the one single greatest philosophical difference between MedPartners and PhyCor, it would be the appetite for risk.

Clearly it is MedPartners, not PhyCor, which has had the big appetite for risk.

I'm referring to risk in two major arenas — risk in terms of spending megabucks, going into debt, for new acquisitions in order to get bigger and bigger; and also risk in terms of getting into global capitation in a major way.

In regard to new acquisitions and new deals, PhyCor is much more conservative than MedPartners. PhyCor traditionally has focused on operating what it has. When PhyCor does make new acquisitions, it's obvious that most purchases are carefully selected, that they are similar in nature, and that they fall into place in a cohesive "pure-play" PPM family that "matches."

Most of PhyCor's affiliations have been with long-term, well-established clinics, many of which have been in operation for several decades. PhyCor basically has demonstrated the point of view when it partnered with physician groups that these affiliations were going to last for a long time, that the relationships had to work, and that short-term problems would be worked out.

Looking at the other side of the spectrum, the MedPartners' mentality has been an aggressive appetite for growth, an interest in diverse purchases and non pure-play, a shoot-from-the-hip philosophy: "Buy it. We'll worry about fixing it later. We're smart enough to fix the problems. We want to get big fast. We never saw a deal that we didn't like — or at least some of us never saw a deal that we didn't like." The adrenaline came from the deal.

As for venturing into the risky business of global risk contracting, there aren't many PPM companies that are heavy into the risk business. MedPartners is thus in the minority in being a large PPM company that chose to dive in very deep water with risk contracting. By contrast, PhyCor is just now beginning to dabble with risk contracting. True to the PhyCor roots and style, PhyCor's risk contracting is taking place in a careful, deliberate, paced fashion.

I think PhyCor wisely has realized it did not have the operating structure to take the cliff dive into risk contracts. And PhyCor wisely has realized that the overall PPM industry as a whole — including MedPartners — has not had the all-important critical information systems that it has needed.

Those information systems, or the absence of them, are at the heart of this "deal-killer" risk issue. Those yet-to-be-developed information systems — and the power they wield in the complex third-party payer/ managed-care environment — add up to a monumental subject — in fact, a subject significant enough for a whole chapter, the next one.

5

"Give Me a Map!":
A Crying Need for Information Systems

IF YOU'RE about to take a vacation trip to a destination in a remote, dangerous area where you've never been, you wouldn't think of starting out without a map to guide you along the way so you don't get lost.

The same thing is true of a business that's venturing into a high-risk area. In such a business, your "map" is your information systems.

These systems serve as a database of key facts, profiles, trends and statistics to use in making decisions to maximize the chances of making money and to minimize the chances of looking at red ink.

If you're in the tricky risk contracting business, you are in a high-risk business. You need the best maps, the best information systems, you can find.

After having worked with physicians and in the physician practice management (PPM) industry for several years, I have learned this: There are some information systems to guide physicians and PPMCs (physician practice management companies) in their business — in fact, many of them. But, as things stand today, the information systems are extremely deficient. These systems do not exist in either the quantity or quality even close to the degree and sophistication that's needed.

I think many people are oversimplifying this task — the task to develop the systems, the operating structure, the resources to deal in the risk environment.

And I think it's going to be one of the most monumental tasks in the history of business to get these tools developed.

The Need for an Overall Information Systems Package

To manage resources you need information systems that can interrelate as a package. What we're lacking in the PPM industry is that no one has created, on a broad basis, an information system package that can be shown, on a large scale, to produce the tangible benefits.

There are parts of systems there — in pieces. But you can't show it as a unit, on a large scale.

The whole package that's needed is not available. We don't have the whole concept in place that allows us to be able to take data and put it into a data repository, and then be able to take the data out and manipulate the data in a way to make health-related projections, and then be able to change health-related behavior on a broad scale.

You might see it done here and there in a few clinics, isolated product lines, scattered diagnoses, and pioneer case-management initiatives. But on a broad basis it just does not exist.

Some Analogies

Suffice it to say that for my part I have found it extremely frustrating to be in situations in the PPM industry where we needed these systems.

So just how strongly do I feel about the impact of this absence of sufficient information systems? How strongly do I feel about the impact that's being made on physicians and PPMCs operating in high-risk contracting?

I'll lay out for you a few analogies, so you can understand my point:

It's like getting into the insurance business without an actuary or a computer.

It's like rolling the dice. I mean, you might as well go to Las Vegas and roll the dice!

It's like going out and building a building and providing a guaranteed price for completing the building, but not knowing what the steel cost is going to be, or what the exact size is going to be, and having the labor cost being variable. You can see that for a building contractor this would be very difficult.

Well, for physicians and PPMCs attempting to venture into the risk business without the crucial information they need, this is all but impossible.

Time and Money

You can't just throw money alone at the systems problem and make it happen.

It takes money, of course — lots of it. It also takes people.

But the major thing that it takes is time to do it. It's not going to happen overnight.

It's going to take time and significant investment until the physician practice management companies will be able to deliver what they hoped, and in many cases said, they were going to deliver in terms of information systems.

In the meantime, in many cases it's going to be a tough sell for a PPM company to go to its physician partners and convince them to pour money from their own patient-care practices into this expensive quest for systems.

You can't go to the physicians and say, "Give me more of your revenue so that I can develop these systems. And give me that revenue for ten years. And then in ten years we're going to have something." The patience isn't there.

So if you're a PPM company that's heavily into managed-care programs and you desperately need these systems, and if your physician partners are pushing you for the systems because you said you could produce them and that has not come to pass, then it falls to the PPMC to fund the systems development.

And quite often for the PPMC there's not enough revenue coming in to support the management requirements plus fund much-more-expensive-than-anticipated systems technology development and make a profit.

That's the bottom line: Where's the money coming from for these expensive systems? Where's the money that allows us to invest in the technology so that five to ten years from now we've got the mousetrap that allows us to manage in this complex managed-care environment?

The Need for Systems with the Managed-Care Product

Many physicians and a few physician practice management companies have ventured into the world of risk contracting.

In my opinion, no one on the managed-care side, regardless of what kind of role he or she is playing in the healthcare delivery system, really has the needed systems to deal well with that risk.

When we speak of risk in terms of managed care, risk refers to the reimbursement system — the system by which you're being paid for the healthcare services you provide. In the managed-care reimbursement system, the whole concept of gamble comes into play. What we're basically talking about with risk contracting is that you're taking a fixed sum for treating conditions, with the unknown being the amount of healthcare resources necessary to treat those conditions. You're not being paid on an indemnity basis; that is, you're not being paid on a fee-for-service, for whatever services you end up providing. Instead, in a managed-care risk-contracting system, you're being paid like the federally-inspired DRGs that came down in the 1980s. It's like this: "Here's X dollars. Now you have to deal with it. If you have to use more dollars to take care of the patients, you lose." It's the opportunity to lose, and it's the opportunity to gain. It's the risk and return from risk contracting.

In this day and age — when healthcare technology, pharmacology and delivery systems make it possible to do so much for so many patient-care diagnoses — if you're taking risks in managed care without the systems you need, you'd better face the fact that you are really taking risks. You might lose a lot of money when you thought you were going to make a lot of money. On the other hand, you might not know if you made money or lost money. That's comforting!

If you're a healthcare provider trying to make a profit while dealing with the riskier forms of "managed care," what you're doing is this: You're taking a chunk (often a hefty chunk) of the premium dollars that are paid for your patients' health insurance coverage, dividing those dollars up to cover the healthcare bills that the patients incur in given areas, and banking on the projection that there will be some dollars left over at the end of the day to serve as a profit for you.

In doing this, you need high-quality information about (a) the health status of the patients you're considering and/or accepting for coverage, and (b) good projections on the amount and types of healthcare services these patients (or members) are likely to use.

Now that preceding sentence above didn't take long to write, and it didn't take up much space. But take a good long look at what it says.

Think of all the insights that sentence is implying you need to know about the health, or lack of health, of the patients with whom you are dealing.

Think of all the predictors that sentence is saying you need to be able to craft about the healthcare services your patients are likely to use.

Unfortunately, the systems that you need to have available to guide you to that information aren't something you can go drag off the shelf somewhere.

Managed care is no different from any other product in that if you run into a problem making money on the product you need to have the systems to pinpoint your exact problems. And this is where I think we're seeing some devastating gaps with the systems we have available today. I frankly don't think we have available to us in managed care the reliable systems which can pinpoint the exact problem or problems.

If you miss your numbers in managed care, what is your exact problem? Is your problem that you had over-utilization of healthcare services? Or was your utilization what was expected, but you priced it too low? Or did you have problems with eligibility of your insured members? Or does your problem exist because you had adverse selection in members? You need to know your problems so you can fix them. And if you can't pinpoint an exact problem, how are you going to fix it?

Physician Impatience about the Systems

A tremendous amount of impatience exists on the part of many players in the healthcare delivery and management industry for workable information systems to become available. Physicians are especially impatient to see those systems "happen."

Those of us who have dealt with the PPM industry know very well that the promise of information systems represented one of the top motivators that birthed this industry. One reason motivating many a physician to say "yes" to a PPMC contract was that he hoped the PPMC could provide systems to guide him through an increasingly complex healthcare delivery-and-payment maze.

Particularly for those physician groups heavily involved in managed care, a big part of what they bargained for in partnering with a PPMC was the availability of systems to enable them to deal in a managed-care/risk environment. They bargained for leverage with the payer.

Where information systems are concerned, I'm not so sure that these physicians, either by perception or reality, have bargained for something that is possible to deliver in the short-term.

Needless to say, information systems were not the only motivator for physicians to partner with PPMCs. Physicians have partnered with PPM companies for many reasons. And I think the partnering with PPMCs has served and will continue to serve many physician groups well with some key benefits other than the information systems. The traditional PPMCs have been and will continue to be value-added extenders of physicians' capabilities. Some of the areas in which I have heard physicians give certain PPMC arrangements high marks include assistance with visionary planning, infusion of capital to aid in purchase of technology, business assistance with collection and billing and other day-to-day operational improvements.

However, the information systems are still a big vacuum for many physician groups and the PPMCs with which they partnered. A lot of physician groups, particularly those deep into the managed-care market, are still looking over the horizon — with growing impatience — for those systems which they have been hoping a PPMC contract would bring them.

Physicians' Need for Help with Declining Reimbursement

Physicians are extremely anxious to have these information systems because they're on the firing line with mounting challenges they're facing with third-party payment and managed care.

Many physicians in today's healthcare market are finding, and have been finding for some time, that their per unit revenue is decreasing virtually with every day that passes.

In decades gone by, if a patient had good health insurance, a physician was likely to do well financially. No matter how big the patient's overall healthcare tab, the physician used to be paid fairly for his services.

In fact, in those days, the more physician services a well-insured patient used, the more money the physician stood to collect from the insurer, the third-party payer.

In those days, if utilization of healthcare services was excessive, and if the payer's premium wasn't enough to offset this, then the payer lost. Historically, in this now-bygone era, the risk was on the third-party payer or the employer.

Well, we don't see much of that anymore. We don't see much of what we call the "indemnity business." What has been happening more and more in recent years is that the payer is shifting the financial risk to physicians, because technically the physician is the only one who really can control utilization of healthcare services.

So the risk is shifted down. And if you are a physician who's dealing with high-risk managed-care contracts and you don't have the systems and you don't have the protocols, and you may or may not have priced your services appropriately, it's a crapshoot!

What Do Physicians Need the Systems to Tell Them?

Let's track some of the information which would be needed by a hypothetical Dr. Jones, who heads a large physician group which is engaged in a risk contract with a big HMO, or health maintenance organization.

Dr. Jones and his group have agreed to care for a given patient population, and it's important for him to understand the "identity" of the population he and his colleagues have agreed to serve.

For starters, there's the information that Dr. Jones needs from the payer, the HMO, about who's eligible for services. The payer has to track eligibility and needs competent systems to do this: What patients are participating this month? Who's covered? Who's paid their premium? Who is eligible to obtain service?

I will tell you that even this basic eligibility information poses a major challenge for systems. The reason is that the information is a moving target. If you think about it, month to month you've got people, beneficiaries, coming and going.

Beyond knowing who's eligible — a complex-enough process in its own right — things really start to get sticky for Dr. Jones.

Dr. Jones needs crucial information from systems which will aid him and other members of his group in pricing their services and planning treatment protocols. In this area, there's really a need on Dr. Jones' part to understand the demographics, the age, the psychographic profiles of the people he's serving. Keep in mind that Dr. Jones and his colleagues are trying to come up with a wide variety of patient-care situations in terms of treatment protocols and pricing.

In developing these treatment protocols, there are so many components with which Dr. Jones and his physician colleagues must deal. And if you really don't understand each component, then it's very difficult to assure yourself that you have priced it appropriately to assure yourself a profit.

The MedPartners Example

MedPartners provides a vivid example of how badly things can go wrong when information systems are not providing the data necessary to make solid financial projections.

This example has to do with losses MedPartners experienced in its global capitation business in California. MedPartners' financial projections were off in California; the information systems were not available. MedPartners' assumptions were too low on medical costs per person.

These missed projections figured significantly into the disappointing fourth quarter 1997 earnings surprise that MedPartners experienced.

That disappointing earnings surprise clearly showed that, in a risk environment, failure to capture relevant information necessary to make accurate projections can quickly flip what was thought to be a very profitable situation into a very negative financial situation.

In a risk environment such as this, it's imperative that your systems be able to capture accurate information to make accurate projections about utilization, changes in benefit plan design or whatever. It's also imperative that when you've missed the mark in certain areas, your information systems be capable of alerting you — quickly!

This MedPartners example points out that with managed care, time can become your enemy — loss of time, that is. You can't afford to go very long operating on faulty projections.

In the case of the missed projections that were reflected in MedPartners' losses in late 1997, this is what had occurred: MedPartners had been moving along on the West Coast taking care of a large population in a global capitation managed-care system, using certain assumptions about medical costs for the given population. Some of those assumptions underestimated the amount of healthcare resources consumed by patients covered under the managed-care contracts. MedPartners did not have systems capable of giving early warning signs so that corrective measures could be taken. By the time they figured out that actual information varied from the projected information, MedPartners already had incurred a huge loss.

Demands for the Physician to Limit Healthcare Spending

There was a time when a physician's main concern was practicing medicine.

That time most likely is gone forever.

In the past 15 to 18 years, we've been seeing growing demands for the physician to take on increasing accountability for how the overall healthcare dollar is spent.

The presence or absence of high-quality information systems plays a crucial role in the physician's ability to meet these demands.

The completeness or incompleteness of these systems impacts the way the physician practices medicine and impacts the physician's pocket-book.

Even if the most sophisticated, workable systems in the world were developed, it would not solve all the physician's problems brought on by these demands for more physician control over, and accountability for, health expenditures.

But there's no doubt that these systems would provide some maps that could help the physician plan patient care that would be more tailor-made for specific patients, run less risk of malpractice problems, and overall be more cost-efficient.

The Physician's Power

The reason the physician is such a target to assume increased account-ability for spending the healthcare dollar is that the physician holds the biggest power as to how that dollar is spent.

There's no doubt that the physician is the key to the healthcare delivery system. You don't have a healthcare delivery system without somebody that's licensed to practice medicine.

If you are admitted to or discharged from a hospital, it's a physician who has to admit you and discharge you. If you have an X-ray or a lab test, it's a physician who orders the test. If you need a prescription medication, it's the physician who writes the prescription. (While there is a movement now to give certain registered nurses prescriptive author-ity, the overwhelming bulk of that prescriptive authority still rests with the physicians.)

Take a look, for example, at some of the statistics that existed when we were setting up MedPartners in the early 1990s. At that time, there was about $200 billion a year spent on physician services in this nation. But that was just the tip of the iceberg when it came to healthcare dollars the physician was controlling.

Take that $200 billion being paid directly to the physicians for services they were providing, and add to that another $800 billion that the physicians controlled with their pens — hospital admissions, pharmacy dollars, ancillary tests, etc.

The Physician's Pressures

In the 1980s and 1990s, all this power held by physicians to control the selection of health services for their patients has in many cases brought the physicians about as much misery as satisfaction.

Although the physicians would not and should not want to relinquish their powers to select and authorize this wide array of healthcare services for their patients, the cost of the services has become such an intense issue that the physicians are pressured on all sides to make decisions about patient care based on cost.

In the past several years, I've come to know hundreds of physicians well. On many an occasion I've looked at a very competent but frustrated physician functioning in a situation where his authority was challenged on matters related to healthcare costs. I've seen physicians frustrated by trying to balance a patient's best interests on the one hand and the cost of meeting the patient's best interests on the other.

I've heard the physicians relate countless examples of dilemmas they faced that involved quality patient care and the dollar sign.

As I've watched these physicians struggle under cost-related pressures, there have been times I've in effect said to myself, "You know, this physician is the most powerful component in the healthcare delivery system. Yet his power is challenged with such force from so many sides that there are times when the very existence of his power makes him so pressured and so vulnerable that he's rendered virtually powerless."

When I speak of these pressures on the physician, what do I mean?

Let's take a look at a hypothetical scenario of the physician who is taking care of a woman who's an elderly Medicare patient in the hospital:

The physician is the one who's responsible for the care of the patient. While trying to keep the patient's best healthcare interests at heart, and also make sure he has covered all the bases to protect himself against malpractice, he must spend countless hours on documentation.

On one side, he has the hospital placing pressure on him to get the patient out of the hospital. On the other side, he has the patient's family placing pressure on him to keep the patient in the hospital.

The reason the hospital is contacting him about resource utilization and length of stay is because it's in the hospital's best interest financially in a Medicare environment to basically provide the fewest resources possible and to have the patient get out of the hospital and back home as soon as possible.

The reasons the patient's family is pressuring the physician have to do with being concerned about the patient's well-being and also worrying about family resources such as money and caretakers. The family is saying, "You can't send Grandmother home, because she's too sick to go home, and we don't have anybody at home to take care of her."

Not only is the hospital calling the physician about length of stay for the patient; the hospital is questioning some of the resources the physician is using or wants to use for the patient while she is in the hospital. While the patient is still in the hospital, the physician is scrutinized about the cost of the services he's ordering for the patient. The hospital is calling him saying, "Don't use this antibiotic," because it costs too much. The hospital is questioning the physician as to "Why did you order this test?" From a financial standpoint, the physician doesn't benefit from not ordering the MRI that may be marginal. At the same time, he could actually run a financial risk (of malpractice) by not ordering a particular test if the patient develops a problem that some plaintiff's attorney convinces a jury could have been diagnosed with the test. Also, if the physician goes ahead and discharges the patient too early and the patient develops complications as a result, then the physician is the one ultimately responsible. He's the one legally, medically and ethically responsible for the care of the patient.

So there's the physician — in the middle, in the box.

In short, the physician has all the responsibility, and everybody else in the world is telling him what he can and can't do.

Getting to the Physicians Financially

As the pressure picked up steam in the 1980s and 1990s to control healthcare expenditures, it didn't take a rocket scientist to know that physicians were the key to the controls.

As the years went by, those holding the big healthcare purse strings focused on the physicians' incomes more and more — basically through three avenues.

First of all, they took the avenue of limitation. With limitation, third-party payers simply tightened up on what they would pay — limiting how much they would approve to pay, and even if they would pay anything, for many types of physician-services. No matter how you cut it, most vestiges of those old-style health insurance plans were gone. And in their place were these third-party approaches that came in the physicians' mail with limitation, limitation, limitation.

Secondly, those holding the big healthcare purse strings increasingly started targeting selected physicians through the avenue of intimidation. With intimidation, big third-party payers launched investigations looking for signs of padded or fraudulent claims and/or unnecessary utilization. Often leading the pack of these initiatives, sometimes with legitimate complaints but often without substance, was Uncle Sam with his proclamation of physician abuse of federally funded Medicare.

And, thirdly, those paying the healthcare tab approached the physician through the avenue of incentive. In this type scenario, those paying the healthcare tab were looking for "deals" with the physicians. They were looking for "packages" in which the physicians would agree to deliver specified healthcare services in a more cost-effective method than these payers had experienced in the past. As these "deals" became more common and more streamlined, many of them came to be known as "managed-care" packages. In many instances, the concepts for these managed-care plans were coming from third-party payers. In some cases, large employers were participating directly in structuring these deals, since they had big bucks at stake in purchasing health insurance coverage for their employees. And then also coming up with many managed-care plan models were progressive physician groups themselves — including groups of physicians actually in practice together, and also networks of physician groups who joined hands for purposes of participating jointly in managed-care programs. As physician practice management companies came into being in the late 1980s, these PPMCs also began joining with their physician partners to structure managed-care programs they could market.

Initially, the physicians were participating in packages that mainly had to do with provision and payment for their own physician-delivered services. As time went on, some of the deals with physicians expanded to include risk arrangements in which the physicians managed utilization and payment for not only physician-services, but for many other healthcare services as well.

It is relevant to note here that although many managed-care plans were touted as positive-incentive overtures to physicians, there no doubt are numerous physicians in this nation who would argue that some of these managed-care plans also came toward them through the avenues of limitation and even intimidation. The reason is that many physicians found themselves in a market in which, if they chose to thrive or at times even survive, they had no choice but to join up with managed care because managed-care plans were claiming such a huge share of patients in their waiting rooms.

However, although it's easy to see how many physicians have felt pressured into signing a managed-care contract they didn't really want to sign, it is true that when a well-structured managed-care plan works there can be financial incentives for the physicians. Appropriately structured and fair managed-care plans can offer to the physicians a better upside opportunity in managing care, because they're then able to participate in cost-savings by keeping people healthy. Ideally this is where healthy means profit, okay? Whereas historically there was no reward to the physician group for healthy patients.

PPMCs and Global Capitation Problems

There has been a perception — among some physician groups and among some PPMCs like MedPartners — that the faster you got into global risk the arbitrage was going to be there and it would be very profitable.

I think the basic idea of global capitation is a good concept — that concept being that if you succeed in saving big bucks for the healthcare delivery system you get to share in some of those savings. However, I think global capitation is good provided you have the following: (1) The right population, (2) priced right, (3) the systems to manage it, and (4) your experience works the way you projected it would work. If you miss on any of those, global capitation can be bad.

As things stand now, without the systems developed to the point they need to be, in my opinion global capitation is dependent on a lot of luck. You've just got to get real lucky. You've got to have great luck with utilization. You've got to have a great contract on the front-end.

Since there's so much luck involved in it now, we all know that you can have good luck or you can have bad luck. As I've mentioned previously in this chapter, with global capitation MedPartners has had some bad luck mixed in with its good. MedPartners and the physicians it's partnering with out on the West Coast already have experienced some problems in missing on some numbers. They've already had the train hit them in some instances. I personally thought it was predictable that that would happen — because they really haven't had all the crucial systems to inform them where they were financially at any given point in time.

Out on the West Coast, MedPartners is dealing with approximately two million globally capitated lives. Because of the size, the magnitude, of that global capitation market in which MedPartners has engaged itself, I think MedPartners faces a monumental task.

Central to MedPartners' ability to manage this huge global capitation market is the availability of the information systems. I personally think that where MedPartners is concerned, the lack of availability of targeted information systems as they relate to global capitation is the biggest problem faced by this particular PPM company.

If There Is a Big Payoff, Who Gets It?

I've addressed the issue of not having the information systems and some of the resulting problems.

But before I leave this chapter, I think I should mention how great it's going to be for the shareholders who get rewarded because they do develop these systems and are able to install them.

Whoever develops and implements these far-reaching information systems to help physicians and PPMCs stands to make a phenomenal amount of money — for providing a phenomenal amount of value.

But, there are looming questions: How do we collect and input the data? Who's going to pay for it? Who owns the data? How do you protect the confidentiality of the data?

Assuming the resolution of those issues, and if the systems should emerge and create savings or additional revenue, there will be an additional set of pressing questions. I'll give you a couple of examples:

Question Number One: How does major cost-savings revenue get split up among involved parties — say, for example, between physician groups and their PPMC partners?

Question Number Two: If the systems produce critical pathways and intellectual capital, who owns these results?

These questions represent the tip of the iceberg in areas that are virtually virgin territory, uncharted waters, areas that are totally unresolved.

I know from my MedPartners experience that many physicians anticipate that incremental dollars in this area will benefit them, while on the other hand their PPMC partners anticipate the dollars will reward them and improve their margins and returns on investment.

I'm sure, if and when these dollars become available, the parties will negotiate a fair and equitable distribution of those dollars.

6

Sizzle Is Not Enough:
Tougher Questions from the Analysts

AT SOME point in time, when you have fundamental problems in a company or an overall industry, there's going to be a day of reckoning.

For the fast-growing company known as MedPartners in this industry called physician practice management (PPM), I think what we saw in late 1997 and early 1998 amounted to that day of reckoning.

It was obvious to me, frankly, that at some point something like this would happen. Considering the size and the complexity and the diversity of the overall PPM industry, I have felt that the tools to manage the industry have been running significantly behind that growth. By "tools" I'm referring to resources such as knowledge base and human capital, but above all I'm referring to the software and other elements that make up those all-important systems.

As those of us close to the PPM industry are keenly aware, it was that proposed merger deal between the PPM industry's "No. 1" MedPartners and "No. 2" PhyCor that turned on the spotlights and set the stage for the day of reckoning.

But I think that day of reckoning would have arrived sooner or later — probably rather soon — even if there had not been a MedPartners/PhyCor crash-and-burn.

What happened with this failed merger and its aftermath no doubt has had the greatest immediate impact on MedPartners.

However, MedPartners was far from being the only company dealt a blow when the deal was terminated. This was much more than a single failed merger transaction. It was an event that turned the spotlight on key problems facing the overall physician practice management industry.

In this chapter, I want to address where I think some of this could be headed — for MedPartners, and for the overall PPM industry.

Facing More Scrutiny

One of the biggest results that will come out of this MedPartners/PhyCor failed deal will be that the analysts will be asking the PPM industry tougher questions.

I was involved with the PPM industry in its infancy in the early 1990s. I remember that then a lot of the analysts weren't asking real astute questions. In fact, some of them were asking superficial questions. The reason is they didn't understand this industry.

Now the analysts are becoming increasingly aware of issues facing this industry. There's an increased level of understanding and scrutiny of the strategies and results of the companies in this industry. Analysts now understand what resources are needed to successfully continue to develop and segment the industry and individual PPM companies.

Analysts are model-driven. Everything they do involves a financial model. And when something falls outside their model they ask questions. They ask, "Why is it this number compared to this number is this, when it's not like this in every other comparable situation we look at?"

In the past couple of years, and especially over the past year or so, analysts have progressed light years in terms of the variables they include in their models for PPM companies.

Even prior to the failed MedPartners/PhyCor merger deal, the analysts had gradually become more and more savvy about PPMCs. But make no mistake about it: What occurred between late October 1997 and early January 1998 with the failed MedPartners/PhyCor merger deal has made the analysts even smarter and stockholders leery.

This matured understanding has enlightened people who need to ask the questions — enabling them to dig deeper, to ask harder questions, to look for evidence to support assertions that were made in times past.

Those who will be evaluating performance of the PPM industry will be doing it in a more detailed way than they have in the past. The SEC will scrutinize much more aggressively than they have in the past. The investor, the analyst, the investment banker will scrutinize at a deeper level.

Just as the questions will get deeper, the answers from the PPMCs better be more specific from now on. For the survivors in the PPM industry, plans need to be better defined and knowledge more accessible. In order to get and keep the confidence of your investors, you're going to have to understand your business and be able to clearly articulate business objectives and financial reporting systems. Even where the more complex systems are concerned, people aren't going to just ask you if you have the systems. They're going to say, "Show me. Show me the evidence."

There was a lot of smoke put out there in the beginning that analysts can see through now. The days are gone when high valuations and multiples can be created with smoke and mirrors.

The Operating Margins

In the early 1990s you could sell the analysts on the idea that your margins came from factors such as economies of scale and from finding fat in operating units or purchasing products and services cheaper.

If you think about it, margins generated from savings are probably onetime events. With per unit revenues declining and all the capital needed for systems to manage information, how can you sustain margins in the short-term? Again, I think it's a timing and magnitude issue.

The PPMCs: Some Stars in Their Crowns

Let's take a look at what created a market for the PPM industry and why it has grown so rapidly.

There clearly was a need for what the PPMCs brought to the table. And the PPMCs have brought many tremendous services to the physicians with whom they have partnered.

At the time the PPM industry was taking root in the late 1980s, a nationwide healthcare reform movement was under way. Some of that so-called healthcare reform came to pass, and some of it did not. However, via a combination of the movement's perception, its threat and its reality, there was born a climate of driving need on the part of the fragmented physician industry in this nation to consolidate. The physicians indeed felt a driving need to organize and develop management expertise and systems and create some leverage.

However, even though the physicians felt these needs, they did not feel that they, the physicians, were capable of organizing the services and leverage they needed on their own. So there was a vacuum. That vacuum was the catalyst that developed the industry.

There's no doubt that the PPM industry in its initial years went through a period of time when we added value to the physicians' practices with which we partnered.

We helped them grow. We improved access to capital. We helped facilitate mergers with other physician groups and helped create leverage.

We helped them understand what was happening to them. We helped them understand different structures, such as IPAs, or independent practice associations. We helped them understand the relationships with institutional providers. We helped them understand some of the buzzwords and relationships that were not in their best interests. For example, I believe some PPMCs performed a tremendous service for some physician groups by showing them the ineffectiveness of PHOs, or physician-hospital organizations. (In today's healthcare delivery market, the interests of physicians and hospitals are not aligned. It's difficult if not impossible for physicians to find an equitable model in joining hands with hospitals.)

Because of the birth, growth and productivity of the PPMCs, there are thousands of physicians in this nation today who are a lot more savvy, capable and confident to face the changing world in which they function and to identify and grasp the opportunities in that changing world of healthcare.

Where Did Some PPMCs Go Wrong?

Some PPMCs became a bit aggressive when it came to helping the physicians with their incomes by encouraging them to venture into that untamed world of risk contracting.

In this area, there were some PPMCs which sold physicians on the idea the PPMCs could develop mechanisms for them to reverse the declining per unit reimbursement. The sell was this: The PPMC could, through risk contracting, help the physicians to pursue dollars that didn't exist to pursue before. There were new sources of revenue.

I don't believe in general this was a matter of PPMCs deliberately misleading the physicians. It is my view instead that there were those super-optimists in the PPM industry who were naive in a sense, who really underestimated the amount of resources and the amount of capital and the amount of time it was going to take to come up with the systems that really would make it possible to create new revenue.

There was also the perception that things would happen a lot quicker than they actually happened. And I believe there are those PPM companies that continue to promise things that they have not delivered and cannot deliver.

As time went on, and as those promised deliverables continued to be undelivered, the physicians' anxiety level and intolerance level and dissatisfaction level went up. When expectations are not met, anxiety and frustration tear apart relationships.

Some Predictions about MedPartners

I obviously have some opinions on why MedPartners got into trouble. And I have some predictions as to steps that will be necessary for MedPartners to reorganize and emerge as a successful company.

Although some of MedPartners' problems resulted from being involved in high-risk managed care without also having the systems to do the job, MedPartners' difficulties also were a product of its inability to manage its meteoric growth.

Before I address some of the things I believe will and should happen at MedPartners, I want to give a summary of this company's rapid rise to success and its crash of late 1997 and early 1998.

MedPartners' meteoric growth propelled it into the darling of the nation's PPM industry and into a young rocket in Alabama's overall corporate structure. At the time the proposed MedPartners/PhyCor merger was announced October 29, 1997, MedPartners was the largest PPM company in the United States and the largest revenue-generating company of any kind in Alabama. In the PPM industry, MedPartners was a model of what aggressive growth could do — with its operations in 40 states, affiliations with more than 13,000 physicians, and involvement not only with physician practices but also other businesses such as pharmacy benefit management. As a revenue producer, its $6.2 billion of revenue was considered virtually unbelievable for a company that had not even celebrated its fifth birthday.

When it was announced that No. 1 MedPartners and No. 2 PhyCor would merge, the apparent Cinderella story appeared to be adding yet another glowing chapter. The merger sale price — $8 billion in stock and assumed debt — would create another first — the largest deal in Alabama's corporate history. In the initial hours after the impending deal was announced, some analysts joined the wave of well-wishers who hailed the deal as golden. One analyst christened it as a "signature deal" in the PPM industry.

But, within a matter of 24 hours after the merger plans were announced, the glitter began vanishing rapidly from this deal initially hailed as so golden. As the dust began to settle, many analysts and investors began to look with a questioning eye. And, as so often is true, plummeting stock values began to stroke their powerful pens in writing what would be the real final chapter about the merger deal. In the first full trading day after announcement of the merger, MedPartners' stock dipped by 17 percent, down by $5.25 per share, as it closed at $25.75 in New York Stock Exchange composite trading. PhyCor has a bad day, too, sinking by 19 percent, or $5.56 per share, to $24 on the Nasdaq Stock Market.

Analysts and investors were nervous about many things. First of all, they were taken by surprise by the merger. This merger seemed to come out of nowhere. Secondly, things just weren't fitting in a package that made management and bottom-line sense to them. PhyCor, five years older than MedPartners but about a third MedPartners' size in revenues, had always been a conservative operator. PhyCor simply did not have the appetite for or experience with growth and risk that MedPartners had. Yet, with PhyCor's price/earnings ratio higher than MedPartners, the way this merger deal was structured from the outset was that PhyCor would be the surviving company in this merger. PhyCor would be left to manage this MedPartners company that was neither of PhyCor's making nor in the PhyCor style of vision, strategy and management.

The investor community obviously was nervous.

Then, as MedPartners and PhyCor went about "due diligence" with a goal of completing the merger by early 1998, leaders of those two companies became nervous.

At the end, on January 7, 1998, it was publicly announced that the merger would not happen.

When all was said and done, both companies got bashed financially in this "mess." But there's no doubt that it was MedPartners that was hit the hardest.

In addition to the announcement of the failed merger deal, MedPartners made a couple of other simultaneous announcements which, along with the failed merger, comprised a growing predicament for MedPartners' investors. There was a warning that MedPartners faced a probable operating loss for the fourth quarter and also an announcement of a onetime MedPartners' charge of $145 million in the fourth quarter.

The day after those announcements, MedPartners' stock fell 45 percent, to $10 a share.

Then, on Friday, January 16, 1998, responding to mounting pressure from the investment community, Larry R. House resigned as chairman and CEO of MedPartners. Concurrent with House's announcement, MedPartners' cofounder Richard M. Scrushy stepped in to replace House. It would be Scrushy who would lead MedPartners during this difficult interim period as the shaken company began its quest for a new

CEO. Scrushy shouldered this load at a time when he still was chairman and CEO of his own highly successful company, HealthSouth Corporation.

Now for some of the things I believe are likely to happen with MedPartners:

It's quite likely some of the "pieces" of MedPartners will be broken off and sold. If this is done, this could make MedPartners a smaller and more manageable organization. If one of those sold-off pieces were to be MedPartners' large pharmacy benefit management operation, the result could be a return to a more "pure-play" focus on MedPartners' original business plan strategy of physician practice management. As things stand now with MedPartners, the company is too complex, too diverse. In my view it's a management nightmare. If it should occur that the company is split into more manageable pieces, it probably would be more valuable right now in pieces than as a whole. And who knows what might happen in the future? At some point perhaps those pieces might circle back together.

I feel MedPartners will be re-evaluating how deeply it continues to involve itself in high-risk managed-care programs like global capitation on the West Coast. Again, as I've already emphasized, the key to success in high-risk managed care lies in having and knowing how to use the systems. There are lots of people out there who have a craving, a yearning, a need for those systems. MedPartners is far from being "The Lone Ranger" in terms of struggling to get those systems in place. One other example which comes to my mind of a company which has suffered the systems problem is a HMO (health maintenance organization) company by the name of Oxford HealthPlans. In some respects, some of the problems that MedPartners has faced with systems have been similar to Oxford's. Oxford had been a very successful HMO company — it grew like crazy — but then it couldn't deliver the systems to manage costs and it got blindsided. When the stock market sustained such a drop that it shut down early on October 28, 1997, Oxford was one of those especially hard-hit. Oxford's market value dropped 63 percent in a day! The reason I'm bringing up this analogy is it's my opinion that as long as

MedPartners is in the real high-risk managed-care business and doesn't have the systems, it's standing out there on the edge of a cliff. With both MedPartners and Oxford HealthPlans, I am convinced those systems — or the absences of them — have been the root of many of the problems. Right now MedPartners is in a position of facing a significant challenge to get a real handle on its operations, especially in the area of risk contracting.

And, finally about MedPartners, I predict you'll see a tremendous shift in MedPartners' management structure. I believe it will end up being more like PhyCor's, that it will become more decentralized, and that it will move toward a smaller corporate overhead. I anticipate MedPartners will have a smaller corporate bureaucracy and a lot of empty offices in its Birmingham headquarters.

Where Is the PPM Industry Headed?

Even with all the problems the PPM industry has been facing, I do not believe the industry will go away. Quite the contrary. Ultimately it will be a good industry. And, along the road to a better PPM industry, it is my opinion we're likely to see the following happen:

- We'll see a restructuring of this industry. As a part of the restructuring, we'll see segmentation — non-managed care, managed care. As a part of this process, there will be many PPM companies that will not survive — because they don't have the management depth, they don't have the understanding, and they don't have a clue as to what value to add or how to add it.
- "Sizzle" is not going to sell well anymore in the PPM industry. Sizzle used to sell. In the past this industry actually was heavily driven by sizzle, and now the sizzle is gone. We're not just promising anymore. We're down to blocking and tackling. We're down to how can you deliver a sustainable value and create a long-term mutually beneficial partnership.
- It will be the "sustainable" that will become the focus of the next phase of the PPM industry's life. The "sustainable" will replace "the sizzle." By the sustainable, I'm referring to the partnership, to

the value-added defined strategy, and to a plan and the execution of that plan.

- Some of the higher-risk managed-care programs such as global capitation have a questionable future in the PPM industry. As I've discussed previously, targeted systems are one of the keys to making this work. If these high-risk managed-care programs do pay off, the payoffs stand to be big. But the losses also stand to be big. At this point, I wouldn't be able to venture a guess as to how long it's going to take for the systems to evolve to control high-risk in managed care. They might take ten years. It might never happen. The investment community might not be patient enough.

- Size will not be as significant a driving force for successful PPMCs in the next several years. The PPMCs that thrive will find that it's important to stick to a core business plan and not to get enamored with size. As the PPM industry goes through this new phase of execution, many companies will see they can be penalized for the baggage that goes with size versus being rewarded for size. You've got to have machines that work. Many will find just because you're a big company does not mean you're a good company. Big ones fall hard. I used to think we were going to see these big, big PPMCs with 20,000 to 30,000 physician members. I now think that will not be the trend. This bigger model is too complicated and unmanageable.

- When physicians are looking around for partners, they are going to be smarter than in times past about "if" and "who" and "why" as they choose their partners. They're going to consider carefully whether or not it makes sense for them to partner in the first place, and, if it does, what they realistically can expect to achieve. They are going to know how to evaluate PPMCs and how to choose the partner that best matches their needs and goals. And, in terms of "why" — in terms of their motivations — there will be few physicians entering into agreements out of fear. Historically, momentum in this PPM industry was developed out of fear and paranoia. Many physicians believed in the late 1980s and early

1990s that a PPMC could be a savior and partnering was a way of protection. I think there's a big question now as to whether or not the PPM structures really can protect the physicians. So, when physicians partner — and there are many other valid motivators to partner besides fear and protection — I believe the partnering will be for the right reasons.

- We are going to experience a rising level of sophistication in the PPM industry. This will occur as involved parties become more educated about PPMCs and as better mechanisms are developed to evaluate PPMCs. As the educational process expands concerning PPMCs, we'll see a streamlining in the communication of PPMCs' real results. We'll see better evaluation tools emerge as the analysts drill deeper and take a lead in developing these tools. We'll see informed people looking not only at the financial performance of companies but also at quality issues and at the tracking of added value and satisfaction. This rising level of sophistication will be apparent with all involved parties. We'll see it within the management of the surviving quality PPMCs. We'll see it with the physicians. We'll see it with the analysts. We'll see it with the stockholders. As the level of sophistication grows, we'll see the quality PPMCs grow and add value. They will be successfully transitioning from the concept stage to the execution stage. The talent pool will get stronger. The market will require performance and reward performance. The industry will shake out. This growing level of sophistication will help the whole industry.

- "Niches" will spring up in the form of start-up companies. These will be single-specialty companies — new companies that have some core traits similar to the conventional PPMC but demonstrate some unique differences, some new and innovative strategies. These niche companies will develop as part of the trend to segment the PPM industry into manageable components. These niche companies will be more narrow and more specialized in focus than the larger general-purpose PPMCs. They will be set up so resources can be more fine-tuned, where the overall operation can be more compact and logically managed. I'm involved with one of those start-ups. I'll introduce you to the company in Part Three of this book.

- The focal point of excitement in this PPM industry is going to move away from the affiliation transaction to what happens after affiliation — to what value is delivered. The focal point is going to move away from the smoke and mirrors. There won't be a valuation based upon smoke and mirrors anymore.

PART THREE:

A Company Called Gēnus

7

The "Quality of Life" Product: A Retail Concept in Medicine and Dentistry

DURING THE initial months after I left MedPartners, I was extremely busy getting my own show on the road — a company I call a "niche player" in the PPM industry. My new company, Genus Aesthetic Medical & Dental Group, Inc., is based on a unique retail concept in aesthetic medical and dental services.

Genus has some similarities to PPMCs, or physician practice management companies, in that it's still a business company partnering with doctors. But it's not a mainstream PPMC. It does not have the third-party payer or managed-care elements. Because of its retail nature, it does have extensive potential to grow revenue that doesn't exist in the mainstream PPMC model. Partly because of this ability to develop a practice via revenue growth, we often refer to Genus as a "practice development company."

By the Fall of 1997, I had managed to put the pieces together to start Genus. I convinced a high-quality board of directors about my idea, raised the $19.5 million in venture capital which my plan called for, and recruited a management team with talent and experience. In early 1998, we opened for business in our new corporate offices in Birmingham, Alabama. We began putting together some partnerships with top-of-the-line aesthetic physicians and dentists in various parts of the nation.

From the time I decided to pursue my own company, I knew I again wanted to create a company that would partner with doctors.

I wanted to pursue this business because I enjoy working with doctors, because this is a business I know can be improved, and because it's a business I feel confident can be a winner for four groups — the doctors, their patients, the company, and the shareholders.

But just as I knew I wanted to create a new company, I also knew I wanted my new company to have some traits that would make it a fit for "today."

I'm convinced the new company we've started is very "today" — very current — in terms of the product we'll offer, the collection of doctors who will provide it, the patients to whom we'll market it, the structure we'll use, and the way our affiliations will add value.

The product is healthcare, focused on improving the quality of life. The product is a self-improvement, youth preservation assortment of health-related services — face-lifts, tummy tucks, nose restructuring, liposuction, hair restoration and hair removal, esthetic dentistry, orthodontics, teeth-whitening, etc. — those services that make you look better and feel better about yourself.

The doctors who are providing the services include both physicians and dentists — in a wide range of specialties and sub-specialties.

The patients to whom we're marketing these services range in age virtually from the cradle to the grave, but we expect a heavy concentration to be in the growing baby-boomer population.

The approach we're using is retail. We are introducing a unique retail concept into the world of medicine and dentistry. In doing so, we are focusing on retail-strategy tools such as brand name, consistency in quality, and promotion. We are taking the high-end approach that's characteristic of an exclusive hotel chain like Ritz-Carlton, a top-of-the-line automobile like Mercedes-Benz.

The method of payment is predominantly fee-for-service, payments made directly by patients to their physicians and dentists. Our success is not dependent on third-party or managed-care plans for reimbursement. It's based on payments from a market made up of a population of consumers who are beginning to understand what they want and who are willing and have the means to pay for quality and service.

A Fund-raising Response to Savor

It was late May of 1997, right after I left MedPartners, when I started raising funding for the new company.

Four months later, as I evaluated our progress on raising capital, I had a dilemma — a complex scenario, but a good situation in which to be.

I was looking at solid interest from multiple sources in amounts far in excess of my projected needs. We found ourselves oversubscribed and I had to turn down some of the money to get this start-up capitalized. In venture capital (VC) funds alone, we had commitments of $30.5 million, and we ended up accepting $19.5 million.

Needless to say, I was extremely pleased with that quick, incredibly positive investment reception; but I was not surprised. This fee-for-service aesthetic medicine and dentistry concept is intriguing. From what we're seeing thus far, I believe we'll encounter on a sustained basis a positive response from the doctors, their patients, and the company's shareholders.

For me, the opportunity is common sense, blatantly obvious, but extremely complex. I don't have to strain to sell it or to make people understand it, but execution will be tricky. In my opinion, this is just a concept whose time had come — a niche that's a natural. If we can execute the strategy we will be very successful.

Genus: Its Meaning and Its Mission

If you look up the meaning of the word "genus" in a commonly used Webster's dictionary, you will find: "A class, kind or group marked by common characteristics . . ."

That definition fits what our new company is all about. Genus is an appropriate name for this endeavor.

So we have created Genus Aesthetic Medical & Dental Group Inc.

What we're doing with Genus is assembling a unique collaboration of some of the world's leading practitioners of aesthetic medical and dental arts.

We're bringing together and extending the capabilities of high-quality

groups of aesthetic medical and dental professionals who all are committed to the same standards: They share the same vision of high-quality
care. They share the same vision of innovation and consistency. They
share a common commitment to teaching. They share the same vision of
having the latest in techniques and technologies available to serve their
patients.

Our vision is to create the laboratory for our affiliated doctors to
develop a high-end, high-quality "brand" on these collaborations, these
services, so patients can easily identify them and associate them with a
Genus standard.

When I explain how we will identify Genus-affiliated physicians and
dentists to the public, I describe the following analogy: Think of a high-
end collection of gourmet restaurants that feature delicious specialty
foods and all belong to one restaurant group — a group that goes by the
name "Chef's Choice." In a given city, restaurants that are members of
this hypothetical "Chef's Choice Group" might be located adjacent to
one another under one roof, near one another in a single neighborhood,
or scattered in different parts of the city. However, the consumer can
easily identify them because, no matter what an individual restaurant's
name might be, if it's a member of this group it will have the "Chef's
Choice Group" logo prominently displayed in front of its location.
When you see this logo, you'll know that the food served by this
restaurant stands for a standard of exceptional quality that has become
the trademark of this brand known as "Chef's Choice Group." Restaurants affiliated with "Chef's Choice Group" are located not only in one
city. Instead, they are located in various parts of the nation — situated
mainly in the more affluent neighborhoods that respond to the gourmet
food market. So, as a consumer who patronizes these restaurants, you
know what you get from Chef's Choice, regardless of the location.

If our strategy is executed as designed, consumers will be able to
identify high-quality, high-service aesthetic medical and dental services
with Genus. Just like the sought-after gourmet restaurants in the hypothetical "Chef's Choice Group," the Genus-affiliated physicians and
dentists will set the standard. Just as the "Chef's Choice" signs guide

consumers to the highest quality in gourmet dining, the Genus experience will guide consumers to the highest quality in aesthetic medicine and dentistry.

Genus Aesthetic Medical & Dental Group is both narrow and broad in focus. It is narrow in the sense that we are dealing only with the part of medicine and dentistry that's in the aesthetic and reconstructive arena. We are not dealing, for example, with doctors whose practices focus on intensive, life-threatening conditions. We focus on wants and not needs. However, the focus of Genus is broad once we get inside the self-improvement and youth preservation arena. We pursue a wide range of services that fall under the umbrella of aesthetic medicine and dentistry. Genus sees a connectivity, an ability to capture the full scope of services and the interrelationships among them.

The physicians, dentists and other service providers with whom Genus will link will represent areas such as:

- Plastic and Aesthetic Surgery
- Esthetic and Restorative Dentistry
- Cosmetic Dermatology
- Orthodontics
- Oral and Maxillofacial Surgery
- Hair Restoration and Hair Removal
- Prosthodontic and Implant Dentistry
- Ancillary Services and Products

Genus will go beyond linking with the physicians and dentists to provide business support and create a network of high-quality aesthetic services. This opportunity is expansive and retail. We must educate and promote. We must decipher and clarify information about aesthetic services for the confused consumer.

As part of this key execution point, we'll be focused on creating a "virtual university" where the most current and best information is deposited, catalogued, and made accessible.

Freedom from Third-party and Systems

One morning in the early Fall of 1997, I was meeting with some investment bankers as part of my objective to educate the investment community about Genus.

During the meeting, I was telling these bankers about the different components of Genus, explaining how the business would work. From time to time they would stop me to make sure they understood a point I had just made, or to ask a question about an issue I had not yet addressed.

These guys were knowledgeable, very tuned in to some of the issues facing many in the healthcare industry.

One of these bankers asked me an interesting question, a very relevant question — a question I was more than happy to answer. Our conversation went like this:

"Bill, what about the information systems Genus will need — to deal with billing and third-party reimbursement?" the banker asked me.

"We don't need them," I told him. "Genus won't need these complex information systems, because Genus won't be focusing its growth and expansion on third-party payers. We are not taking risk. We will need basic financial systems to consolidate financial reporting and create operating statistics and reports, which you can do very simply and in a non-capital intensive manner. Genus is not a claim-form, referral-authorization business. We don't need all the superfluous paper."

The banker paused and thought a minute, reflecting on the needs of fee-for-service, direct patient-care payment.

"You know, Bill, you're right. You are dealing directly with patients, clients, consumers. You're not going through third parties," he said. "You are not complicating the purchase decision."

He obviously was pleased with my answer.

I can't tell you how pleased I was to be able to give him that answer. I felt that I helped him "break the code" in understanding a core element in our strategy.

It is my opinion that one of the problems with healthcare in general is the third-party involvement. It complicates the equation. I believe the more dependent you and your company are on a third party, the more complicated and unmanageable it gets.

On the other hand, the more direct a relationship you can have between purchaser and seller — where patients and doctors have clear expectations and responsibilities — the higher opportunity you have to add value and increase the understanding of the purchase transaction.

This freedom from the third-party, managed-care element is one of the key reasons I saw Genus as such an opportunity. Understanding the elements of a direct seller-purchaser decision creates a unique opportunity in the healthcare arena. In this retail aesthetic medicine and dentistry market, I really like that one-to-one, doctor-to-patient aspect — where you don't have a third party making decisions and complicating the once-revered doctor-patient relationship. Here we have come full circle. Back to the relationship — the patient; and the person who provides the service, the doctor.

When I was working at MedPartners, I was aware that I was involved in some pioneer initiatives that were making history in this young industry. I knew I was part of the laboratory which had positive impacts on physician-practice structure, patient care, and shareholder reward. I am proud to have been a participant at that pivotal time when the PPM industry still was in its infancy.

But even with all the good, that third-party issue still loomed heavy for me. There were days when I felt we were beating our heads against the wall chasing that declining dollar in a managed-care environment, with the third-party element in the middle, and the lack of systems to guide us along the way. It's difficult enough having to deal with third-party and managed care under any circumstances. It would be onerous had we had excellent, targeted information systems to serve as a map. But those systems were not and are not there to the extent that's needed, as I discussed in Chapter 5 of this book.

I saw, plain and simple, that the systems we needed didn't exist, that the systems had to be developed, that it was going to take a significant time to develop them, and that while you're developing them the leverage is still held by the third-party payer.

I know Genus will face its own sets of challenges and opportunities that are distinctly different from traditional PPMCs. Many of the challenges we will face will be the kind you find in the retail business. I'm ready for the retail challenges.

The Retail Concept

The most intriguing aspect of the Genus vision and strategy is the retail aspect. That's the main thing that excites me, drives me, and puzzles me.

Within this retail vision and strategy, I think our biggest challenge is to create and sustain the "brand," to establish Genus firmly as a brand preference, a trusted seal of approval.

To be successful in retail, you have to differentiate yourself from everybody else. You have to carve out your own unique niche and communicate that niche to the consumer. The name you give your niche, the identity that you place on that niche, is your brand.

Our brand name is Genus. Our vision is to make that brand name a symbol for very specific traits. We want Genus to stand for the standard in high-end, high-quality aesthetic medicine and aesthetic dentistry. When a consumer thinks of aesthetic medical and dental services, we want that person's mind to turn to Genus in the same context that he or she would think of a Mercedes-Benz or a Lexus as a top choice for an automobile or a Ritz-Carlton hotel suite as a premier choice for lodging.

What I envision is a situation in which a consumer selects a Genus affiliate because he or she trusts that a Genus affiliate has proven, state-of-the-art technology, that the provider is well trained, and there's a high service standard.

There's a tremendous opportunity here in aesthetic medicine and dentistry with this "service standard" and "trust" element. Many of our affiliates and potential affiliates have defined standards of quality and have focused on customer service. We feel their experience and leadership will be one of the keys in our success. As consumers, we all want the guys who "wrote the book" to establish the quality of the product and we want it delivered to us in a certain way. Our vision and strategy for the Genus service standard is for every Genus client to feel "special" and "catered to." Our Genus service standard is one in which the client feels that his or her individual needs, questions, and expectations are addressed both with competence and caring. Our vision and strategy is to have a Genus service standard in which each client receives the kind of personal attention you would expect if you went into an exclusive upscale clothing boutique or hair salon. A growing dissatisfaction exists among American consumers in reaction to the depersonalization that has accompanied the mega-supermarkets, expansive department stores, and rambling discount houses. At Genus we want our clients to receive exceptional care and attention. At the same time, we also want them to feel they are in a very special, personal place — where everyone around them takes pleasure in anticipating and meeting their needs and fulfilling their expectations.

To establish and sustain Genus as a brand, we will invest in training on a significant and ongoing basis.

In the retail arena of aesthetic medical and dental services, I think there's room for a high-end provider. I want Genus to be the trusted company.

The Market

We see a domestic market size of at least $35 billion a year spent on the services that Genus has targeted. Our plan is to understand and tap into that market heavily, and to grow considerably our share of that market.

According to the difficult-to-assemble research data, the current tab of $35 billion can be broken down into approximately $18 billion on plastic surgery and related services and some $17 billion in the aesthetic dental arts field. I've studied this "data" closely and I feel the estimates are very conservative.

The consumers who are pursuing these services fall heavily into the baby-boomer population — those in their 40s and 50s. They fall heavily into the more affluent socioeconomic groups — the middle-class, upper middle-class and the wealthy. Although women still make up the majority of consumers, males are the fastest growing segment.

What we're seeing here are three key trends that are converging at the same crossroads:

- The aging of the huge baby-boomer population — a population which as a group already has displayed a concern for youth preservation and self-improvement. This population contains a healthy chunk of people who are willing and affluent enough to seek out aesthetic services and spend money for them.
- Phenomenal progress in technique and technology which has made it possible and safer to perform a wide range of services to make people look better and feel better.
- A growing public-image acceptance of accessing these services. This has become an era in which it's increasingly commonplace for a man or woman to consider some aesthetic procedure as having a valuable place not just in someone else's life, but in his or her own life.

An Attitude, a Lifestyle

Needless to say, I've done a lot of thinking and analyzing over the past several months about what has brought this $35 billion industry to this point and how we can help grow it further.

I view this aesthetic medical and dental market as a major retail opportunity looking for a place to happen. There's growth potential here, tremendous growth potential. I foresee, within a matter of a few years, that this will be a huge industry — so big that it will make that $35 billion figure look pale by comparison. There will be more and more of us who'll be out there picking our smiles out of books and writing checks to make those bags under our eyes disappear. As a nation, we're getting older. Longevity statistics alone tell some of that story. And, as the years roll by, we are becoming increasingly aware of effective procedures available out there which can take years off our appearance, making us look and feel younger and enjoy a better quality of life.

We also are aware that all this is not just an appearance issue; it also can be a performance issue as well. If we feel better about ourselves, we often perform better in our various roles in life — in our work, and in our social and romantic relationships.

This whole market is being driven by multiple components. It's demographic. It's psychographic. It's an attitude. And gradually, for many people, it's becoming a lifestyle.

The lifestyle of which I speak is being the best you can be, looking the best you can, feeling the best about yourself you can possibly feel. It's not just a product-specific or procedure-specific issue we're talking about. It's a mind-set.

Our goal with Genus is to harness this attitude — to expand the number of people who pursue a "look better-feel better" lifestyle, to adhere to a standard that builds trust in Genus to help make such a lifestyle a reality.

Using the "look better-feel better" lifestyle mind-set as a foundation, we're also trying to direct the potential consumers toward Genus. We are creating the perception that Genus is special; we are making that perception "the real thing" by creating an assemblage of the world's best people sharing a common vision.

When I think of the concept of a product being "special" and being central to a lifestyle, I think of Nike. Is Nike just a tennis shoe or a sportswear line? It's true that Nike makes a great tennis shoe and it makes a great sportswear line. But what's behind Nike is more of a lifestyle. It's not just a tennis shoe, not just a sportswear line. It stands for something beyond the tennis shoe. Nike is an attitude, a thought process.

That's where we're headed with Genus. That's what's so challenging in this whole branding concept. We are focusing on the perception that Genus in terms of quality and high-end is on a level with the Nike brand, the Mercedes-Benz brand. We are creating this image, this quality, this standard of performance and service with which people can identify and which they can trust.

Not Just Accepting the Inevitable

This "look better-feel better" product is a concept that's consistent with so many perceptions and experiences to which baby boomers were exposed during the particular era in which they grew up in America.

These people grew up in the 1950s and 1960s. It was a time when America was having an industrialized and technological boom. The

Space Age was evolving and the nation was putting men in space — in fact, making it possible for men to walk on the moon.

Baby boomers grew up with the "can-do" attitude, with the concept that things could be better, that situations could be improved and often totally "fixed" by technology and technique. They came up expecting technology and technique to make their lives better. After all, it was post-World War II technology and technique that ushered into their lives the fancy automobiles, color televisions, home appliances, designer clothes, chic hairstyles, youthful cosmetics, and healthcare drug and surgery miracles.

The whole concept of aging came to be viewed so differently by baby boomers than it typically had been seen by their parents and grandparents before them. In decades gone by, men and women in their 40s or 50s or 60s were more likely to somehow accept looking older and acting older as a product of inevitability. They were likely, at around age 40 or so, to begin to give in to the aging process and settle for living "the youth thing" vicariously through their children and grandchildren. However, the baby boomers didn't grow up thinking that way. As the baby boomers themselves became moms an dads and a few years later entered their own 40s and 50s, they still bought the designer clothes and got the chic haircuts and watched their weight and went to the gym to work out. So, when aesthetic medical and dental services began to be increasingly available, it was just a "natural" for the baby boomers to go a step further and consider enhancing parts of their bodies which were sagging, wrinkling, fading, thickening, thinning, missing, or doing something else they didn't like.

After all, they had seen firsthand since childhood that so many things in this life are possible, that you don't have to sit back and accept the ravages of time.

The Fastest-growing Market — Men!

I find it fascinating, and quite exciting from a market-size standpoint, that men are the fastest-growing consumer segment of the aesthetic business.

Men were understandably much slower than women to find some of these aesthetic procedures acceptable. But they've seen what these aesthetic procedures can do for men. They're seen men who have benefited — seen them in the movies and on TV and in the magazines and also have seen aesthetic benefits among men they know.

Gradually over the past couple of decades, other trends and other products have influenced men to think it's okay for a man to be concerned with his appearance. For example, it was only 15 to 20 years ago when blow dryers still weren't "cool" for men. You weren't a "real man" if you used a blow dryer. And, a decade or two ago, men used only the most basic of masculine fragrances. Look at those male markets today for fragrances and blow dryers, and aggregate dollars spent.

Similarly, I predict that we're going to see an absolutely phenomenal rise in the demand by men for aesthetic medical and dental services. This same guy who is driving the Lexus and wearing the Rolex watch and collecting fine wines and smoking expensive cigars is going to want it all. He's going to want his appearance to match everything else in his "good life."

Some Typical Customers

Let's take a look at the types of consumers who already are partaking of what's out there for them in aesthetic medical and dental services:

It's the kind of "look better-feel better" attitude and mind-set that already has helped this industry reach the current $35 billion. It's the kind of thinking that will help it to continue to grow:

- A woman just entering her 50s is still very attractive. However, she decides there are a few things she will have "fixed" — the chin that's sagging a bit, some facial wrinkles that are deepening, a few spidery veins that are marring her bathing suit look, a smile that could use some enhancement. So off she goes to the world of aesthetic medical and dental services to launch her "overhaul."
- A man in his 40s knows he's dead-ended in the corporate structure where he now works. He decides to look elsewhere for a better job opportunity. In addition to getting his resume up-to-date and

taking inventory of job opportunities to explore, he decides to take ten years off his appearance by having a procedure to remove the bags under his eyes and lift his drooping eyelids, and another procedure to fill in his balding spot with hair replacement.

And, as we're well aware, there are many, many consumers of aesthetic services who are not baby boomers — who are considerably younger or older. These are a few typical profiles of other potential aesthetic-services consumers to whom we'll be marketing Genus services:

- A 14-year-old girl is very self-conscious about her large nose. Her parents decide a perfect birthday gift for her will be a "new" nose — one shaped by plastic surgery.

- A 28-year-old young man is doing well in his career and is reasonably happy with his social life. However, despite his broad-shouldered build and nice features, he does not have a good feeling about his appearance. His crooked teeth are the problem. His parents could not afford orthodontics when he was a child. He has seen excellent results with adult orthodontics, and he decides now is the time to address this issue in his life.

- A young woman in her mid-20s has been self-conscious ever since her teenage years because she is extremely flat-chested. After reading about women who have been very pleased with the results of breast augmentation surgery using the newer technology, she undergoes the procedure. She's happier with the results than she ever dreamed possible. For example, a whole new world of choices opens up to her in clothing that she now can wear very becomingly. As often is the case with women who undergo breast augmentation, this young woman opts to go a couple of steps further and to have more aesthetic work. She finds herself smiling more now because she feels so good about herself, so she has cosmetic dentistry. She's happier with the way her figure looks from a side view, so she decides to enhance her facial profile by undergoing a procedure to deal with a chin she has never liked.

- A young woman in her early 30s has given birth to three children. She still has a size-8 figure. However, a combination of childbearing and just getting a bit older has deposited a couple of extra inches around her middle. So she opts for liposuction.

- A 65-year-old woman has been a widow for a couple of years. In the initial months after her husband's death, she went through a difficult grieving period and stayed to herself a great deal. But, in recent months, she has begun to come to grips with her loss. She's getting out more — is involved with community and church volunteer work, has taken a couple of trips with friends, and is meeting new people. She has just reached the decision that it's time for her to seek still another kind of "lift" — a face-lift.

The Challenge to Educate and Direct Consumers

I was talking recently to a well-educated professional young man, telling him about our focus on aesthetic medical and dental services.

He said this to me: "You know, if I were having something like plastic surgery, I wouldn't know what to look for. I'd really need someone I trusted to give me quality information about what can be done and who I should see to do it. If I had somebody who could logically take the confusion away and communicate to me what's good and what's bad, what defines quality, and what would be 'right' for me, I would feel much more confident and be more inclined to undergo plastic surgery."

This young man is far from being alone. Even though there is a growing market for aesthetic medical and dental services, there still is a tremendous amount of ambivalence and confusion among potential consumers.

People are confused because they don't have the kind of information they need about aesthetic services. And they don't know where to go to get the information. Many had been misled by an over-sensationalizing media which likes to focus on catastrophes.

I think there exists a real opportunity to sort through this confusion for consumers, to educate people as to what is possible and to direct them toward quality providers. It is our goal at Genus to both educate consumers about what's possible and then guide them to quality providers.

In the midst of this confusion, I have heard consumers asking these types of things in particular:

One question facing many consumers is simply "What's available?" There's a lot of information out there — in newspapers, magazines, on the Internet, etc. But I'm convinced that many people have heard a little bit of this and a little bit of that and they don't really understand the big picture. They don't understand the technologies and the techniques. They don't really know the ins and outs about the lasers and microscopes and the new aesthetic materials. They're confused about the various options for a specific type procedure which interests them. They don't know if they've heard all their options. They don't know what to expect.

A second consumer question that comes to my mind is "What provider should I select to perform an aesthetic service for me?" Advertising and promotion of these aesthetic medical and dental procedures have been so undifferentiated that many consumers don't really have any idea as to what provider does what. Many people don't understand which providers are educated and trained and licensed to do this or that. They don't know how to evaluate the quality of the providers and the level of their credentials. They don't know what's safe and what's not safe. They don't know the right choice for their own particular needs. They hear all the sensationalism, sometimes good, but too often bad.

And a third question that no doubt goes through the minds of many considering aesthetic work is "Should I even bother to do this or just leave things as they are?" There no doubt are many, many people who have the desire to have aesthetic services but who just haven't had anything or anybody motivate them to take that step. Or, perhaps they haven't seen the data which confirms that better-looking people have a competitive edge.

Our goal and challenge with Genus is to develop and implement some very targeted educational and promotional campaigns aimed at answering for the consumer these questions of "What's available?" and "What provider should I choose?" and "What value is there for me to really decide to do this?"

Our goal and challenge is to take some of this latent interest in aesthetic medical and dental services and, with the help of consumer education, to convert latent interest into happier people.

This is what I believe the marketing challenge is for Genus: To take this large and growing population, educate them, and motivate them to move in a direction that is beneficial to them, beneficial to our physicians, dentists, and other specialists, and beneficial to Genus.

That's the consumer-education formula we're looking for. It has never been done on a broad scale. It's the core to this retail aspect of the Genus strategy.

8

The Shared Vision: Aligned Incentives for the Doctors and the Company

YOU MEET a beautiful woman and start seeing her socially. You like her, and she likes you. Then you start considering marriage. So you talk about more serious issues. You share your plans for the future, and she shares hers. To your disappointment, you find that what's important to her doesn't have a real priority with you, and vice versa.

So, where do you go from there with this relationship? The way I see it is this: You can like one another, you can see one another. Maybe down the road, if your mutual priorities come together, you might even marry one another. But for right now, you don't have aligned incentives. You don't have a shared vision for the future. And it probably doesn't make a lot of sense to get married.

That's how I see it with the physicians and dentists we're talking to about partnering with Genus Aesthetic Medical & Dental Group.

We tell them up front: What we're talking about here is a common vision. This is long-term. Companies and doctors in this partnering environment are looking to do long-term transactions — with the same permanent element people look for when they're thinking of getting married. So if the doctors and the company don't have the same view of where we're headed, we shouldn't get married. Period. Shake hands and move on.

From my years of experience in the doctor-partnering industry, I would strongly advise both doctor-groups and management companies to place an up-front, number-one, top priority on making sure they have a shared vision before they spend the time, effort and money pursuing an agreement for their future.

To have a shared vision when you're embarking on a partnership, you must have a common set of goals and you must have an effective dialogue between the company's leadership and the leadership on the doctors' side. You must have a clear mutual understanding as to what you are trying to accomplish.

Reflecting back on my experience at MedPartners, in situations where the doctors and the company share this common vision, those relationships tend to work very, very well. In situations where there is not the common vision, it's not going to work and you consume many nonproductive hours and waste resources.

The Three-legged Stool and the Seesaw

When a doctor-group and a management company form a partnership, each side of this partnership has far-reaching "powers" and huge responsibilities that go along with those powers.

The doctors are responsible for the patients.

The company is responsible for the checkbook.

Both are responsible for establishing systems which meet each other's needs. That's what makes the relationship a true partnership rather than a mere "arrangement."

Jointly the two partners develop the vision of where they're going and the strategy of how to get there. Jointly they develop the vision and strategy that relate to services for the patients and resources needed to provide those services, handling the staffing and money management, and creating new opportunities of mutual benefit.

In going forward as partners, you have to have a balance in your relationship if you are to have this "shared vision."

By "balance" I mean a balance of power, a balance of ideas and motivation and input, and a balance of respect for one another.

You can't have the management company going in with the approach that everything the doctor-group has been doing previously was wrong and needs to be restructured — "throwing out the baby with the bath-water" so to speak. You can't have a doctor-group dictating to the management company as though the company's people are neophytes. You can't have either the doctors or the company coming up with all the ideas and timetables for the future and stuffing it down the throat of the other.

You've got to have a balance in which each partner is willing to carry his weight and willing to allow the other partner to carry his.

It's like the three-legged stool.

It's like the seesaw.

It has to be a symbiotic relationship or it will unravel.

At MedPartners, we used the "three-legged stool" analogy to illustrate the need to balance a physician's role in the healthcare system. At that time, we were referring to the need for a physician to have a balance of power with the other two key players in the healthcare system — the hospital and the third-party payer. That analogy still applies today for doctors in the traditional healthcare environment. It is the hospital which controls much of that physician's work environment and partici-pates in a major way in caring for his patients. It is the third-party payer which pays that doctor most of the money he receives for the patient-care services he performs. For the doctor to have a balance in his work life, the three legs of that stool have to work together in equilibrium. The stool needs to stand strongly on all three legs and be mutually beneficial to all three components. If changes are being made at the hospital that are in the hospital's interest but are bad for the doctor, you've got a conflict. Because if the hospital ends up "owning" the doctor, the doctor's leg of the stool weakens and could totally collapse — thus leaving only the hospital's leg of the stool and the third-party payer's leg of the stool intact. The same is true if the third-party abuses the doctor's interest. If the payer extracts more from the equation than the payer is entitled to, if the physician is being punished economically because the arbitrage is benefiting the payer to an excessive degree, then here again the physician's leg of the stool becomes weak.

When it comes to a doctor-partnering relationship, the roles of the management company and the doctor-group differ considerably from the roles in the "three-legged" stool analogy about the doctor, the hospital, and the third-party payer. However, the message about the need for balance is the same.

The seesaw is another analogy that comes to my mind when I think of balance in a doctor-partnering relationship. Neither a doctor-group nor a management company wants to be on one end of a seesaw that's out of balance with the partner on the other end of the seesaw. No one wants to be stuck on the ground or up in the air because he's on a seesaw ride that's like having an elephant on one end and a mouse on the other.

The Big Six

A "recipe" for setting up a doctor-group/management company partnership that has a shared vision is to have your priorities in order when you're creating the partnership.

I have six priorities I think you need to consider in deciding whether and how to put together an affiliation. I call them "The Big Six."

One of those six priorities is money, the economic potential for both parties in the transaction.

However, in my opinion, where a lot of people make their mistake is that they incorrectly put the economic issue first when they're involved in early negotiating and planning. They're primarily and often excessively focused on how much money is involved, what the multiple is, the economic considerations of the business model. Some people tend to be totally absorbed and preoccupied with this money issue to the exclusion of everything else.

Money is important. I'll talk more about that later. However, if you put a top priority on the money in front-end discussions, I view this as a potentially damaging reversal in proper ordering of priorities — a reversal that could blur your ability to do a good job with the other five priorities.

In addressing "The Big Six" on my list, I actually like to list the money last. I'd say to either a doctor-group or a management company: "Make sure you look at the first five before you look at number six." I don't leave the money issue until last because it's the least important. I leave it to last because it's very important and deserves to have the first five priorities sorted through early on to protect and ensure it.

Here are The Big Six:

1. Do your "due diligence" on one another — to find what makes one another tick and see if you think you have a match.

If you're a doctor-group looking at a management company, ask these questions: "Why was this company founded in the first place? What is the company's mission and how is it set up to meet this mission? What types of doctor-groups does this company serve best and what can the company do for these groups? Does the mission of this management company fit the needs of our particular group? What kind of management talent does this company have? What is the track record of the people in this company? What kind of depth do they have? Does this management company have the potential to add significant value to our doctor-group, to make it stronger and more profitable than it could be on its own or by partnering with another management company?"

If you're a management company looking at a doctor-group for possible partnering, your due diligence should include the asking of these questions: "Is this a doctor-group which would add credibility to the company? Is this a doctor-group to which our company could add value? Is it a doctor-group whose culture and needs and opportunities match with our company's resources? What is this doctor-group's history, its reputation, its style, its market? What are this doctor-group's strengths and weaknesses? In light of the group's market and its competitors and present realities and future likelihoods and possibilities, what does this group want to become and are its expectations realistic? Can we help this doctor-group to meet its potential?"

2. Share your ideas in terms of your vision and your strategy — here again, to see if you have a match. (Actually, this sharing of vision and strategy will be a natural and crucial extension of your due diligence on one another.) I've found that individuals in leadership positions sometimes tend to put their own spins on what they mean by these terms of "vision" and "strategy."

My definitions are pretty basic and rather unromanticized. I see vision as using your imagination to conceive long-term objectives. And I see strategy as coming up with plans and methods to meet those objectives. To me, vision and strategy are so closely related that I often talk about them as going hand in hand and even sometimes refer to them as a single unit. I guess that's because I'm an impatient guy who likes to see results as soon as possible. I'm not comfortable with sitting around for months or years contemplating what your vision is going to be before you start coming up at the same time with some plans for how to make that vision a reality. Thus, the term "strategic vision" suits my purposes. I think if you're a doctor-group and a management company who are considering "getting married," you need to get to know each other in relation to your "strategic vision."

You need to know if you're seeing eye-to-eye on these issues. These are questions for both the doctor-group and the management company to address as they have initial talks about strategic vision: "What ideas do both parties have to help a doctor-group define its vision in a way that spots key opportunities? Where do the doctor-group and the company stand in terms of style and attitude and resources and talents to implement strategy? What are the long-term goals and timetables envisioned by the two potential parties? And, very important — again, I'm an impatient guy who likes to see results — what are some short-term initiatives that are going to make this new partnership valuable?" Now, before you start putting your signatures on any lines in a partnership agreement, you as the doctor-group and you as the company need to recognize that, where your "marriage" is concerned, vision and strategy are more than just well-worn business terms. These are your maps for deciding where you want to go, your vision, and how you plan to get there, your strategy.

3. Evaluate the "fit" of the management company's business model with the doctor-group's business plan as they apply to a partnership.

Ask yourselves a few key questions: "Does this particular doctor-group fit the way it should into the business model being used by the management company? Does the management company fit the needs and goals addressed in the doctor-group's business plan? What kinds of alterations, tailoring, and modifying can be done by either party to make this relationship a more workable one?" I'm a firm believer in tailoring business models and business plans to fit individual situations.

I also believe there are appropriate and inappropriate ways to go about doing this. For one thing, when obvious problems and non-fits are spotted with a business model or a business plan, address them up front rather than ignoring them and just hoping things will work out on their own. A second rule: In addressing and tailoring some of these situations, be professional. State your differing viewpoints clearly, but state them with respect and an open mind. Don't just talk; also listen. On the one hand, don't fail to address pressing issues because you're afraid of hurting someone's feelings, of bruising an ego and crashing a deal. At the same time, don't go out of your way to be critical and abrasive if you think some constructive changes are in order. If the two of you as potential partners can't talk respectfully to one another early on about details in a business model and a business plan, you're sure to run into communication problems down the road.

And a third rule: If you try doing some alterations and you still don't come up with a "fit," don't strain yourselves to the point that you remake your group or company into something that you don't want or need to be. Sometimes it's just better to back off and not pursue a transaction right then if the business model and the business plan place you too out of sync — and if further alteration doesn't seem the thing to do. I've seen cases in which two parties came out feeling good about their due diligence on one another, had a good experience with preliminary talks about strategy and vision, but then ran head-on into unresolvable differences when it got down to the nuts and bolts of the "fit" of the company's business model and the doctor-group's business plan. If you hit a roadblock and decide the fit isn't there, it's like that relationship with the beautiful girl: Postponing a marriage for right now doesn't necessarily mean saying good-bye forever. You might return and find that things work better at a later time.

4. Make sure your partnership can be structured so that the two parties are mutually incentivized. You must be incentivized in the same direction. Ask yourselves: "Do we have a situation here where what's 'good' is good for both, and what's 'bad' is bad for both?" If the answer is "yes" and you indeed are mutually incentivized, then you have increased your chances of having a partnership that's structured toward a win-win experience for both parties.

5. Add value to the doctor-group on a sustainable basis. If you don't think you can answer a heartfelt "yes" to the questions in this category, you probably should not engage. The questions are: "Is this something that can help both parties profit on a long-term basis? Is this a partnership that can make it possible to bring sustainable growth, operating improvement, and marketshare improvement? Is this a partnership that can accomplish those goals not just on a temporary basis of a few weeks or a few months, but over a period of years?" Both parties need to be focused on added value that has staying power, that will last. I'd compare this to the professional singer who has a "one-song hit" but then quickly disappears into entertainment oblivion, as compared to the professional singer who has the creative vision, lasting talent, untiring commitment, and rich song material to build a singing career that can be sustained over a period of many years — hit song after hit song.

6. The Economic Model. The money issue.

The Money

Much of the long-term success in a doctor-group/management company partnership boils down to what ends up in people's pockets.

If a management company is not able to show evidence of value on doctor incomes, the partnership won't stay together on the long-term.

At the same time, in a mutually incentivized model, if the doctors aren't doing well financially, the management company isn't doing well financially either. It's called: What's good financially for you is good for me, and vice versa.

In my experience in the doctor-partnering business, I've found that some of the major joint celebrations between doctors and the company have been due to economic progress. The opposite also is true: When friction brews between the doctors and the company, the most common source of problems is money.

You can establish relationships built largely on trust, and relationships that are built on momentum. However, you won't be able to keep these relationships together long-term without economic success. The bottom line in these relationships' survival indeed is money.

The honeymoon period to see positive economic results is relatively short.

The Valuation Process — More than a Formula

PPM companies have different ways of approaching the "valuation process" for determining the purchase price of an individual practice.

Variations in the basic economic model portion of the valuation process can occur on details such as percentages, multiples paid for goodwill, amounts paid for hard assets, etc. Also, variations in this valuation process can occur to the degree that a PPM company uses a "formula approach."

In terms of the basic economic concept, these PPM companies generally buy a percentage of the doctors' ongoing revenue stream. In addition to paying the purchase price, the management company is adding value to the doctors with a package of management resources and access to capital for technology improvements, efficiency improvements and expansion.

In the valuation process used by Genus Aesthetic Medical & Dental Group, a multivariable equation is the guide.

We are buying a minority interest in the earnings stream of a practice, and this earnings stream is projected on a set of factors. We are not using a rigid formula approach.

I think it can be a real problem in a PPM transaction if the valuation process becomes too "formula-driven." By that I mean it can become a real problem if you use a formula approach that focuses solely on economic-model factors such as the multiple, the earnings, etc. — an approach that can overlook other significant factors that also strongly impact valuation. If you are going to understand a transaction, the valuation process cannot be just a formula.

In my view what's going to happen is the successful PPM companies are going to get better at using valuation approaches which are multivariable. As a result of this multivariable approach, I think we're going to see the successful companies creating stronger long-term relationships with their partners that will be characterized by more aligned incentives, consistency and direction. As a result of this multivariable approach, the successful PPM companies will be looking at businesses not just with current conditions in mind, but futuristically.

At Genus, in taking the position that valuation is a complicated decision, we've tailored our valuation process to look at components that add up to the true value of the enterprise: You have to look at historical trends of the practice. You have to look at issues like capacity and marketshare. You have to look at management. You have to look at the balance sheet. You have to look at issues such as capital investment — how much capital investment is needed to expand the revenue. You have to look at how the management company can increase the value of this business.

All those things have to be factored in. You can do justice to a valuation process only after you have taken this multivariable approach with a significant amount of due diligence, financial modeling and pro forma development.

You need to share with your partners-to-be the information you gather during this process. This information-sharing is consistent with alignment of incentives, with enabling you and your "partners" to share the same strategic vision.

It's imperative to link this valuation process to sharing the same strategic vision down the road. I know from years of observation and experience that the actual purchase produces psychological benefits that last from a few minutes to maybe 60 days in the minds of the seller. Beyond the purchase, the real test rests with the ongoing economic condition and trends for the mutually incentivized parties to those transactions.

The Doctor as a Businessman

One of the biggest misconceptions in the world is that doctors are bad businessmen.

I just don't buy that position. I think it's about as accurate as the statement that country lawyers aren't smart. I think often doctors are pretty damn good businessmen, and it's not uncommon to see doctors who in fact are excellent businessmen.

In the past decade and a half, I've earned my living by dealing closely with doctors. Over the years, I've observed among doctors the same range of capabilities and skills that you'll run into in any profession. I've seen enough to know that it is a real mistake to assume a blanket stereotype of doctors in the role of inept businessmen.

It was while I was with MedPartners that I got a healthy taste of how wrong this stereotype really is. At MedPartners we would often go into physicians' practices with the goal of improving business functions, only to discover that there was not much opportunity for improvement in areas we had anticipated improving. We held some original assumptions that we would encounter evidence of waste in the doctors' practice, that we would find fat, where a lot of costs could be eliminated. In practice, we discovered instead that a lot of these doctors were pretty good at what I would call "expense management." I'm defining "expense management" as managing costs well, making good decisions about matters such as supplies and salaries.

In addition to making good decisions about managing costs, I've also observed another real business-trait "positive" among doctors. I've found that doctors tend to be very good at making decisions period! Maybe not always the right decision. But I'll take someone who can make a decision, right or wrong, over someone who can't. The key is not making a wrong decision often. Good decision-making capabilities are not only desirable but indeed necessary talents for an effective leader to possess. However, even some executives in high positions in the general business world tend to have trouble with decisions. That's definitely not the case with the majority of doctors with whom I've dealt. Doctors are not afraid of decisions, and they don't have to muddle over things forever before they make decisions. But then that shouldn't be surprising if you really think about what a doctor and his work are all about. Doctors are well trained and tend to be very intelligent. As a daily part of their professional lives, they shoulder enormous responsibilities which entail numerous decisions. They are called upon to make one decision after another, frequently under intense pressure, often when a patient's very life or quality of life hangs in the balance. This ongoing experience doctors have in making decisions well and in a timely fashion definitely places them in a good position to deal effectively as a partner with a management company.

The Doctor as a Strategic Planner

If a lot of doctors are so good at business skills such as managing costs and making decisions, then why do they need the help of a management company?

How could a doctor benefit from having a partner who thinks the way a businessman thinks?

My answer is: The typical doctor needs a lot of help with strategic decisions. Often, it is a "time" factor. Strategic decisions require research, analysis, etc. The busy doctor could well benefit by having a partner who can bring research and analysis to the table for critical decision-making events to take place.

Along the same line, the doctor needs business help in overcoming some of his own habits and attitudes that can interfere with his being a good strategist.

As a rule, doctors in my opinion simply are not good strategic planners. I've said many times: "Businessmen by their very nature are strategic. Doctors are not strategic."

In today's competitive healthcare environment, if a doctor does not think and act strategically, he gets left behind. He can miss out on opportunities to maintain and expand his patient base and build organizations which are positioned for the future. He can miss out on options to merge with other doctor-groups. He can overlook and/or turn his back on valuable business opportunities that could serve him and his patients and family well.

Just because a doctor has not been strategic in the past does not mean he can't learn to be. I've interacted with doctors who in the past had never thought much about strategy one way or the other but who have turned out to be great at it. I've seen doctors who have had a lot of fun acting strategically, and have had even more fun seeing what well-thought-out and implemented plans could do for their lives and their businesses. However, learning how to plan strategy and how to implement strategy is like going to business school and studying under the case-study method. In essence the goal here is for the doctor to engage with people who have seen and lived through more business situations and circumstances than he has. That's where the business partner performs.

Reworking Outdated Doctor Attitudes

For a doctor to be good at strategic planning, he has to do more than learn how to identify business opportunities and negotiate deals.

The doctor has to learn more about himself and the way he traditionally has thought and acted all his professional life — especially how he has thought and acted in dealing with other doctors.

He has to take a look at his attitudes and his actions and his habits as they relate to strategic planning. This is especially true for the doctor moving more into the "retail" end of healthcare, for these concepts are not taught in traditional medical and dental school curricula.

(NOTE: Although my sentences are structured with the indefinite "he," I'm actually referring to "he" and "she." We all know the medical and dental professions are far from being a "he" society.)

I am identifying four primary trends in doctors' behaviors and attitudes that are enemies of good strategic planning. These are behaviors and attitudes which traditionally have been commonplace among doctors. They also are behaviors and attitudes which I firmly believe now are luxuries doctors no longer can afford if they are going to be good at business.

1. Doctors tend to tell their business secrets to everybody, and especially to other doctors. They tend to go into doctors' lounges and spill their guts about everything they're doing. Doctors get together and compare notes, and as a result everybody knows what everybody else is doing. If someone is doing a deal, then the other doctors know what that deal is — financial details, the whole thing. It doesn't matter if it has a diluting effect on a doctor's own shareholder interest or not; he's telling about terms and conditions. This has been the way doctors have interacted for decades. This is partly a holdover from the days when there was less competition among doctors for marketshare, when there was less competition among the hospitals and HMOs and other entities with which these doctors have affiliations. However, even though times have changed, doctors' habits about sharing their business secrets have not changed that much. I ask you this: Would a good strategic businessman go to a Rotary Club or Chamber of Commerce meeting and tell all his competitors basically every strategic move he is about to make? No way. His board and his shareholders would have his head.

2. Doctors tend to seek "consensus" among fellow doctors. Not only do many doctors tell other doctors what they are doing; they want the other doctors to approve of what they're doing. As an example in point, allow me to share with you a memorable experience I had almost a decade ago with a doctor's need for consensus. This was an experience in which I witnessed firsthand how this doctor-consensus thing can strike deathblows to strategic planning and proper execution of a plan.

The time frame I'm talking about is 1989 and 1990. In the several years prior to this, I had put together and was in charge of an organization which created a network of primary-care physicians for a large healthcare system. As an extension of that role, I became the leader in trying to get an innovative medical mall project off the ground in Birmingham, Alabama — a first-of-its-kind project for Birmingham and one of the first such medical malls in the United States. This was a project which was physician-driven and centered around patient convenience and non-duplication of services.

To explain how the doctor-consensus issue became so significant in this deal, let me give you a little background on the medical climate in Birmingham at that time. As many of you reading this may know, Birmingham is a city which for decades has been known for its booming healthcare industry. It's the home of a huge, long-established, diversified, and very successful group of healthcare enterprises. The Birmingham health scene is broadly based, with a first-class academic health center and not-for-profit and for-profit health systems which have spread their tentacles far and wide. However, as successful as this city was and is in the healthcare arena, Birmingham also has a history of being a conservative city which was a bit slow to warm to some of the entrepreneurial healthcare concepts. Over the past several years, Birmingham-based entrepreneurial companies like HealthSouth and MedPartners, and national for-profit companies with local links such as Tenet, have changed this climate tremendously. However, when I was trying to build doctor-support for the innovative medical mall concept back in 1989 and 1990, I faced a significant challenge.

On the one hand, the medical mall project had tremendous support — lots of physicians interested. The project also had a great deal of opposition, with some of the more conservative doctors looking at it as a threat to the status quo. Ultimately, I'm sorry to report that this medical mall project fell through; it never happened. I don't like being a player in failures, and fortunately I haven't experienced many of them. But that medical mall project was a failure — not in terms of concept or structure, but in terms of execution. I remember it well. And I learned from it. (I've found that you tend to learn a lot more from your failures than you do your successes. But I'm also convinced that you need to limit learning that way.)

There were several factors that figured into the failure in implementation. I'm going to talk about other factors in a "lessons learned" section later on in this book. However, there's no doubt in my mind that one reason this project never became a reality was the doctor-consensus issue. There was a physician working closely with me to put this project together who believed so strongly in consensus that it was a natural compass in his daily life. He was a fine man, a specialist with a reputation as an excellent clinician, and a doctor who was well respected among his peers.

But he was not the businessman-physician I should have had involved in this project. He did not have the "intestinal fortitude" or "transmission" to act strategically and decisively because he was so consumed by the political ramifications of every action we were taking. He was focused on wanting to set up meetings and invite local doctors and tell them everything we were doing, to make sure they all had an equal opportunity to hear the plan firsthand. Some of the doctors he wanted to involve in these meetings were known to be our opponents in this deal, were never going to agree with us, and instead were at risk to use inside information we supplied them as weapons against our project. Like I said, this doctor working with me was a great guy. But his style was to make everybody happy. I would say to any doctor who's interested in becoming a good strategic planner: You can't do anything cutting edge that's going to make everybody happy. You just can't do it. That kind of scenario doesn't exist. If you're consumed with consensus, you'll never make a good strategic planner.

3. Doctors often allow their egos to get in the way of good business by being jealous of other doctors and by not working with doctors who could help them. Now, doctors don't have a corner on the market in being jealous. There's widespread jealousy in many other professions as well. But I don't think it's any secret that the physician world is filled with more than an average amount of ego and jealousy. The way I see it, that kind of goes with the territory. It stands to reason that a great deal of drive and ego has to exist in the first place in most young men and women who decide to become doctors. They would have to believe intensely in their own capabilities to undertake the rigorous training they face and then to function daily in a profession that demands of them such incredible quotients of high performance, time, responsibility, stress and pressure.

Understandably one of the by-products would be and has been a high degree of competition and jealousy among doctors. However, the implications of ego and jealousy can be extremely negative in some of the newer business-related situations in which doctors find themselves today. Many doctors are now entering business arenas they've never entered before in which the existence of some of this jealousy and over-competition can cost them money and opportunity. Many jealous, competitive attitudes will have to be curbed among many doctors who now decide they want to be effective strategic planners. For example, a doctor in today's world might find it's more in his interest to cooperate with, rather than compete with, business-savvy doctors whom he formerly has shunned.

In the past, prior to today's business/doctoring "marriages," it was much easier for a doctor to turn his back on another doctor he thought was overly aggressive in a business sense. In today's world, by contrast, a doctor might find it's in his best interest to take a more open-minded look at some of these doctors who are stepping forward as facilitators and leaders on good business initiatives. I've seen well-structured opportunities make bedfellows of past enemies.

4. Doctors tend to be afraid of criticism which could come their way if they show businesslike streaks. I think in decades gone by there was a line of demarcation drawn that many people thought a doctor was not supposed to cross. To comply with this image pattern, a doctor was supposed to stick closely to his role of taking care of patients and not cross the line into the role of also being a strategist and a businessman. The doctor was not supposed to venture outside the box and do anything related to reaching out for a new business opportunity. It was as though the role of a doctor and the role of a business strategist were mutually exclusive. If the doctor became involved in a healthcare venture that obviously was set up both to take care of patients and to make money, the doctor often was viewed as having his mind only on making money and not also on caring for and about his patients.

Some of this kind of sentiment traditionally has been rather widespread. In light of this, it has been understandable that many doctors who have possessed natural business talent have been reluctant to step forward and use that talent, for fear that they would be criticized. But the pendulum is swinging. The pendulum is taking a big, wide swing. And it's moving fast. We're seeing in this nation the emergence of a way of thinking that's totally on the opposite side of the spectrum. We're seeing a trend for knowledgeable people to respect a doctor who understands both medicine and business. I would say to any doctor who has an interest in learning more about strategic planning: Before you become too afraid of the image that goes with this, make sure you're taking the temperature of public sentiment with a current thermometer instead of an outdated one.

Fear: The First Big Motivator

It was that all-powerful emotion of fear that drove many physicians to join up so rapidly in the late 1980s and early 1990s with the pioneer companies in the new industry known as physician practice management, or PPM.

Let's take a look at the unfolding of the healthcare-reform drama which fed that fear element.

The backdrop for this drama was painted when the days were simpler for the doctors, before all this so-called healthcare reform. In those days, most of the doctors were doing real well. A doctor came out of medical school, he hung his shingle, and he was immediately successful. Not too far down the road, he could buy himself a Mercedes, maybe two of them. As long as he worked, it was hard to lose. He basically was out there without a lot of financial risk, a machine in a market with plenty of demand.

But then, beginning in the early 1980s, all that began to change.

In one development after another, many physicians began to feel fear

— fear that their financial security and position in the healthcare order were eroding.

The turmoil was centered in Washington, D.C. And it was bipartisan. Both the Republicans and the Democrats were taking aim at healthcare costs. They were doing so in light of mounting concern because an increasing percentage of the gross national product was being claimed by healthcare expenditures.

The early 1980s marked the real beginning of what would be a chain of developments taking aim at what was paid out for healthcare services. Although hospitals were the first to take a direct hit, there was no way hospitals could be affected without doctors also being affected.

It was in a Republican Administration, the first Ronald Reagan Administration, when this system called "prospective payment" came into being to cap the rate of growth on hospital expenditures.

Then, before that rule was fully implemented, we got "DRGs," or diagnostic related groups, which totally changed the thought process and economics of the hospital business for governmentally paid-for services. Instead of more healthcare services being better, the Washington-endorsed goal suddenly was that less was better.

When you think about it, what was the concept behind DRGs? The concept was that the federal government, a big healthcare payer, was saying, "Time out! We're sick of paying the entire bill. We've accumulated all this data. We're going to shift some of the risk to the healthcare institutions. This is what we're going to pay, and only this. You guys (the healthcare providers) work it out. If you can't make ends meet with what we pay, you lose." So the risk was shifted.

This caused a big reorganization in hospitals. We began to see a major change in how hospitals did business. All of a sudden, hospital operations were inundated with business people and cost-accounting systems looking for a better way and a means to keep score.

In 1992, about the time I was involved in writing the initial business plan for MedPartners, the same kind of squeeze that already had come to the hospitals was tightening up on the doctors. They were experiencing risk, declining reimbursements, exclusion from plans and some capitation. They were experiencing increasing situations in which the risk was being shifted down more from the payer to the doctors. In many instances, the doctors were experiencing an instant replay of what already had been happening in the hospitals.

MedPartners was incorporated in January 1993, the same month that Bill Clinton was inaugurated for his first term as President. Even before the Clinton Administration went to work, the nation's doctors already were feeling the impact of mounting third-party payment limits, HMO initiatives and the escalation of this thing called managed care. Then, it seemed that no sooner had Bill Clinton taken the oath of office than the Clinton Administration began marching toward a goal of massive federally legislated healthcare reform. As a first step toward that goal, First Lady Hillary Rodham Clinton was named to guide the work of a much-publicized healthcare-reform task force. And the nation's doctors were saying, "Now we've already got all these mounting financial pressures, and here comes more of the same. Here comes a legislated healthcare reform. Hillary is going to make all this even worse. What the hell are we going to do?"

It was in this environment in which MedPartners began operation. We became partners with thousands of America's doctors during a period when this nation's medical community was experiencing its highest level of fear and unrest in history. Fear accelerated our success.

The strategy of MedPartners at this crucial time was this: Organize the physicians. Create this "clinical enterprise" that can engage, and let the company provide the infrastructure to help the doctors create equilibrium, as we discussed with "the three-legged stool." As we were starting MedPartners, we were thinking things like, "Hey, wait a minute. We've already been seeing healthcare reform. Now we're seeing threats of massive federally legislated healthcare reform. We see 650,000 physicians out there. These doctors are overwhelmed with change and risk. The doctors are incapable of managing risk because they don't have the infrastructure. The doctors are undercapitalized to take on new initiatives. When you add up all the healthcare services that the physicians control with their pens — doctor-services, hospital care, prescription drugs, etc. — we're looking at a doctor-controlled industry of $800 billion. Yet the doctors are the most fragmented and powerless piece of this equation. We see total fragmentation. And nobody is facilitating any kind of consolidation. PPM companies like MedPartners can help the doctors organize themselves effectively — something the doctors have never done." What an opportunity.

Although ultimately the Clinton Administration did not realize its full-blown legislated healthcare reform package, the healthcare-reform ideas projected by the Clinton Administration nevertheless had their impact. The ideas and issues raised by the First Lady's task force overflowed into the private health insurance sector and trickled into the chambers of Congress and State Legislatures, influencing and triggering changes both significant and subtle, both rapid and gradual. We already were having market-based healthcare reform anyway, and some of the ideas from the Clinton Administration fueled this even further. So healthcare reform was in place in America, in a big way and in a lasting way.

Simultaneously with the big-boom rapid-growth era for this new industry called physician practice management, another attempt out there trying to organize the doctors was the PHO movement, or "physician-hospital organization" movement. These PHOs were set up as organizations allegedly through which physicians could join hands with hospitals for mutual goals and benefits. The whole premise of this PHO concept is flawed on the front end, because doctors and hospitals have so many conflicting interests that there's no way they can create and enjoy this arrangement I call "a shared vision." The economic interests of a hospital and the economic interests of doctors who are in private practice and work at that hospital are not aligned. I don't hold back much in speaking my mind about the PHO concept. I think it's about the most ineffective mechanism ever thought about in healthcare, and I personally have never seen any evidence in the entire United States that a PHO has ever really worked. The bulk of the third-party payment system doesn't even recognize the PHOs. The PHOs did, with all due respect, make many lawyers, accountants and consultants rich.

When the physician practice management industry was gaining such rapid steam on the national medical scene in the early 1990s, many doctors considered PPM companies, (PPMCs) because they already had experienced an unproductive run with a physician-hospital organization, or PHO. A lot of these doctors saw a business company like MedPartners as someone they could link with who didn't have the conflicting interests they intuitively observed with hospitals. I've talked to many doctors who were turning away from a PHO and toward a PPMC whose view was: "With a physician practice management company as a vehicle, we can align with an entity that can help us through this tough period. These business people are on our side. Unlike hospitals, the business companies don't have hospital beds they want us to fill, or surgery centers they want us to support, or diagnostic facilities they want us to utilize for our diagnostic tests. They're basically going to add resources to help us deal with this complex situation in which we find ourselves."

MedPartners was not the first physician practice management company in the United States. However, MedPartners was destined to grow rapidly into the nation's largest PPMC. We had a CEO, Larry House, with an insatiable desire for growth, and a market waiting for us. I think we were very fortunate with MedPartners as to when we hit the market. Timing can be everything. And in the case of MedPartners, there's no doubt that timing was a factor in the company being able to move so fast in consolidating the doctors. There's no question that the fear factor was the major motivator in bringing about that consolidation.

Bringing in the Business Specialist

Although Bill Clinton had not yet been elected President in late 1992 when I was organizing some of the original MedPartners business plan, much of the handwriting was clearly on the wall.

The talk of escalated Washington-backed movements toward legislated healthcare reform was rampant in this election year of 1992. Also, the nation's doctors already were feeling the brunt of what for several years had been coming down the pike from Washington and also from private-sector healthcare-payment initiatives. These changes were affecting the doctor's ability to have two Mercedes and his freedom to practice medicine as he saw fit.

As I thought about ways we could reach out to physicians through MedPartners, I examined how physicians routinely work and function on a day-by-day basis. I thought of ways to assist doctors that would be natural and comfortable for doctors to accept.

By this time, I had worked with doctors for several years — first as an assistant hospital administrator and then later as a healthcare system senior vice president and as chief executive officer of a company which developed a primary-care physician network for this same healthcare system.

My mind focused on particular aspects of how physicians are trained, how they function and how they think: When a physician faces a patient-care situation which is out of his realm of expertise, it's just a natural for him to call in a specialist. If you're going to a general practitioner physician and he finds that you need heart surgery, what does this GP do? He calls in a specialist, a cardiovascular surgeon, to perform your heart surgery.

Well, in my mind it was logical that doctors would be likely to accept quality outside business help in dealing with some of these escalating business challenges that they felt were out of their realm of control. If a GP will call in a cardiovascular surgeon if his patient needs heart surgery and the GP doesn't do heart surgery, doesn't it stand to reason that the doctor would call in a business specialist if he's confronted with all these business issues and he doesn't have the training or track record to deal with them?

So this need for a business specialist — a need intensified by an awful lot of fear among doctors in the 1980s and early 1990s — was a driving force in the birth and the success of such early PPM companies as MedPartners. And, this need for a business specialist to help the fear-plagued doctors also was a guide for me as I sat there putting together some of the components of MedPartners' initial business plan.

Being Proactive — Today's Big Motivator

I think if you talk to doctors today who are seriously seeking partnerships with management companies, most could tell you quite honestly that fear is not their biggest motivator.

Increasing numbers of doctors — physicians and now also dentists — have an interest in partnering. These doctors have an interest in bringing in a business specialist. But they are experiencing this partnering interest during times in which doctors are not feeling the same anxiety levels and fear that haunted so many of them in the early to mid-1990s.

Today's doctor climate is more settled, more thoughtful, than it was a few years back. Also, many realize that management companies, as diverse as they are, are not a quick fix. The times simply are not as frenzied and emotion-ridden as they were a few years ago.

Doctors no longer have a fear that their world might change, because they know that their world already has changed and that it's going to change some more. For the most part, doctors in today's environment have confronted and accepted the fact that practicing medicine and dentistry will never take on the open, freewheeling style that was characteristic of the 1950s, 1960s and 1970s. The good old days are gone.

Even when changes occur that are not welcomed by a given group of people — and that's the case here with the doctors and many of the changes they have faced in recent years — there's nevertheless some kind of settling-down that can come from knowing something is a reality and that it has to be dealt with.

Along with facing that the doctoring environment indeed has changed, more and more doctors have made themselves knowledgeable as to what they can do about it. They have made themselves more knowledgeable about how they can organize and mobilize and partner with others who share their vision. They have made themselves more knowledgeable about what they can do to limit the negative impacts of change. They have made themselves more knowledgeable about how they can take a step further and make change a positive for them and their patients.

In today's environment, when doctors are looking around for a doctor-partnering agreement, they're more likely to be doing it for positive reasons — like market positioning — than for negative ones — like retrenchment and insulation purposes.

Doctors in the late 1990s and on into the 21st Century are more likely to be looking for partners to help them be proactive. They are saying, "We don't want to have to react to the environment that's dealt us. We want to help structure our own environment."

The doctors who are sitting down with us discussing partnering agreements are mostly men and women who want to step up in a proactive fashion to take more control of their own destiny.

I hear doctors saying that these are the things they want in a business partner: They want a business partner to help them tap into opportunities that exist in changing market conditions. They want a partner to be a facilitator, a negotiator, a mediator, a capital source, additional arms and legs. They're looking for access to information about circumstances in different markets, and information at different stages of the development of their own doctor-group.

Many of today's doctors who want doctor-partnering also are looking for ways to augment the humdrum and enjoy the practice of medicine or dentistry — to expand their choice of opportunities for an improved "Quality of Life" for themselves, too. Many of them are stimulated by new approaches and feel reinvigorated by the positive forces of change. They don't want to be in a professional situation in which they have invested years of training and thousands of dollars only to be taking a pessimistic, gloom-and-doom attitude they hear from some of their professional colleagues. They want to capitalize on the positives in today's healthcare market. And there are a lot of positives out there on which today's doctors can capitalize, providing they make good decisions.

The Issues are Much the Same

In my early days with MedPartners, I spent much of my time traveling around the eastern part of the United States forging agreements with physicians who were affiliating with our new PPM company.

When I was out beating the streets and talking to doctors about how we could help them with their problems back in the early and mid-1990s, I was hearing some of the same things from doctors in various parts of the nation.

It didn't matter if I was sitting in Miami talking with the doctors there, if I was up in Raleigh in discussions with a physician-group in that North Carolina city, I was fascinated, amazed, at how many markets I went into where they were talking about the same things.

For one thing, I was hearing physicians in various parts of the nation talk of problems with fragmentation. I was hearing them talk about problems in information transfer from point to point. I was hearing about the doctors' quest for linkages to help with the connections they needed.

Now as I'm traveling around the nation talking to doctors in my role as president and CEO of Genus Aesthetic Medical & Dental Group, again I'm hearing them discuss similar problems, no matter where their practices are located. Many of the problems and needs I hear them address are the same as they were in the early 1990s: The fragmentation; the need for linkages; the need for new opportunities which will help them control their own destinies.

To me there are messages here: One, despite the diversities which do exist from market to market in various parts of the nation, many of the basic challenges doctors face in their practices have been — and still are — much the same all over the United States. Also, a well-structured management company with depth in experience and resources can develop and utilize tools with common denominators for addressing the market opportunity and a doctor's needs, regardless of where this doctor might be located.

Strategic Alignment within a Doctor-Group

For the various members of a doctor-group, it's imperative they share a strategic alignment that enables them to convert their joint visions into reality. Not that each is identical. What is more important is that they be compatible. Every successful partnership involves some "give" and "take."

If a doctor-group agrees to go forward with a partnership with a PPM company, that's a "big picture" — a vision — a composite vision gleaned by pooled intellectual capital.

To make that vision of a partnership crystallize and become productive, the members of the group must pursue a "strategic alignment" approach for structuring and implementing the partnership.

Having the common vision for entering into a partnership is the big leap. It's like a view from 100,000 feet. Once the doctors decide to take the leap, they must delve underneath that vision to define their specific objectives that feed into the accomplishment of their goal. The overall group agrees on a set of key objectives that are consistent and understood by everyone in the group — not unlike an athletic team in which team members bring different but valuable skills to the table. The successful teams have the right person playing in the right position. All can't be pitchers, quarterbacks, etc.; yet, on a good team, all are winners. It's also like in a company, where it's important for everyone to contribute his or her pro rata piece towards the accomplishment of a special goal — via adhering to mutually understood objectives.

Those objectives are what I call a set of "strategically aligned objectives."

For a doctor-group, I think a relevant analogy is for the group to have a vision of making a trip from Birmingham, Alabama, to attend a medical meeting in Buffalo, New York. You and your partners in the practice decide you want to make that trip — your vision. Then you decide the components of your plan for getting from Birmingham to Buffalo. You decide whether you want to fly or drive. If you elect to drive, you decide what route to take, how much distance you want to cover each day, and where you want to stop for the night along the way. Those various components of your plan are your strategically aligned objectives.

As a doctor-group uses strategically aligned objectives to move smoothly through planning and implementing a partnership with a PPM company, it's important up front to establish an environment in which this approach can work.

If you are a physician in a leadership role in a medical practice going forward with a partnering process, my first suggestion to you in establishing a strategically aligned environment is that you and your doctor-partners make sure you share the same agenda within your own organization. Examine, honestly, which skills each brings to the table and look at how you, as a group, can provide the "best" product to the patient/client. Ultimately, everyone wins — the patient, the doctor, the group, the company, the stockholders. A business partner with aligned incentives can facilitate this process and help the doctors rethink how and why they do what they are doing, and help them implement the kind of change which does indeed improve the quality of life for everyone who participates.

What we're talking about here is consensus in the minds within your own doctor-group so that you cohesively can pursue some new objectives. Partnering with a business company entails objectives decidedly different (but, perhaps more gratifying) than those encountered in a traditional practice of medicine or dentistry.

Before a doctor-group goes looking for a management company with which to partner, it helps to get far down the road in making sure the doctors within the group share the same vision and goals — or at least that they can compromise and focus on a clear plan.

Now it stands to reason there will be times even after you launch discussions with a management company that you will have a few issues to resolve within your doctor-group. However, I can't tell you how strongly I would advise you to get those "philosophical differences" — those big internal issues — addressed, and at least set up to be resolved, before you bring in an outside party.

Don't go into partnering negotiations wearing a big set of rose-colored glasses about the individual goals of all the doctors in your group. If problems exist with conflicting goals among you and your doctor-partners, at the very least become aware these conflicts exist and be willing to confront and resolve the differences.

I want to describe some issues I've encountered along the way while participating in over 120 doctor-group/business-company transactions.

I refer to these types of issues as "internal governance" issues — issues related to the internal governance of the doctor-group.

Generally and contractually speaking, it's not supposed to be the role of a management company executive to deal with a doctor-group's internal governance issues. However, it has been my experience that in actual practice I've spent a great amount of time on issues related to internal governance of the group. I'm talking about issues such as compensation plans, prioritization of business objectives, and conflict resolution mechanisms.

To put it plainly and simply, there have been many transactions where during the negotiation phase I've spent more time and energy on internal governance issues than anything else. There have been many times when I've felt like Henry Kissinger, trying to iron out everything from subtle underlying differences of opinion to open hostilities and hatred among members of doctor-groups. I've seen differences of opinion so strong they threatened to break up well-established entities.

These are not minor issues. I can't tell you how risky they are to handle. You don't want to go into a situation and see that group become so fractured that the group "blows up" because of issues such as internal distribution of wealth, influence, control and greed. It becomes important to us to facilitate an environment and an internal growth process so that we can deal with doctor-members as one. We have one contract, not individual contracts with each member.

I've seen some rough days in dealing with internal governance issues. Some of the doctors with whom I've dealt have seen trying days. But so far so good.

Maybe it's because I've reaped benefits from my years of negotiating and dealing with these egos. Maybe it's because I really do like dealing with human behavior and emotion and feel comfortable in that role. Maybe it's because I've been lucky over the years. Maybe it's a combination. But so far when I've encountered differences of opinion among members of a doctor-group, I've never had a group disintegrate as a result.

While many factors have changed considerably in the doctor-partnering arena in the past several years, there has not been a big change in this area of internal governance issues. There's always a lot of issues to be worked through in many doctor organizations — no matter how long the doctors have been together, no matter how deep their mutual professional respect and personal friendships appear to be.

From our standpoint as the management company, in order to go forward with an affiliation we need to be convinced we are dealing with a doctor-group entity which is acting as a single unit. We need to be dealing with XYZ Group. It's true that within this group there typically are several (maybe many more than "several") individual doctors, and that each of these doctors is a "shareholder" in the overall group. But from our perspective, when all is said and done and the ink has dried on any partnering agreements, our responsibility as a company is to XYZ Group, not to Dr. X individually in the group, or to Dr. Y individually, or to Dr. Z individually.

If we encounter internal governance conflicts before we execute final agreements, the conflicts can relate to a wide range of factions, personalities and agendas as described in the following hypothetical scenarios:

- **The "I'm different, I'm special" issue.** You can find yourself dealing with two or three doctors who have split off from the rest of the doctor-group and are promoting their own agendas to the exclusion of, and sometimes also at the expense of, the agendas of other members of the group. Sometimes you find a situation in which one doctor in the group is so strong and dominant that he alone drives the process. The challenge is to tactfully identify the decision-makers and the expected ramifications of various actions/ decisions.
- **The "grow-marketshare" versus the "status-quo" issue.** This issue arises in a situation in which there are doctors in a group who want to venture out and try new things, contrasted by other members of the group who think things are functioning quite well as they are. These differences in goals can come because of several factors: It's common for management companies to deal with doctor-groups

whose members have conflicting agendas because they are at different points in their careers — with retirement being earlier for some and later for others. It's also common to run into groups in which some doctors had rather keep things as they are no matter what their age might be and regardless of whether they're planning to retire soon or a couple of decades down the road. Let's look at the different agendas for commitment on the part of members of one hypothetical 15-member doctor-group. Say you have ten members of this group who are primed to "go for it," to take advantage of new opportunities. But you have five guys who are happy with things the way they are. These five don't want to work any harder, or give anything up, or take any risk. They don't want to take on a management partner. Their strategy is: "I don't want to take any risk. I don't want to go to the bank. I don't want to sign any kind of personal guaranty for any capital for expansion. Neither do I want to partner with a management company in order to bring in business support and capital. I just want to practice medicine the way I've always practiced it until I'm ready to wind down."

• **The money issue — the distribution of funds.** This often has a secondary agenda of pitting the senior guys in a practice against the younger guys. Where a doctor stands in relation to when he plans to retire often is very much a factor in this scenario. Assume the management company is making a purchase price offer to the practice. This offer is being made to purchase a minority interest in the ongoing revenue stream from the doctors — a minority percentage of the doctors' income after operating expenses come off the top. And let's say we're talking about a 20-year partnership. So we're proposing to give this doctor-group an agreed-upon purchase price to enter into this long-term agreement. We're agreeing that the management company will perform certain services during that 20 years, and the doctors are agreeing they will pay the company a percentage of their earnings (after all operating expenses) during this 20 years. So we go to the doctor-group and make the formal offer on the purchase price. And then the entity has to decide how the pie gets split. This issue alone often polarizes the members of the group. The company and the doctors might have been talking for weeks, even months, with discussions apparently going smoothly. But then when the money figure goes on the table, all hell can break loose. It can go like this: I put the money offer on the table and say, "Okay, guys, now you decide how you're going to split it up." It would not be an uncommon scenario for the older guys in the group to say to the younger guys, "Well, this really is our business. You know, we older guys really developed this business. We've been here the longest. The goodwill that's being purchased here is really ours." But then the younger guys in the group are saying, "Well, wait a minute. We are going to have to pay the management fee for 15 years longer than you are, because you older guys are going to retire in five years or so. The younger guys really should get the larger portion of the pie."

When company representatives are dealing with these serious internal governance issues, they know the issues have to be resolved before the partnership is completed. You can't leave major internal governance issues out there festering. If you do, the operating group that assumes responsibility for adding value is doomed from the onset.

I can't get comfortable with paying the kind of money we're paying a doctor-group to do an affiliation with major discontent existing among the shareholders. I don't want the kind of discontent that could mean I'm left in a couple of years with an entity that's a lot smaller than it is when we do the deal. It goes against the plan for consolidation and significantly discounts what we valued.

It's important to be astute enough to gain an up-front understanding of the governance and the long-term ramifications of the governance. Prevention early on and proper contingency planning to deal with various "what-if" scenarios can save a lot of time, effort and money down the road.

Avoiding "Arranged Marriages"

I strongly feel that the PPM industry has had some real problems with what I call "arranged marriages."

In this scenario, two sides of a new partnership are pushed together to actually sign a long-term partnership agreement before the people involved even get to know one another!

When this occurs, the new still-unfamiliar partners have already signed a deal and now they start trying to address important issues together. They're attempting to address issues jointly when they don't have a mutual understanding of a joint strategy. They're trying to create opportunities and resolve problems while at the same time they're trying to get to know the people and the organization they've married — something that should have been done earlier in the pre-agreement discussions.

I've seen "arranged marriages" occur in several ways:

One way is when one doctor who's leading a doctor-group becomes overly aggressive and rams the idea of a partnership down the throats of his partners without informing or involving them. In a situation like this, the majority of the doctors in a group feel and act like they were railroaded down the path into an affiliation with this management company they don't even know. That starts everyone off with two strikes.

Another way to easily end up in an arranged marriage is to involve a broker. I don't even pretend to have an open mind about most transactions between doctors and management companies which are put together entirely by a go-between broker. The reason I feel this way is, as a general rule, the broker has no real motivation to personalize the transaction so people on both sides of the affiliation really know one another. In fact, a broker usually doesn't even know the people involved well enough to have the capability to personalize the transaction. I'll concede you might occasionally find a broker-negotiated deal that works well long-term. However, I know firsthand that some pretty dismal results can occur when the brokers facilitate an economic transaction which has nothing to do with substance, the people or the plan. In a case

like that, the transaction gets done and the broker goes away. After the
broker leaves, here are the management company and the doctors
looking at each other like the strangers they are and in effect saying,
"Well, one side paid its price, and the other side got its price. Now what
do we do?"

A third way to run into problems selling a plan effectively is to lack a
clear and concise strategic vision and specific plan to sell on the front end.

So what's the ideal situation to prevent the arranged marriages? What
steps should be taken to make sure the parties do indeed know one
another? What steps should be taken to effect a transfer of ownership of
this new doctor-partnering approach?

In my mind, you do three things:

1. Develop a clear and concise strategic plan. You've got to know what
you're doing and where you're heading. Then, through some effective
mechanism that's set up, that clear and concise strategic plan has to be
sold to all doctors in a group, top to bottom. Everyone has got to buy into
it. In shaping this plan and in selling it, that's where you flush out
leadership in the doctor-group, issues related to governance in the
doctor-group, resource allocation, and an implementation timetable
among the particular parties.

**2. Engage directly with your prospective partners. If brokers are used,
they can participate as well.** In cases where a broker is involved, take
every precaution to make sure that personalization occurs. In a traditional PPMC model, a broker puts together a package of information on
the doctor-group that is his client. This package of information is called
"the book," and "the book" gets distributed among PPMCs interested in
making a proposal. The PPMCs submit their proposals back to the
broker. The broker evaluates the proposals and then "short lists" the
potential companies for his client. A thorough broker will provide his
client, the seller, with some analysis on PPMCs which have made
proposals. With Genus, it's going to have to be a very targeted, well-
structured situation in which we can use a broker. The reason is that our

strategy is so retail, so service-oriented, so high-end, so focused on the integration of the physician into the leadership of the company, that you can't have just "Here's the book of information." From the view of our potential affiliates and from our view, you can't have a serious discussion about a marriage in which you have never seen the bride. Both parties in Genus discussions will be very unreceptive to arranged marriages. Genus is different from the traditional PPMC. We're not a managed-care player; we're not just an access point into a system for a managed-care plan. In our situation, the company and the doctors have to meet face-to-face in order to drill down deeper to see what are the motivations, drivers, strategic visions and shared values. That's important for both parties. Very early in discussions, both parties need to be able to look one another in the eye. Organizations are made up of people. The doctors need to know who they're dealing with, and we need to know who we're dealing with. The doctors need to get comfortable, as we do. If both parties are serious about a Genus affiliation, we need a head start on an opportunity for a symbiotic relationship. I'm not saying that we won't in some cases use brokers as an entry point for discussions that quickly become more personalized. I am saying if there are brokered deals in our segment, then somehow the brokers are going to have to expand the information to deal with some of the core things that we look for. The commitment we have to our affiliates will require that.

3. Understand clearly the decision-making process. Make sure you know who the players are and what makes them tick. Agree to a timetable and keep commitments. When I'm structuring these types of transactions, what I try to do in the beginning is quickly assess how decisions are made in this doctor-group. I often ask the questions: "How does your group make these types of decisions? Do you take it to an executive committee? Do you turn it over entirely to an outside lawyer or consultant? Does the majority of your board make decisions? Do transactions like this have to be unanimous?" I think it's very important to understand how they make decisions. In companies, you pretty much know, because their structures are fairly consistent — chairman, president, chief executive officer, chief financial officer, etc. But in a lot of these medical businesses, you don't have this type of structure. So you have to understand or assess this group's particular decision-making process, so you can present yourself, your company, your proposal, in the proper form. Otherwise you can spend a lot of time and effort presenting to the wrong audience.

(NOTE: It's crucial that a "transfer of information" exist not only with doctors in a group, but also with members of their staff. I'll discuss that in the next chapter.)

A Relationship of Trust

If a doctor-group and a management company expect to enjoy a shared vision and accomplish their mutual goals, they have to build and nurture a relationship of trust.

Trust is not something that just happens. It's built on real things like keeping your word and getting results.

I'll tell you from experience that it doesn't take a long period of time for two parties to know whether or not they are building and enjoying the benefits of trust.

Results either happen or they don't. People either keep their word or they don't.

Speaking from the viewpoint of the management company, these are several trust-related tenets I think the company has to live by with the doctors:

- **Make sure that you can deliver on commitments you made during the sales process.** I can't emphasize this enough — how important it is that a company manage the gap between expectation set by sales and the reality that can be delivered on the operating side. That's a key source of where your credibility comes from. This is true when it comes to keeping financial commitments. It's true when it comes to keeping other types of commitments. If a commitment of time and effort has been made, it's just as important to make good on that as it is to make good on financial commitments.

- **Honor your commitments on "spirit-of-the-deal issues."** What I'm referring to here are issues which often are crucial to your discussions with the doctors but which might not show up in the formal documents you sign. Even though these issues might not have made it to black and white, they often are more important to the doctors than anything else. If you as the company really are a good partner to the doctors, if you're the kind of partner the doctors can trust, you must make it a priority to live up to any commitments you made in this area. You must never-ever even think of telling your doctor-partners that these issues are not in the formal documents and you really don't have to address them. One of the prime examples that comes to my mind of "spirit-of-the-deal" issues has to do with mergers. After the ink has dried on the documents and the partnering has begun in earnest, a leader of the doctor-group might say to a company exec: "You said during the sales process that you were going to help us grow through recruitment of other groups. Specifically you said we were going to pursue a merger between our group and John Doe's group. I know it doesn't say that in the document. However, that was part of the reason that we did this. We're interested in it. Where are you in this process?"

- **Remember that your relationship is that of partner and not consultant.** I don't have anything against consultants. I've met some consultants who do good work. But the role of the consultant tends to be a more detached one, a more temporary one, than does the role of partner. In my mind, the consultant does not have to build that long-term level of trust, loyalty, and continuity that partners must build. A consultant has not invested financially, whereas a management company that's a partner with a doctor-group has invested risk capital in that doctor-group's future. The company stands to gain or lose financially, depending on how successful these doctors are. The company has a chance to impact that level of success. As a partner to a doctor-group, a management company has both the opportunity and the responsibility to get in the trenches with the doctors. There are some consultant situations in which a consultant comes in and gives a little advice, blows some smoke, does a nice slide show, writes a report, goes away and moves on. The consultant doesn't usually stay around long enough to understand the big picture. And he doesn't have the responsibility of being an operator. He doesn't deal with the day-to-day, the nitty-gritty, the crises that can have folks' heads on the chopping blocks. However, the management company does deal with these things. As a partner to the doctors, a management company has made a long-term pact of trust with the doctors to respond to them, to get answers for them, to open doors of opportunity for them.

- **Use diligence and candor to solve problems, and don't deny problems.** I think the style that partners use in approaching problems can impact as much as anything toward making the partnership work or not work in getting results. Along the same lines, I think the style that partners use in problem-solving can impact as much as anything toward building up or breaking down trust in a partnership. The two tools I stress as crucial in an effective problem-solving style are diligence and candor. The diligence is pretty obvious: Work at it. No matter how much effort it takes to solve a problem, keep at it until you have it resolved. The other tool, candor, has to do with admitting your mistakes and being willing to take the heat, and then going on to correct the problems at hand. People aren't expecting you to make the right decision 100 percent of the time. But they are expecting you to be candid and forthright with them when you have not succeeded. If you fail, confess that you've failed and then spend your energy on fixing the problem. Don't take up everybody's time and frustrate them further by denying it or pointing fingers at other people and looking for someone else to blame. If you try to take the escape route, why should someone trust you? I firmly believe that taking responsibility and being accountable for the negatives as well as the positives in problem-solving are central to building a relationship of trust.

Run TOWARD That Fire!

Some doctors seem to have the mistaken idea that one of their goals in business partnering is to save them time from business details. The doctor who subscribes to this line of thinking is telling himself: "Well, I'm going to get someone else in here to deal with all these management issues. Then I'm going to spend all my time taking care of my patients and seeing my family and playing golf. As soon as my new business partner starts to work, I'm washing my hands of all the business details."

That's not the way I see a good doctor-partnering transaction evolving — that is, if the doctor indeed does get the most out of the transaction.

This is true partnering! And I would say to the doctors, "This is not running away from the fire. It's running toward it and jumping into the fire."

In the most effective doctor-partnering arrangement, the doctors bring in a business specialist to work with them on strategic planning, on streamlining business operations, on setting the stage for future success. If these endeavors are really pursued, it may take more of a doctor's time rather than saving him time.

A lot of doctors who go into partnering find that for the first time in their careers they are developing and implementing strategy. They find they are looking at business opportunities that fit their practices. They are looking at the strengths and weaknesses of their organizations. They are understanding the threats to their market and the opportunities in their market.

I know there still are doctor-partnering companies out there saying, "One of the big things we have to offer is we're going to take these business responsibilities off the doctors." In my mind, this is plain bunk! If they succeed they have shortchanged the doctors because they have cheated them out of the opportunity to really be full partners. Actually, I think these companies are selling the wrong thing, that they are six years behind and obviously inexperienced. I don't think a company can serve a doctor-group well with this approach.

I think if you would poll doctors who have been involved in effective partnering they would tell you that after the partnering agreement they spent more time on business issues than they did before. But I think a great percentage of these same doctors would tell you that they don't regret the time spent. In my years in the physician practice management industry I've seen many doctors take to all this like some great adventure. This is new and exciting and it's building up their world and it's making them money. Doctors by nature are bright, well educated and curious. A lot of them have just never had access to a business specialist who could teach them more about their own business as it relates to financial analysis, marketing information and strategy. The doctors find themselves exposed to people and resources and organizations that they haven't been exposed to before.

As a matter of fact, I run into many doctors who, after getting involved in partnering, discover they like business, are drawn to it, and have a knack for it. They like understanding things to which they've never been exposed in detail. They like the interaction with business people. They enjoy seeing their practices prosper. They're having fun!

I do not want a partner who has the perception that my company is going to come in and do bookkeeping for him. I don't want to just manage status quo and count the nickels and dimes and hope the nickels and dimes continue to be what they have been historically.

Instead, I want to enter a relationship with a doctor who wants to be a partner with me with a goal of adding value to his practice. I want our company to join hands with a doctor and his partners who see this as an opportunity to build up an organization with them. That's a different ball game. To do that, the stimulation needs to work both ways. We need to stimulate the doctors. But we want partners who are interested enough in the process also to stimulate us. I want to partner with doctors who are interested in all this, who respond to it, who learn from it and give us input and participate. I want challenging doctors as partners, people who are engaging, not people that you have to drag along. I want people who are going to put forth effort, who are going to take issue with us and debate us on certain things, who will candidly tell us how things are from their point of view. I want doctors we can stimulate into exploring things they haven't looked at previously. I think this kind of partnership is better for everyone, where everyone is part of the process, where everyone has a part in creating and implementing a plan that works.

"Intellectual Capital" of Genus Affiliates

Our plan at Genus, although rather unique, is to aggressively integrate physician leadership into the strategic management of the company.

There is a tremendous amount of "intellectual capital" out there in the minds of the successful physicians and dentists which needs to be mined and infused into building the culture of the company. It's the key task, however, a complex one.

I'm talking about sharing the common vision. I think a key role for us at Genus is to facilitate the development of a "fraternity" of the men and women physicians and dentists with whom we affiliate. By facilitating the development of this fraternity, we will be facilitating a collaboration of intellectual capital and talent. This collaboration can help drive the direction of and impact the decision-making and development of the company.

The opportunity to be part of this collaboration of intellectual capital is, in my opinion, one of the reasons people are affiliating with Genus. They see the opportunity to participate in the early stages of developing their organization. It's not just someone else's organization. It's also their organization.

This whole "intellectual capital" arena is a key area in which I think Genus is different. Doctors all over this country have had experience in having some kind of affiliation with organizations which gave them little or no opportunity for real input. Take a hospital situation, for example. A physician sells his practice to a hospital and becomes a hospital employee. Now, if you're employed by a hospital, and you're one of 2,000 employees, even though you're a physician, how much say-so do you really have in the decision-making of the organization? How much input do you have in how the hospital performs and what technology it uses or whatever? Granted, all kinds of committees are set up in the typical structure. But is the doctor really an influential participant in all this? Does he or she really have an opportunity to contribute with ideas, assessments and leadership? The answer is "no."

Through our plans to integrate doctors' intellectual capital into the leadership of Genus, we plan to give our affiliates this opportunity. It's an opportunity which could bring very positive results for the affiliates, the company, and the clients and patients we serve.

"Circle Your Wagons" Through Genus

"Circle your wagons to grow your business" is a core facet of the "shared vision" of Genus Aesthetic Medical & Dental Group.

This is central to the opportunity that Genus is offering high-end physicians and dentists who specialize in a wide range of aesthetic-related services.

In Genus we are entering into partnership agreements that in some ways offer a bit of a different opportunity from the conventional partnerships.

As I've explained previously in this book, this big difference is that we're creating the "retail concept" in aesthetic medicine and dentistry. We're doing this complete with emphasis on a high-end product, creating a brand name with which people can identify, and promotion and education.

This concept is different from the norm because we will be able to grow the total volume of services. We're able to take this retail approach because we're offering an array of services and aesthetic products that are primarily elective and paid for directly by patients, as opposed to "sick-care" services primarily paid by the third-party payers.

Through Genus affiliations, we will see many high-quality providers drop their ridiculous competitive boundaries and instead circle their wagons in a cooperative arrangement to corner some markets.

I think some of these practitioners who previously have shunned one another are going to join hands after asking themselves, "Hey, how can we do a better job working together? We're actually in the same market. Why don't the quality people get together, make use of a management company's human and financial resources, and dominate markets? If we can do this, if we can dominate growing markets, then doesn't everybody win?"

(NOTE: There are several approaches we are employing to make this happen. I will discuss this in Chapter 10.)

As aesthetic providers circle their wagons to join Genus, two of the cornerstones of that shared vision affiliation will be cooperation and education:

1. Collaboration of Genus affiliates. Take some of the really good plastic surgeons and dermatologists, for example. Some have drawn their rigid territorial lines and think of one another as opponents — because of turf arguments over issues such as who does certain procedures in some of the facial work. However, some of the high-end providers in these specialties are going to find they've been fighting the wrong people for the wrong reasons. They will find that, by collaborating as Genus affiliates, they stand to gain more in terms of self-satisfaction, productivity, and financial reward.

2. Maximizing Genus affiliates' strong track record and expertise in education. Genus is interacting with top-tier plastic surgeons, dentists and other aesthetic providers who already have a strong background in contributing to the educational process. We are forming partnerships with providers who have made significant academic contributions, who already are educational leaders by virtue of having conducted symposia and/or written books and articles on the latest developments in their respective fields. These providers see Genus not only as an opportunity for taking their practices to the next level, but also as a major educational opportunity. They see the potential, through the Genus vision and strategy and capitalization, to bring together a now-fragmented collection of high-end aesthetic providers into an unprecedented collective pool of intellectual capital. These providers see the opportunity for Genus to enable them to focus their already-proven educational abilities in two directions — toward educating patient populations in a consumer-education and marketing strategy, and toward clinical education for their professional peers. As a part of the Genus commitment to education for our affiliates, we are consolidating our educational and training resources. This consolidation is a focus that's truly high-end, that's truly based in education. It's not based on taking potshots at other providers who aren't as well-trained and who are not as successful. It's a proactive versus a reactive approach. We're interacting with clinicians who understand the Genus strategy as their opportunity to participate as leaders and contributors in developing innovative educational campaigns that will truly differentiate the high-quality providers.

At Genus we know people are evaluating us closely. We're also evaluating them closely. As I said earlier in this book, we want only the top-tier providers because that's what the Genus brand name is going to stand for.

If a doctor decides to affiliate with Genus, this is what he gets: He gets an opportunity to leave his impressions on the company, today and in the future. He gets someone with whom he can share his strengths, opinions and successes. He gets someone willing to invest in his future. He gets money. He gets a partner that can help him acquire technology, help him with management, help him with marketing, help him grow the number of providers with whom he has a relationship, and teach him how to grow his marketshare. He gets a partner who can help him grow his volume, grow his total business — key to the retail element. He also gets an identification with a Genus brand name that's in the type of high-end category associated with Mercedes-Benz and Ritz-Carlton. For "fulfill-ment" of these kinds, professionals have always had to turn to their professional associations and medical/dental societies. Yet no profes-sional association can offer what a business partner can in this arena. Professional associations must be all things to its members. Restraint of trade laws prohibit associations and societies from excluding marginal practitioners. A company can choose to partner with whomever it chooses. A good corporate partner can develop targeted market strategies and contractual relationships which benefit itself and its doctor-partners as well. So what does all this mean? It means that many doctors will be turning more and more to corporate partnerships rather than to association memberships for guidance and help. And, that provides the right niche for a company like Genus that is poised to fit the void.

We believe this unique retail medicine and dentistry concept is a win-win-win "shared vision" for the Genus patients, the Genus affiliates, and the Genus company.

9

Bringing Employees into the Loop:
The Key to Decentralization

A 15-MEMBER group of doctors has been looking for a management company with which to partner. The group decides that our management company might be a fit. We at the management company take a look at the doctors and agree there's some real potential. So we start preliminary meetings to get to know one another better.

The discussions go well. The doctors are comfortable with how well they really do fit into our company's business model. As we delve into the doctors' business plan, we see how our company can bring substantial added value to their practice.

So it gets close to working out the final points of a partnership.

Our discussions become more detailed. We focus on the nuts and bolts of how this doctor-group handles its day-to-day operations. We begin zeroing in on how specific people in our management company can plug in.

I find myself pleased with how these discussions are going, except for one big problem.

What's bothering me in this scenario is what I call the "empty-chair-that-should-not-be-empty" syndrome. It's the empty chair in the conference room that I feel should not be empty.

In my mind, that empty chair should be occupied by a specific key individual who is going to play a pivotal role in this partnership we're creating.

That key person is the man or woman who is employed by these doctors to oversee the day-to-day business operations of their practice. The title given to this person sometimes is "clinic administrator," sometimes "business manager," sometimes "office manager." Regardless of the title, this person is the one who's in charge of the business operations of the medical practice. This individual really is the one who should function as the right arm of these doctors.

I'm talking about a person who oversees operations which have to do with managing employees, employee benefits and employee in-service training; patients' billing and collections and patients' records; legal matters; purchase of supplies and equipment, and payment of rent, insurance, utility service, etc. The job description of a clinic administrator will vary somewhat from one doctors' group to another. However, some doctors for years have empowered their administrators not only to supervise employees in the office but also to interview, select, hire and fire the employees. In many medical practices, these clinic administrators not only do bookkeeping on office expansions and renovations and relocations the doctors have handled; instead, these administrators often handle these initiatives themselves. It's not uncommon to find a clinic administrator who for years has been the one to select office sites, negotiate leases and real estate deals, and interact with architects, builders, and interior designers to decide everything from office layout to the color of wallpaper and sometimes even actual building materials.

In short, the clinic administrator might be a person who has great insight into the management issues we're discussing with the doctors as we work out details on an impending affiliation agreement.

By having the clinic administrator claim this "empty chair" in early meetings between the doctors and the management company, the administrator often can function as a treasured source of information and guidance to help transition the new partnership smoothly. The administrator can help lay a foundation for the management company to interact in a positive fashion from the outset with the employees in the doctors' office. The administrator can help position a team-building mentality — something you have to have if you're going to manage change effectively in a doctor-group/management-company partnership.

I would advise those involved in creating a doctor-group/management-company partnership to evaluate early on whether the doctor-group's administrator is likely to remain with the practice after the new partnership transaction is complete. If the administrator is qualified and likely will want to stay on, I would suggest involving this person in the partnership planning discussions at the earliest possible time. Don't keep your management leader in the dark. Don't let your partnership suffer from the "empty-chair-that-should-not-be-empty" syndrome.

The Reason the Chair Is Often Empty

There's no question that the clinic administrator usually will be the most important person in the day-to-day working relationship between a doctors' group and a management company.

It is the clinic administrator who most often is the one to serve as the go-between between the company and the doctor-group.

So, if this clinic administrator is so important in the workings of this partnership, wouldn't it be a natural that the doctors would invite the administrator to planning sessions with the management company early on?

Not necessarily.

In my early years in the physician practice management (PPM) industry, it actually was unusual for the administrator to be included until a transaction was already complete or on the brink of being signed. Historically it was almost typical for the administrator, who ultimately would have an all-important go-between role, to be left out of the partnering transaction. It was rare for the doctors to bring the administrator into the loop.

The reason for the "empty chair," for not including the administrator, generally was that the doctors didn't want their employees to know what was going on until everything had been settled and we were ready for partnering functions to be implemented.

In our new company, Genus Aesthetic Medical & Dental Group,

we're strongly encouraging the doctors not to let this happen. We're explaining to them that they stand to gain a lot more than they stand to lose by bringing in that administrator early. As a rule these doctors have entrusted the clinic administrator with a multitude of other confidential information over the years. Why not entrust the administrator with this information and make use of the administrator's extensive knowledge?

There's only a limited window of time when confidentiality is an issue. I advise doctors to be realistic in assessing what their employees know or suspect when partnering discussions are in progress. They usually know or suspect a lot more than the doctors would like to think they do. These employees tend to be savvy folks. They are in the patient-care business, which is a strong "people-business." They tend to be able to pick up on things when people are interacting in some kind of different fashion. Most employees know something is up when they start seeing these men and women in business suits come in and out to meet with the doctors.

Selling It on the Front End

The challenge of a new partnership does not end with the execution of an affiliation agreement. The challenge intensifies after you sign the agreement.

Crucial to the management is how you communicate this new partnership to the employees in a doctors' office — how you sell the new partnership to the employees on the front end.

I've thought an awful lot about this. Having served for several years as a chief operating officer of a large physician practice management company, I've spent a tremendous amount of time dealing firsthand with these issues. I've spent time in the field, interacting with doctors and their clinic administrators and the employees in their offices. I've spent time playing go-between on issues involving the employees and managers in the doctors' offices and corporate people.

I think as much as 60 percent of the problems that we see implementing a new affiliation with a doctor-group are a result of the affiliation not having been communicated well on the front end to the clinic administrator and in turn to the employees in the doctors' office.

I advise doctors who are partnering with a management company to take steps to avoid some of these problems that fall into that 60 percent. To do this, place a high priority early in your discussions on working with the management company to develop a coordinated transition — a plan of how to sell this affiliation. I'm referring here to a transition for selling this affiliation in-house — first to your clinic administrator and then, with the administrator's help, to your other employees.

Bring those employees into the loop as soon as you can. Get them hooked up as soon as possible. Don't feed anxiety levels.

If you communicate the new partnership well on the front end, you have a much better chance the employees are going to "buy in" to this idea, this concept. You run less of a chance they will resist both the doctors and the corporate people as the partnership moves forward. Your overall chances of success with the affiliation go up exponentially.

Timing is important here. It's not only what you communicate to people. It's when you communicate it. With the employees in a doctors' office, it's best if you can give them good information very early.

By developing this "sell plan" and implementing it with your employees, you can prevent damage. If you don't do this, it can cost you and the management company time and productivity down the road in damage control. You can spend a lot of time dealing with misconceptions and hostilities — troublesome negatives that you enabled to get a head start, because you did not communicate to your employees early and effectively.

Decentralization is the Goal!

Bringing the employees into the loop can put you firmly on the path to decentralization — straight out of the shoot.

There's no way I can stress how strongly I believe that decentralization is the right way to go.

In Chapter 4, I expressed my belief in decentralization. In that chapter, I was comparing the decentralized style of the PPM company PhyCor to the more centralized style of the nation's largest PPM company, MedPartners. In making that comparison, I explained that I felt more comfortable with PhyCor's decentralized strategy. I alluded to situations during the period I was MedPartners' chief operating officer-East when I took issue with the company's CEO, Larry House, over centralization of billing and collections.

In recent months, as I've been getting Genus off the ground, my belief in the decentralized style has become even stronger.

My whole belief in decentralization is based on my concept that you don't push decisions down from the corporate office to the field just because it's the "corporate thing" to do.

For this decentralized system to work, it has to be an approach subscribed to and adhered to both by the doctors' offices and the company. The ideal in decentralization exists when the employees in the doctors' offices really do view the company as additional arms and legs and resources they welcome as facilitators, versus employees looking at corporate as "Big Brother" who wants to control everything that they do.

If you go to a Webster's dictionary and see what Webster says about decentralization, this rather long word takes on a much simpler tone: "The dispersion or distribution of functions and powers from a central authority to regional and local authorities."

For our purposes here, the "central authority" is the corporate office, and the "regional and local authorities" are the doctors' offices.

So what are the nuts and bolts of how "decentralization" is applied to a doctor-group/management-company partnership? I think a doctor-group/management-company partnership is better served if you place as much control as you can with the employees who actually work in a doctor's office. The people who are dealing directly with those all-important patients are the employees in the doctors' office — not the people who work in some distant corporate offices of the management company. I don't see how the average relationship with a patient can remain as personal as it should be and can be if you create a partnership and all of a sudden you transfer the majority of the business-function control to people in the management company's corporate offices.

In my mind, you especially need to be decentralized if you're involved in a geographically dispersed business like the one we have. How can you really have a personalized business if you have someone in a corporate office in Birmingham, Alabama, making all these decisions that so drastically impact doctors and their patients and employees in doctors' offices that are located many miles away in Texas or New York?

This lofty-sounding goal of protecting the personal nature of doctor-patient relationships is something you hear many healthcare professionals idealistically espouse as something they want in health-related businesses. However, this personalization in dealing with patients is not just something optional we might like to have at Genus Aesthetic Medical & Dental Group. This personalization in dealing with patients is something mandatory, that we must have, to make our personalized Genus retail brand-name concept work. We cannot nurture that personalization and that consistent brand-name image if we don't have the clinic administrators and the employees signed on with us. They are less likely to sign on with us enthusiastically if we don't inform them early and keep them informed about what's going on. They are less likely to continue to work with us cooperatively on the long-term if we don't practice a decentralized style of management. At the end of this chapter, I'll address more in depth some of the Genus retail implications as they relate to employees in the doctors' offices.

The Payoffs of Decentralization

An entire book could be written on the payoffs of decentralization. As applied to a doctor-group/management-company affiliation, these are four payoffs of decentralization that I consider key:

1. Decentralization's biggest single potential payoff is that it stands to increase your chances of having a higher job performance level among employees who work in doctors' offices. Part of the problem I see with some of these partnering agreements is that a management company arrives and takes away all the authority and decision-making from the employees who work in the offices. So you have people who in the past have been accustomed to making these decisions and all of a sudden they are told they can't make these decisions anymore. When that happens — and it does happen when you practice a more centralized style — I think employees' commitment and accountability can go down drastically.

2. Decentralization speeds along the decision-making process and I think makes for better decisions in the long run. If you use a centralized management approach which prevents the empowering of doctors'- office employees to make day-to-day decisions, that doesn't mean those decisions aren't there to be made. Somebody still has to make the decisions. Under a structured centralized approach, they could mean that all of a sudden you're letting the management company's corporate people make the bulk of day-to-day decisions necessary to manage a doctors' office. I've seen such an approach in operation, and I've witnessed some resulting delays in decision-making. I have seen cases in which even some very bright, talented corporate people felt very uncomfortable when they had to make some of these decisions that traditionally had been left inside the doctors' offices. And I've seen the frustration level go up with everybody. So what I recommend is to continue to empower the employees in the doctors' offices to make decisions, and then hold them accountable for making good decisions.

3. Decentralization aids a good working relationship among employees who work together in the doctors' offices, helping them to work better as a unit toward meeting the needs of the doctors and their patients. A centralized style of management is high-risk to trigger problems not only between doctors' office employees and the management company, but also among the employees who work side-by-side there in the doctors' office. I think decentralization decreases friction among employees by clarifying who's job it is to do what, avoiding delays in decision-making, and preventing general uncertainty due to lack of communication. Also, I feel that decentralization is more of a protector of the bonding and comradery among employees at the local level.

4. Decentralization is core to building trust between employees in the doctors' offices and the people who work in the corporate offices. Trust is crucial if you're going to have a partnership that works. You can't write a policy and mandate that somebody respect you. Employees are more likely to respect people at "corporate" because they actually believe in what they're saying, because they believe the corporate folks indeed have come to understand the issues and have identified with the issues. These employees in the doctors' offices are more likely to respect the people at corporate when they feel the people at corporate return that respect for them and their work. I think using a decentralized style is a corporate message to employees in a doctors' office that speaks for itself in saying: "We respect you and the work you have done in the past; we're entrusting you with this responsibility for the future and believe you will do a good job."

The Practice (Clinic) Administrator as the "Point Person"

Why should the practice administrator be the "point person" in this role of selling the partnership to the employees on the front end?

Why is the practice administrator such a key person in managing the transition?

A key reason is the practice administrator has the experience and insight to understand the doctor-group practice. An effective practice administrator already has the trust of the doctors and has a track record working with the doctors. An effective clinic administrator already has rapport with the employees who work in the practice.

Let's take a look at a clinic administrator who might be working with the hypothetical 15-man doctor-group that I'm using as a model in this chapter. As is the case with this hypothetical doctor-group, this clinic administrator I will describe is a profile I've created as a hypothetical model for purposes of illustration. This profile is a composite, embody-ing some of the positive professional traits I have observed in qualified clinic administrators I've seen serve medical practices well.

This hypothetical clinic administrator is a woman we'll call Margaret Jones. She has been working with this particular doctor-group for 10 years. When she came on board to manage the office, there were five physicians. She has seen the number of doctors in the practice increase over the decade to 15. Likewise, she has seen resources expand to meet the changing needs of this growing practice — more employees under her supervision, more office space and equipment to keep track of, etc. One of the few things that hasn't changed during the decade is that Mrs. Jones has been in charge of the business operations for this medical practice from the outset. Mrs. Jones arrived with a strong background of training and work experience in accounting and human resources management. Over the years she has availed herself of ongoing continuing education to keep her knowledge and skills current. Her abilities have expanded to keep pace with the expanding practice.

In my ideal scenario with the hypothetical Mrs. Jones relevant to structuring a doctor-group/management-company partnership, she in her role as clinic administrator is included in the partnering discussions from very early on. It would be important not to miss out on the benefits of the depth and knowledge of a clinic administrator like Mrs. Jones. It would be ideal not to have to be concerned about the "empty-chair-that-should-not-be-empty" syndrome. In the ideal situation, Mrs. Jones would soon come to understand and be enthusiastic about the opportunities in this new partnership that's in the process of being created. As the affiliation discussions progress, Mrs. Jones would begin contributing her own valuable input that would enhance this partnership's success.

Also in this ideal scenario, Mrs. Jones would assist the doctors and the management company in accomplishing two major tasks:

She would help manage the anxiety of the employees and bring them into the loop.

She would function as an ongoing go-between — to be this partnership's bridge, its link between what's going on at the doctors' offices and the management company's involvement at the corporate level.

When Employee Anxiety Becomes a Nightmare

Before I address what can go right when you do a good job managing the transition into a doctor-group/management-company affiliation,

I'm going to discuss how wrong things can go with the employees in the doctors' offices when the transition is not managed well.

If employee anxiety is not addressed and channeled to positive ends, it can rage out of control very early in the partnership. If the anxiety level gets a considerable head start, your chances of ever totally achieving some of your objectives with this particular group of employees might go out of the window for good.

Instead of bringing employees into the loop with information, you can have employees turn against the company — and even turn against the doctors — as a result of unaddressed anxiety. You can find yourself having to manage an adversarial situation.

The result can be that much of your management time in the early days of the partnership can be spent managing resentment, resistance, foot-dragging, inertia, and just plain crisis.

In short, you can have a nightmare on your hands.

I'll share with you my own scenario of such an anxiety-fed nightmare.

I developed this scenario based on a composite of attitudes and developments I have encountered in my own experience and also what I have been told by others. Some of this came from my experiences out in the field in the PPM industry. Some of it came from talking with other doctor-partnering management folks. And much of it came from candid discussions I have had along the way with employees and clinic administrators in doctors' offices.

This scenario also addresses the need for a decentralized approach. I'm demonstrating here a case in which employees are kept in the dark and also in which the management company is using a centralized style.

This scenario actually begins when those initial planning meetings commence and proceed between the doctors and the management company, prior to an agreement. As the meetings continue, and as a partnership agreement gets closer and closer, all the employees — including the clinic administrator — are left in the dark.

The employees are doing their jobs. They know something is in the works. But they don't really know what. They see people wearing suits coming in to see the doctors. They see increased "activity." They hear rumors. Their anxiety level goes up. They don't know what's going to happen.

A big issue with each employee here is the natural one: "What's going to happen to me?" That's a common and valid employee concern. When change appears to be in the making and the atmosphere is filled with mystery and intrigue and uncertainty, nearly anyone would think to himself or herself: "What's going to happen to the jobs here and to the people who hold these jobs? Will my position be eliminated? Will I be eliminated?"

Then the official announcement is made — that this doctor-group has entered into a new partnership with a management company. When this happens, the anxiety level goes off the map with the employees! What does this mean? How does this relate? Why is it being done? How is it going to benefit the doctors' practice? How is it going to benefit the individual employees?

For purposes of discussion here, let's assume that the announcement of a partnership is made quite tersely, with little elaboration and virtually no effort to personalize the communication of the change to each employee.

Things get worse.

Put yourself in the seat of one of the employees, and see how these feelings and emotions play out:

You've been an employee in the doctors' office for several years. You've been told many times you do a good job, and you know you do a good job. You enjoy your work; you like the environment and the people around you. Then you start hearing rumors that management changes are in the making. You come to work one day and there's this announcement concerning a new management affiliation. It's a done deal. No one bothers to translate this announcement to you. So you translate it on your own: "The doctors that I work for just sold an interest in their practice to an outside company that's based off in some other city. No one really has talked to me about anything or explained anything. I wonder if anybody really cares what I think or cares about what I do here."

A few weeks go by after the announcement, and this is where you stand on information: The clinic administrator and the doctors you work for don't give you any details about what will happen. The people from the new management company don't give you any details about what will happen. No one addresses those things that are on your mind. You're told you should just do your job and not worry, that nothing much will change.

Well, that part about nothing changing soon proves to be all wrong. All of a sudden, bang! Here comes all this change. Here comes a brand new employee benefit plan. More policies. More requests for information. More observation. All kinds of scrutinization from various people. These management people are coming in and tagging your equipment and looking at the forms you use. There's just all this activity.

It gets worse and worse. In the doctors' offices, the phones are ringing off the hook with calls from the corporate offices of the management company. You're helping to answer calls from people in all kinds of specialties at the management company's corporate office — from leasing, from legal, from accounting, from accounts payable, from all these areas. It's like, "Send me this!" and "Why are you doing this?"

All of a sudden it's chaos. And it's interfering with seeing patients. It's disruptive. It's not a positive. It's a negative.

It didn't have to be this way. Clear information provided to employees in a timely fashion, plus use of a decentralized approach in implementing and managing the new partnership, could have created a transition that was a positive investment in the future rather than an obstacle.

Managing Employee Anxiety toward Positive Results

Anxiety is not an unnatural response to change. It's as natural as the day is long.

Anxiety can actually be the birth of something positive instead of something negative — if it's addressed in a constructive way in the beginning. Let's take a look at the anxiety level in a doctors' office when a new partnership is announced and implementation begins:

You cannot go in and start making changes in a structured environment like a doctors' office, where they've been doing business in a certain way for years, without creating some anxiety among the employees. It's ridiculous to deny such anxiety exists. It's more ridiculous not to address the anxiety in a constructive fashion. I strongly feel we in this doctor-partnering industry must do a better job of managing the anxiety level among employees than was typically done in the early years of the industry. I also think we can do a better job now. Experience is a great teacher.

First of all, we need to think about the very nature of anxiety. As I've alluded to earlier, there actually can be some positive things about anxiety. The first positive that comes to my mind is that it's impossible for somebody to be anxious about something if the person is not also curious about it, interested in it. So if someone is anxious, you usually have someone who is willing to listen to what you have to say.

The challenge here is to capitalize on that curiosity and interest to a positive end while the anxiety is still in the very early stages. You do that by giving the employees the information they need and deserve, early on. Don't make them worry and wonder and fester. Don't let their information feed on fear and rumor.

Let these employees know how this change is going to benefit them. Let them know how they can participate in this new partnering process. Learn what each employee contributes through his or her work. Let the employees know they are both understood and appreciated. Allow these employees to be involved in the process and to help. This creates and nurtures a decentralized system.

This is where an informed and cooperative clinic administrator — an administrator such as the hypothetical Margaret Jones — can help tremendously. Mrs. Jones knows the employees. The employees know Mrs. Jones. The employees are accustomed to listening to Mrs. Jones, accustomed to respecting and following what the clinic administrator has to say. At the same time, Mrs. Jones knows what's going on with this new management partnership. She's not having to depend on guesswork and hearsay for her information; she has been sitting in that all-important "chair" in the planning sessions.

The clinic administrator can help the management company to get to know the employees in a way that can better ensure a decentralized style of management.

If you have someone like Mrs. Jones who can be the link between the employees in the doctors' offices and corporate out of the shoot, what's likely to happen is that employees in the doctors' office and management people in the company will actually get to know one another, respect one another, and complement one another.

What's also likely to happen with help of a knowledgeable, cooperative clinic administrator is that it won't take "a rocket scientist" to set up this decentralized structure. It will naturally evolve.

Practice Administrator as the Ongoing Go-between

The pivotal role of the clinic administrator doesn't stop with helping to "sell" this partnership on the front end.

Quite the contrary. The administrator has an ongoing role as the all-important go-between that links the company and the doctors.

By the very nature of how this partnering business is structured, the clinic administrator will report to a board that has representatives from both the management company and the doctors. That board sets direction and policy, representing the doctors' interest and the company's interest. Then the board looks to the clinic administrator to help implement that policy.

In interacting with this board through the decentralized approach I favor, one of the key roles of the clinic administrator would be to function as a kind of "prime minister" for decentralization.

It's worth noting that the board shouldn't have a hard time selling the clinic administrator on decentralization. This idea of decentralization generally isn't hard to sell to a clinic administrator or to other employees who work in the doctors' offices. Decentralization works to the favor of qualified employees, because it entrusts them with responsibility and rewards them for handling responsibility well.

In a partnership agreement managed with the decentralized approach, the clinic administrator would take a leading role in conveying this corporate-office message of decentralization to the employees in the doctors' office: "We want you to have input and independence, and we are not going to dictate to you every step of the way how you perform management functions in the doctor's office. That means making decisions happen as much as possible inside the doctors' office, where the patients are being served. That means having our corporate people in the role of supporters and facilitators, not folks who come in and usurp the functions of everyone at the doctors' offices."

Five Setup Steps of Decentralization

In getting decentralization firmly entrenched in the new partnership implementation, I think five initial steps are crucial. Some of these steps take place in the doctors' offices. Some of these steps take place in the management company's corporate offices. Some are a joint endeavor.

With the steps that take place in the doctors' offices, it's helpful to have the assistance of an experienced clinic administrator to work with the management company in laying this foundation for decentralization.

In the event that for some reason the clinic administrator is replaced, then the successor in this position takes the leading role in assisting corporate with these steps as this partnership goes into the implementation phase:

1. A priority is communicating to the employees in the doctors' offices not only the responsibility that they have but also the accountability they face. It is imperative that all employees have it communicated to them clearly what is expected of them in their jobs in light of the new partnership. Then it's important it be communicated that corporate is willing to give them room to do their jobs. In a decentralized approach, this is corporate's message that we are asking the administrator to help us convey to employees: "We are giving you leeway. We are saying we believe in you and your abilities. We have a high level of expectation of your performance. But part of the deal here is that we expect you to perform and carry out those responsibilities. You will be held accountable." I strongly believe if you empower competent people to make good

decisions and get out of their way, they will make good decisions. This can be a win-win-win situation. It can be a win for the doctors and their patients, for the management company, and for employees and the clinic administrator.

2. At the same time the clinic administrator is helping corporate to communicate this responsibility/accountability balance to the employees in a doctors' office, there are some attitudes that must be re-enforced and re-emphasized by leaders of the management company in their communications to key people in the corporate offices. I think mature "corporate attitudes" are so crucial to success that they're worthy of re-emphasizing at the corporate level relevant to every single new affiliation corporate enters into.

I've mentioned some of those attitudes earlier in the book, in Chapter 4, and I think they are worthy of mentioning here. I believe that management people in the corporate offices need to understand and believe that they are there to serve the field — the doctors' offices — and not that the doctors' offices are there to serve the corporate office. Corporate people need to remember that revenue is generated in the field, not in the corporate offices. This means as long as the employees in the doctors' offices are competent and doing their jobs and making good decisions, corporate must not interfere with them. When corporate intervenes, it must be to bring in resources and support that add value, not to interfere or subordinate or unnecessarily second-guess.

Corporate staff have it incumbent on them to make sure in this regard that they are not into what I call "empire-building" and "silo management." I've seen situations where corporate employees got carried away by measuring their worth based on how many people reported to them and how much power they had and on building these little towers, or silos, aimed at management in a vacuum. All this can be very detrimental to the spirit of decentralization.

On the other side of the coin, if the company has access to a good, strong clinic administrator in a new affiliation that's being implemented, and the company listens to and works with that clinic administrator, we're a step ahead of the game in this regard in letting decentralization function smoothly.

3. With the help of key individuals from the doctors' offices, "processing" approaches must be set up that make it possible to meet the doctors' needs quickly and smoothly. The goal of a partnering agreement is to correct old problems and to create new opportunities. The goal is not to create "processing problems" that set up roadblocks and create more hassles for the doctors than they had before.

I'll tell you from experience that 90 percent of problems in getting things done quickly can result from lack of communication between the doctor's office and corporate about process — setting up the right ways to do things. I saw firsthand at MedPartners that this is extremely important. When I think of "process," one area that's very important is that the management company needs to listen very closely to the clinic administrator when it comes to the processes for adding and replacing employees.

Let me give you my scenario of an example of a wrong way to respond to a doctor's immediate need: A nurse who is working for a doctor in the group has to leave suddenly, with no notice, due to personal problems. The doctor has to have a replacement, and quickly. If this doctor is dealing with some folks at corporate who are using a "process" that's slowing things down, it could go like this: "You need a nurse? Okay, fill out a request form. Then we'll put an ad in the newspaper and screen the candidates. And maybe in a couple of weeks you've got your nurse." So the doctor is standing there scratching his head saying, "It's going to take me 14 days to get a nurse? And in the meantime I'm out of business? So what value is there in this process. And how much is this process costing our practice? We hired you guys in the management company to move us faster, not slow us down."

Now the moral of this story where the clinic administrator is concerned is that if the administrator had been involved from the beginning, the administrator likely would zero in on the urgency of getting the nurse. The administrator likely would have some valuable guidance as to what process should be used to get the nurse. The administrator might even know exactly where to get this nurse — in fact, maybe even a quick transfer of a nurse who is already working in some other job within the doctors' organization.

4. Information must be obtained early on to provide the corporate office with guidance and advice concerning the reasons the people at the doctors' offices have been doing things a certain way in the past — such as buying from certain vendors and using certain service people. I can't tell you how valuable this information is, to keep corporate folks from going off making changes just for change sake. The goal here is make changes only when they are in order, and only when they are wise changes. Sometimes the wisest decision is to leave things the way they are.

Our goal at corporate here is not to make things different; the goal is to make things better. The goal is not to make changes which tend to "throw out the baby with the bath-water." When you have access to an experienced clinic administrator who has worked a long time with this practice, the administrator knows how things were done in the past, and why they were done that way. We at corporate don't know that. We need the administrator, or whatever appropriate persons at the practice possess this information, to communicate all this to us at corporate and to guide us accordingly.

One reason this whole issue is so important is that the purchase of supplies and the selection of service people is one area that will be approached very differently under a management partnership than it was before the doctors entered into a partnering agreement. Prior to the affiliation, these decisions about where to buy supplies and services were made there in the doctors' offices, usually by the clinic administrator or someone who worked under the administrator's direction. Historically, if they needed to buy something in the doctors' office, they just bought it. With the new partnering with the management company, this changes.

Now the management company is revisiting all these vendor and service relationships. Some of those old relationships will remain intact; others will be discontinued. If the management company doesn't take a look at the "big picture," some vendors and service people could be discontinued that should not be discontinued. In my opinion, here's where an experienced party like the clinic administrator really can come in. The administrator has the ability to factor in not only how much money is being paid out but also relevant factors such as loyalty and quality and trust. I mean, here's where someone like the administrator needs to speak up and where it behooves a management company to listen.

For example, you might cut out some guy who's been servicing certain equipment in that doctors' office for years and save a few cents or a few dollars a year by going to a national service contract. But what do you stand to lose? Will this national company come to that doctors' office on short notice to service the equipment? Can you depend on a national company to come quickly when you need emergency service in the middle of the night or on a holiday or when there's an electrical power failure? If the management company decides to make a change that results in a little money-savings but you lose the true service aspect of the purchase, then what you're left with is true economic cost that's significantly more than the savings you generated by a volume discount or whatever. Those are factors to consider in the partnering. The clinic administrator and/or other knowledgeable employees in the practice can provide valuable guidance.

5. We want the practice administrator to work with the corporate office to take advantage of areas where he or she can "pull down" corporate resources to help the doctors in the practice. This is an area where this partnership agreement can sing! It's an area where it can bring value, grow the practice. All of a sudden the clinic administrator and the doctors have available to them business resources they didn't have previously. During the early negotiations the administrator needs to take inventory of what the corporate resources are, and the company needs to take inventory of all the functions the administrator handles and where

corporate resources could plug into these functions. There's room for tremendous creativity here.

I'm talking about the administrator reaching out to corporate and pulling these resources toward him or her to meet needs and add value. I'm not talking about shoving these resources at the administrator and the other employees, of forcing them on the practice in a centralized fashion. I'm talking about assistance the administrator will be glad to have and which will benefit the doctors. I'm not talking about a scenario in which someone at corporate is pushing this on the administrator and saying, "Get out of the way. We're corporate. And we do it this way."

Let me give an example: Let's say the doctor-group has a pending real estate issue — to do with expansion, acquisition, construction, whatever. The clinic administrator should be able to pull from resources at the corporate office, to take advantage of corporate talent that can assist in this real estate deal. Another example: Maybe the administrator has been asked by the doctors to look at some purchase of technology. The administrator should be able to pull down expertise from corporate experiences in negotiated pricing, to augment this decision-making. In this area of pulling down corporate resources, there is unlimited potential to add value to the doctors and their practice.

Training Employees in "The Genus Standard"

The doctors' office employees with whom we deal through Genus will be involved in an extensive and exciting Genus staff development and training program. Genus Aesthetic Medical & Dental Group will invest heavily in employee training and development with a goal of introducing employees to consistent Genus approaches that must be practiced by Genus affiliates everywhere.

I refer to this set of consistent approaches as "The Genus Standard."

Creating the Genus Standard is necessary in our strategy of establishing and promoting a Genus brand name as part of the retail concept. This Genus brand name is part of our strategy in growing our particular market.

Although each Genus affiliate will retain its own autonomy in practice operations, each affiliate will help create a Genus brand presence that links it in a public- perception sense with all other Genus affiliates across the nation. Because of this linkage, each and every Genus affiliate must consistently provide the same level of quality patient service.

In creating a brand name we are saying to the public: All of the physicians and dentists who partner with Genus adhere to the same high standard. All of the employees who work in the offices of those physicians and dentists from coast to coast will become an integral part of creating a unique experience.

As we develop this consistency, Genus patients will expect the service experience wherever they engage with a Genus affiliate.

It is our goal that the Genus brand name will stand for high-quality service to patients and clients not only in terms of the best in technique and technology but also the best in attitude. When I say "attitude" I'm talking about elements such as friendliness, concern, confidentiality, and follow-through.

To make all this happen, we will be investing heavily in the component of training people as to what's expected.

I'm describing a training program that expects the same kind of service elements that Disney demonstrates. When you go to Disney World, you encounter employees who all seem to have the interests of the customers at heart. Every detail of the Disney experience is thought through carefully and in detail — the way Disney employees talk to people, the way they transport them from one place to another, the way they serve them. Why can't aesthetic healthcare be delivered this way?

I mentioned earlier in this chapter that I have a very special interest in this whole issue of "personalized" dealings with patients. I have a special interest in that personalization because this is going to be a mainstay of our standard. No one should ever feel like just another number, a nameless face, or part of a "herd of cattle." The patient experience on a consistent basis must be individualized, personalized, understood.

As I mentioned earlier, this personalization in dealing with all aspects of a patient's experience with Genus is not optional. It's mandatory. Each Genus patient should finish a Genus experience feeling like a special, catered-to individual whose care and experience were personalized by the doctors and the employees.

People should feel this personalization with every Genus contact — in interacting with the doctor, the nurse, the technician operating some of the high-tech equipment, the receptionist, the person handling the financial arrangements.

For the patient who'll experience Genus, the lasting impression will not come from the look of the facade of the building. Instead, the patient's lasting impression will mainly be formed by the people the patients encounter inside the building — by how these people interact with the patient and how they interact with one another. If the staff members are not coordinated and communicating with ease, it will reflect negatively on their interactions with the patient. There has to be a smoothness in the employee interactions — a smoothness and ease that will create trust in The Genus Standard.

This retail and service approach in many respects creates a different style from the conventional doctor-partnering model in the PPM industry. In the conventional model, there is no brand name with which all the affiliates are associated. In the conventional model, there is no major national promotion that has the goal of growing understanding and awareness.

The reason we're able to do this is we're not depending on third-party decisions and sick people. Instead, Genus services will mostly be elective and performed for healthy people.

My vision for Genus is — through training and development of Genus-affiliated physicians and dentists and their staffs — to create a positive "experience" for the typical patient that differentiates this company and its affiliates from mediocrity.

To make all this happen, it's crucial for Genus to have the buy-in and enthusiasm of employees interacting with clients.

We must remember that people "want" our services. They don't necessarily "need" our services. Our goal is to create an experience that makes each Genus patient glad he or she was exposed to The Genus Standard.

10

To Start and to Sustain: The Birth and Performance of a Company

I HAVE a vivid memory of the first time I walked into a conference room to make a presentation to raise VC, or venture capital, funds.

This presentation was in 1992, and it was for the initial venture capital funding for MedPartners.

The scene was this: I walked into the conference room and in front of me was a big table. And there on the table, stacked about as high as I could see, were business plans. Business plans all over the place!

I took my seat with these really bright people, these VC guys who held MBAs from places like Harvard. They were all rather emotionless. And it seemed they were all talking to me at the same time — firing questions at me about our business plan for MedPartners.

The tenor of their questions was focused on shooting holes in our plan: "Why is it the way it is in your plan? If this ratio changes over here, what happens over here? How does this compare to someone else in the industry?"

We were successful in getting our funding for MedPartners. So the ultimate outcome of our initial MedPartners' courtship of the investment community was a positive one. However, I'd be less than candid if I didn't admit that for me that first VC presentation was a grueling experience. As I sat in that room — with a host of business plans from other competing start-up companies stacked up all over the place, and these highly-educated business guys firing away at me — I was intimidated. Fortunately, I wasn't smart enough to be scared.

Since this was my first time out with a VC presentation, I didn't really comprehend the subtleties of what was going on. Later on as I looked back to 1992, I realized I had been naive. I should have perceived that what I was seeing was a negotiation tactic in action. It was the goal of these guys to make you feel like you were one in a million, to make you feel they didn't need you. It was part of a game.

Having all those business plans stacked up in front of me was like a stage-setting or window-dressing part of the game. Later on, as I understood this process better, I knew this represented an unspoken message from the VCs to me that was quite clear: "So you think you're unique because you put together a business plan for a start-up company? Look here! We've got lots of business plans from which to choose in deciding where to place our venture capital."

It's also part of the game to shoot questions at you, to communicate that your plan has all kinds of flaws. What this can do, if you don't respond well and you don't hold your own, is allow them to dilute you, to own more of your company. The game plan is this: The more holes they shoot in the plan, the cheaper they can buy an interest in the company. The game is negotiating how much of the company gets sold to the investors. If the investors can weaken the company's plan, through questions and challenges and shooting holes in assumptions, then essentially — if they are interested in your plan at all — they can buy into the company at a better price. They can get a better deal than if they had said, "Hey, you've got a great idea here. We don't find any problems with your business plan. How much money do you want?"

The Second Time Around

It was easier the second time around. It was easier to go in and face the VC guys. However, it was an even tougher environment.

It was tougher because the VCs became much more savvy about the PPM industry during the five years that elapsed between my first and second time around.

When I was raising money for MedPartners in 1992, the VCs were shooting a high volume of questions at us. However, the content of their questions did not reflect much in terms of their having a real understanding of the physician practice management industry. At that time, the PPM industry was still so new, such a different concept, that the issues involved still were foreign to a lot of people, including the VCs and us. As I presented to VCs in 1992, even though I was a bit taken by the challenging and rapid-fire nature of their questions, it was still clear to me that no one had PPM experience.

That was not the case in 1997, when I was facing the VCs again — this time raising venture capital money for Genus Aesthetic Medical & Dental Group. By this time, the newness was gone. Some people had been burned. During the five years that had gone by, hundreds of companies had raised money to start companies which were partnering with physicians and dentists. And, as more and more business plans had come to VCs, and as they monitored how these companies performed over the long-term, they knew more about the opportunities and they knew more about the problems. Their questions were a lot tougher.

I was glad in 1997 that it was not my first time out. I was glad for having had that experience five years back with the stacked-up business plans and the roomful of interrogators. I was glad for my experience as a chief operating officer inside the PPM giant MedPartners during that five years. And I also was glad we now had a business plan with Genus that contained new and different retail medicine and dentistry components which struck a quick, positive cord with the VCs.

Five years of hardcore experience in a booming and fast-changing industry can infuse you with added respect in many arenas. By the time I faced VCs in 1997, I had developed a seasoned respect for the responsibilities VCs face. I had a higher respect for why the VCs were playing such a tough "game" with me back in 1992. These guys have a tremendous fiduciary responsibility to the people who invest in their funds. Venture capital people typically are looking to make four to five times their investment. If they put up $1 million they want to realize a $4 million to $5 million value in a relatively short period of time. And the competition for the VC money is monumental. These VCs have a host of new ideas and new business plans from which to choose. They must ask the tough questions in order to choose wisely.

When the VCs are sizing up a new business plan, they look at the horse and they look at the jockey. The horse is the idea, the concept, for the company — as explained through the business plan. The jockey is the leader who will head up the company. In a sense, I think many times they tend to look even more closely at the track record of the jockey than they do the specific traits of the horse.

It's not some deep secret or hard-to-understand formula that the VCs use in evaluating a horse and a jockey. The VCs' inventory of questions basically covers this territory: They look for market, to see if the market is there and if it's growing. They look for a unit model — that is, have you developed a unit model for doing business that makes sense and can be duplicated in different geographical locations? They look for whether the company's top leader is experienced with a solid track record. They look for whether this jockey in turn has recruited a strong board of directors and a well-incentivized management team that has relevant training and experience. They look at whether the valuation is reasonable — the amount of the company that they are buying and projected returns.

The path of questioning they follow is not a mystery. But you'd better be prepared to answer questions to the VCs' satisfaction if you expect to raise the funds you need.

When I was seeking VC funding for Genus in 1997, I received incredibly great response. In four months' time, I received offers for $30.5 million in VC monies to start up Genus. We were substantially over-subscribed. I ended up accepting $19.5 million in VC money to start up Genus Aesthetic Medical & Dental Group Inc.

Since the competition for the VC money is so stiff, and since the questions with our industry are getting tougher and tougher, I knew this positive response to Genus was a solid endorsement.

I knew this horse called Genus was a good one to ride. And I knew, from having lived the experience, that I — the jockey — had paid some dues and earned investor confidence.

Some Memories of a Jockey

The excitement was riveting at MedPartners from the time we hit the ground running.

Sitting in a pivotal chief operating officer slot and spending the majority of my time and effort doing development, I had a chance to help direct nonstop frontline action as MedPartners quickly made its way to the top as the largest PPM company in the United States.

Deals came fast. I learned something new from each and every one of the 120 or so doctor-group/management-company transactions in which I participated. Every affiliation had its common denominators but then also had its unique elements with people and structure. I learned something about myself, too — that I love doing deals. I like doctors; I like the business. Actually, I had found myself at home in the healthcare industry from the time I went to work as a young assistant hospital administrator back in the early 1980s. When it came to MedPartners, no one could have been a better mentor than MedPartners' founding CEO, Larry House. Larry was a talented deal-maker — in fact, a consummate deal-maker. Maybe too much of a deal-maker.

In the early days at MedPartners, as we were putting together these partnerships, there was not a lot of understanding among the doctors about what we were doing. As I've said, this whole physician practice management concept still was in its infancy. So there was a learning curve that had to be developed on the other side. As we met with the principals — the physicians and their advisers — there often was a hell of a lot of coaching that had to be done to raise the level of understanding for all parties. We not only were doing a lot of deals; we were doing a considerable number of smaller deals.

On the operations side, I learned in the field and in the corporate offices. I spent a lot of time on the road, traveling thousands of miles and spending hundreds of hours with doctors and their staffs in the offices where they worked.

The escalating level of operations activity that existed at MedPartners during that rapid-growth period is something a person would have had to actually be involved in to believe! Some of the people who worked for me did a little tracking of the activity during the time I was there as chief operating officer-East. We grew so rapidly at MedPartners that, at the height of the activity while I was there, we were averaging 150 calls a day coming into my office alone! These calls were coming from the 100 to 110 physician groups, representing more than 800 physicians, that I was dealing with in locations stretching from South Florida to Texas up all along the Eastern Seaboard to Connecticut. These practices were diverse in size and specialty. There were groups in which the members were all in one specialty, and there were groups in which members were in a wide range of specialties. They ranged from a three-man dermatology group to a multi-specialty group of 140 physicians. I was getting various transaction-related, negotiation-related calls from the doctors and their lawyers and accountants and also from our own MedPartners people.

Again, along the way during that exciting period, I learned a lot from MedPartners CEO Larry House. One of the things that Larry effectively communicated to me was the investment of time, hard work, and overall commitment that you as an individual must make when you're participating in a start-up company. Larry understood the sacrifices you have to make, and the volume and intensity of work you must do. It's something that no one who hasn't been there can understand.

As we went forward with MedPartners, it didn't take me long to develop my own "big picture" about what it's like to sit in a key seat in this situation. This is the way I see it: Being involved in an investor-owned company in a new industry is like living with a revolver at your temple with the hammer pulled back. It is intense. I came to feel that you're only as good as your worst deal. I mean, it's like this: You screw up big-time and your brains can get blown out — not literally, but professionally. However, on the other side of the coin, if you do well, you stand to do real well.

Suffice it to say that doing something like this is not for the faint of heart. You've got to be ready to step up. You've got to be willing to take your beatings when your beatings are due. You have to learn from your mistakes and learn how to correct those mistakes and move on.

There's something about this kind of challenge that gets my adrenaline flowing. I love it! I like the fact that you can't go to a shelf and pull out a textbook that will tell you how people before you have done what you're doing now. Instead, in what we're doing we are the ones who are writing the textbook. Some people thrive on the unstructured nature of that environment. I'm one of those people.

I was aware while I was deeply involved at MedPartners that, if my experience was productive, it was an experience that could prepare and qualify me as a "jockey" to go out and ride my own horse — to move from being a No. 2. guy in MedPartners to starting up and heading my own venture. That was my plan all along. MedPartners for me was a productive experience. And Genus became my own horse.

Why This Horse Will Ride

I think you know when something has a good feel to it.

When we were putting together the components of the Genus business model, I knew that the opportunity was there.

It didn't surprise me when the venture capital guys embraced Genus. I didn't have to stretch to find some pieces of the Genus plan that they would like. I knew before I went in to make the VC presentations that the pieces all fit together like a unit, like a complete puzzle. And I knew what the VCs liked about this horse:

- **Our "niche" in the healthcare industry** — bringing together the physicians and dentists who perform aesthetic services on a "wants" versus a "needs" basis.
- **Our pioneering** — introducing a unique high-end retail concept into aesthetic medicine and dentistry.
- **Our unit model** — our Genus unit model that can be duplicated in high-end markets all over the nation where the whole is greater than the sum of the parts.
- **Our payment-for-services base** — focusing mainly on patients paying directly for services rather than third-party intervention.
- **Our minimal need for information systems** — the fact that direct patient payments rather than third-party payments meant we

would not need the complex information systems which have muddied the water in the more conventional physician practice management industry.

- **Our product** — "look better-feel better" aesthetic services provided during an era when new developments in technique and technology are creating more and more possibilities.
- **Our market** — taking an offensive marketing approach focused on the middle-income to upper-income, especially targeting the more affluent baby-boomer population that knows what it wants and is willing to pay for it.
- **Our sales strategy** — emphasizing building critical mass in targeted markets, our "rifle approach."
- **Our sales tools** — using a Genus brand name as a standard and a "label" to promote the concept and set the standard, training doctors' office employees and even the doctors themselves to provide a consistent Genus product, and educating patients about aesthetic services and directing them toward Genus providers.
- **Our founding board of directors.**

The Founding Board of Directors

As soon as the Genus vision took form in a detailed enough fashion to enable me to communicate it clearly, my immediate goal was to identify outstanding leaders who would join me in sharing this vision.

These were the leaders I asked to join with me in becoming founding members of the Genus board of directors.

There's no doubt in my mind that the diversity and strength of the Genus board have helped Genus to build immediate momentum.

Besides myself, these are the founders on Genus' board of directors:
- **Abraham D. Gosman.** Involved in healthcare for some 40 years and a leader in companies such as Meditrust, Mediplex, PhyMatrix and CareMatrix. Abe Gosman has a strong Wall Street record and has successfully taken six companies public. He is truly a visionary, a healthcare/business icon.
- **Dr. Charles A. "Scotty" McCallum.** Retired president of the

University of Alabama at Birmingham, Dr. McCallum also is a former dental school dean — an oral surgeon with degrees from both medical school and dental school. Dr. McCallum brings to Genus an internationally recognized clinical presence and the knowledge of how to educate.

- **Bruce A. Rendina.** As president of DASCO Companies, Bruce Rendina is a leader of the company that's one of the largest medical real estate office-building developers in the United States. As Genus' real estate needs emerge, Bruce Rendina's depth in the healthcare real estate arena will aid tremendously.

- **Barry P. Schochet.** Executive vice president for Tenet Health System, Barry Schochet is based with Tenet in Dallas. He holds a key position in what next to Columbia is the largest investor-owned, acute-care hospital company in the nation. He brings to Genus great insight in overall healthcare operations and familiarity with multiple markets.

- Serving in board positions to represent the investor interests are representatives from the co-leads among our five venture capital partners. One of these representatives is **Scott F. Meadow,** a general partner with Sprout Group. I have known and respected Scott Meadow from my early days at MedPartners, when he was with a VC company that became an original MedPartners investor. The other investor representative on the board is **Jack Tyrrell,** a former investment banker who now is a partner with Richland Ventures. (In addition to Sprout and Richland Ventures, Genus' other venture capital partners are Chancellor LGT Private Capital, Oak Investment Partners, and Skyline Venture Partners.)

The Challenge: To Sustain

Earlier in this book I expressed my strong view that "sizzle" is on its way out in this PPM industry and that it's being replaced by operational performance. We're seeing a trend where interested parties are looking beyond the smoke and mirrors to see what's real and what's not real. It's not blowing smoke anymore.

The PPM industry has created such a stir, and in many instances has made people so much money, that there have been new companies cropping up right and left. Some of these "new kids on the block" are in the mold of the more traditional physician practice management company, or PPMC. Others are what I call the niche companies, which have cornered off some "piece" of the PPM market with physicians or dentists or both.

Well, the "neighborhood" is getting a little crowded. This doctor-partnering neighborhood that in the early days was mostly upscale and high-quality is now being infiltrated by some doctor-partnering companies which are building rather shoddy houses that few live in very long or very happily. In short, there are so-called PPM companies moving into the neighborhood which are just creating critical mass and have no value to offer.

It's shakedown time. We are seeing a period in which a lot of these companies simply are not going to make it because there is no depth to enable them to produce results, to have "sustainability."

For several years I've been deeply involved in development and operations in this industry. I've circulated among the cream of the crop in the investment community as I've made my fund-raising rounds to start up two companies, five years apart. I've heard the talk, and I'm seeing the results.

It has become commonplace that, in addition to the capable people who are running already-established quality PPM companies and starting stable new ones, there also is an unrealistic collection of people promoting doctor-partnering concepts. Included in this group are people who have just looked at the glamour side. They have just looked at the glitz of being involved in the creation of a public company — looked at how they think this thing they are doing is going to skyrocket and they are all going to get rich. In this group are people who are failing to see the realities of their transactions and what it means to sustain.

Some of these unrealistic people already are and will continue to be impacted by today's negative reactions to sizzle and "the three shells and a pea."

In fact, the way I see it, this trend away from sizzle and smoke-blowing indeed is creating two levels of "cuts" in this doctor-partnering industry that has grown so fast. Unrealistic folks in doctor-partnering will continue to fall victim to these "cuts."

The "first cut" level I see is that more companies are going to have trouble on the front end raising the investment money they need to start up a company. As I said, investors like these VC guys are just getting tougher on the details and on the long-term outlook.

The "second cut" level I see is a failure to thrive and survive among companies which are not able to perform well and sustain themselves after they go into operation. If a new start-up does not have depth and sustainability, the fluff is likely to fall out sooner or later — these days, I'd say more likely sooner than later.

There are some companies that will somehow make it through the first cut only to fall victim to the second cut not too far down the road. For the most part, these are the companies which somehow procure enough money to go into operation but which are not able to produce results after they get into operation. Most of these companies will fail because they lack a good business plan, because they don't have a management team capable of executing their plan, or because they are not capitalized well enough — or a combination of these reasons. In the capitalization arena, there are companies which lack enough pulling power on the front end to attract major VC funding but nevertheless start up on a shoestring budget — sometimes with the help of maybe one private "angel investor" who got sold on their concept. There are a few among this group that do well long-term, but they are very few and far between.

Once a company is in business, it indeed is "sustainability" time and not "sizzle" time. By sustainability I mean whether a company can deliver a sustainable value, whether it can create that long-term mutually beneficial partnership, whether it can bring value-added. By sustainability, I mean whether or not a company can interact with the doctors in ways that make money for the doctors and the company. The doctors expect to make money after entering into an affiliation with a management company, and they should expect to make money. But the doctors also want — and have a right to expect — that a management company not only help them financially but also assist toward other goals. They have a right to expect the management company to help them build marketshare with a practice that's on the cutting edge of what's going on in the medical or dental profession.

Sooner or later if you're going to sustain a company you've got to do more than talk. You've got to produce results. You've got to implement. You've got to execute. There has to be some evidence of tangible results. If you can't turn your business plan into something of benefit, then everything else is going to go out the window. If you can't produce, vision is just vision. If you can't take a concept and move it to implementation and reality, what you're looking at is just junk!

I mentioned earlier that we're seeing people get a lot smarter among the analysts, the VCs, the general investment community. Others also are getting smarter. Those people who are the key players in individual doctor-partnering transactions are getting more sophisticated about the industry. The physicians are getting smarter. The dentists are getting smarter. The lawyers and accountants representing the various parties are getting smarter.

These people have learned a great deal about how to look beyond the smoke and mirrors and separate what's real from what's not real. These people are getting more savvy in spotting the copycats in this doctor-partnering business. They're getting more savvy in spotting the people who have no substance.

But, at the same time, these interested and involved parties also are becoming more savvy in how to work with those doctor-partnering companies that do have the plan and the power to add value and sustain.

On My Genus Menu

I feel we have four key things in place that give us a running start with "sustainability" at Genus.

First is the quality of our business plan, the quality of our business model.

Next is the strength of our capitalization, which I think places us in a position to take advantage of business opportunities that can create a solid foundation on which we can build and grow.

Next is our board of directors.

And next, and very importantly, is our management team. We've put together a top-notch Genus management team. Members of this team represent track records in diverse businesses all related to what we're doing, and these are top-tier people I'm confident can execute our business plan.

Beyond this, I have a few priorities for our company's "sustainability" that are high on my Genus "menu." They have to do with:

- Integrating intellectual capital.
- Creating momentum by showing value-added results soon after an affiliation is closed.
- Implementing "profitability" systems aligned with quality control.
- Concentrating on "growing" a culture.
- Educating consumers about quality.

Creating Momentum

It's my feeling that once an affiliation is closed you need to create momentum by getting the doctors focused on something new and exciting from the onset.

That's one thing I'm stressing at Genus.

Not long after signing a partnering agreement, the doctors and the company should start doing something positive together.

In my mind, if the doctors and the management company take part in joint initiatives from the beginning, this can represent "step one" in their relationship in several respects:

It's step one toward getting everyone focused on the joint strategic agenda.

It's "step one" toward doing something positive and proactive to get the value-added ball rolling immediately, rather than spending valuable time worrying about something negative. If you agree to be partners with someone and then time goes by without any activity, you can become anxious and concerned and develop negative energy instead of positive energy.

And it's "step one" in focusing on how to function well within the partnership, on getting accustomed to working well together as partners.

Again, it's no different from a marriage. It's not really a comfortable marriage if you get married and your life does not change in a positive way. It's not really a comfortable marriage if the two of you don't start accomplishing goals jointly that you could not accomplish separately.

The nature of these first initiatives will differ from one partnership to another. A first initiative for one doctor-group might be some technology the doctors haven't used before. A first initiative for another doctor-group might be an expansion or a merger.

Regardless of what form the first initiatives take, timing is important. These initiatives need to start taking shape very soon after an affiliation is closed.

The Importance of Team-building

When I was growing up, I played a lot of ball, including baseball. I think there are a lot of similarities between building and coaching a baseball team and building and leading a company.

With both a team and with a company, it's important that you identify and recruit the right people for the various positions. It's important that these individual "players" are able to interact and function as a unit — as an effective team.

It's a challenge — albeit an exciting one — to put together a high-quality team for a new company. In recruiting the best people for key company positions in areas such as development, operations, promotion, etc., the process really is similar to the baseball team-building of selecting the pitchers and catchers, putting together the infield and outfield, and making sure there's a strong batting lineup. Everything's got to make sense. Everything has to contribute. It's all got to fit, to interface with the other pieces.

Once you have recruited your company's initial team, the way you proceed strategically to reach your company goals also can draw analogies from the game of baseball. As you first begin moving your company's business plan from concept into execution, it's like you're in "Spring training" — getting ready to compete in that first season. As you launch the season, you have game plans, tactics, strategy for getting where you want to go. And, like in baseball, you have that overall vision of where you want to be headed. For me, the vision of where I want to go with Genus is like embarking on the road to the World Series.

As you get the right team in place — making needed adjustments and changes as they become necessary — you'll soon find that the team spirit, the team success, will begin to drive your company like a unit. You'll find that, through team-building, a company culture is taking root.

The Company Culture

If we look in a commonly-used Webster's dictionary to see what is meant by "culture" as it would apply to a company, we find that Webster is really saying our culture is our "customary beliefs, social forms and material traits." In short, our culture is really what we stand for.

It's crucial to me that a company I'm heading develop a culture that stands for high values and consistency. It's a top priority with me to see to it that the Genus culture is communicated to everyone in the company. It's crucial to me that the people who work in that company understand and adhere to the company's "culture."

When you have a new company like Genus, you have a wonderful opportunity in that you're building the company culture from the beginning. You're not coming into a company that has been in existence for years where you might not agree with what the company stands for — and then you either have to adjust or try to change things.

However, the culture-building is still a challenge. For one thing, I think in a fast-paced industry you can have so many tasks that the company might not pause long enough to build a culture.

I'm determined that this will not happen at Genus. I want Genus to have a clear mission, clear "social forms" of how we interact with people, and a clear set of beliefs and traits and goals. And I want each and every person who works for Genus to understand this company's mission and to understand the Genus beliefs and traits and goals.

If you don't have a real culture in your organization, you can end up with people working for the company who don't even know what the company does!

I have been exposed to organizations which suffered from this. I have been inside companies where I'm convinced you could have this scenario: I think you could pass around a sheet of paper to all the employees and tell them to write down in 100 words or less what the company does, and the majority of the employees would not have a clue where to start!

At Genus, we are going to have a "cultural tie" with our doctor-affiliates that is closer than what is customarily seen in a more conventional doctor-partnering relationship. The reason for that unusually close cultural tie is the Genus brand name — a brand name that's going to link us all in a unified "label" of being associated with high-end aesthetic medical and dental services. This is a "label" tied to a standard and defined by a culture.

I find that brand name to be a real strong plus in building the culture of the company called Genus. I find that brand name a plus in linking the goals of our affiliates with one another and in turn linking our affiliates' goals with us at the corporate offices. We all are working under a common standard — to improve the Quality of Life for everyone who encounters a company called Genus.

There is no way to separate the issue of the Genus brand name from the issue of the Genus corporate culture.

Each of our affiliates will retain its own cultural separateness, but at the same time this Genus brand and standard will link us together.

As for how this Genus brand name should impact our people in the corporate offices, if corporate employees really understand what the Genus brand name stands for, then they've gone a long way toward understanding the overall culture of this company called Genus.

I have a fervor about doing things the right way to develop the people in our corporate offices and also develop the people in the Genus affiliate offices to honor the high-end, top-quality, and consistency traits which the Genus brand name represents. To do this, we must have top-quality training that runs the whole gamut. This includes training in hospitality and advocacy, management training, clinical training, sales and presentation training, etc. — all geared toward patient/client satisfaction.

The whole key to this puzzle is to create the culture. We must do this through training and development. And then that has to tie into the incentive system.

If we can do this — if we can establish, promote and live up to the Genus brand name — we'll be great. If we can't do that, we'll be no more than an aggregation of pieces spread out — with no consistency, no brand, no service standard, no way to differentiate.

As I look at the culture issue, as I look at the brand issue, it really boils down to the piece that has to do with training and development of the people. It's not the money. It's not the technology. It's the experience. It's how we all treat one another and in turn how we all make sure the patients are treated and served when they are drawn in by the Genus brand name and served by our Genus affiliates.

That's all central to our Genus culture.

Checks and Balances

In the physician practice management industry, be it a traditional model or a "niche model," you're trying to accomplish several goals concurrently that relate to different arenas and different audiences. There's a real business challenge in this.

This challenge is: How can you grow quickly, maintain your vision, not compromise your quality, and add value to your affiliates and your shareholders — all simultaneously?

I'll be honest with you: I've not seen a PPM company really hit on all of these the way I think it could or should be done. Most, I believe, have not focused on the needs of all the parties who come to the table. Perhaps a missing link has been getting the doctors to buy into valid quality control systems which relate to clinical outcomes and profitability.

If you've got a good shot in this PPM industry at succeeding with these multi-track goals, you must have a company structure that's set up with checks and balances.

At Genus, we're placing high priority on establishing and utilizing five core approaches: Number one, integrating the intellectual capital and experience of our affiliates into the growth and development of the company. Number two, focusing the strength, responsiveness and commitment of management toward adding value to our affiliates. Number three, remaining responsive and flexible with regard to changes in market conditions and opportunities. Number four, developing (with the doctors) systems to improve "closure-rates" when consulting with new patients, making more efficient use of operating and follow-up schedules, and generating higher percentages of repeat business. Number five, assisting the doctor in developing his/her "dream practice" — such as one in which the doctor spends his/her time doing the things he/she does best.

Educating the Consumer

When I say we're implementing a Genus retail concept to grow the volume of and elevate the gratification ratios of the business for the doctors who affiliate with us, I'm talking about the use of strategies to educate the consumer. I'm referring to strategies to educate the consumer on what services are available, who performs them best, and how to make decisions which improve their chances of better outcomes.

As we focus on growing the volume of business for the physicians and dentists who are our affiliated aesthetic-services providers, we are using approaches that are more familiar to the world of retail than to the world of medicine and dentistry:

- **Brand preference.** I'm sure I've communicated by now that one of the most challenging things I see with Genus, and I think one of the biggest opportunities, is creating a respected brand. We're talking about separating out, setting a service standard, creating a revered label. This is our goal: We plan to use this brand to address this confusion in the marketplace about aesthetic products and services. We plan for our physicians to create a high-end brand that consumers and clients and patients will recognize as being consistent with quality — quality in technology, technique, service and outcomes. I think that's achievable, and that it will allow us to grow our businesses, because this is exactly what the public is looking for. I think we can take advantage of some of the leverage we can develop over a multi-market base, using very prominent, well-respected people already identified as "experts" in their respective fields.

- **Expanding products and services.** There's a lot of opportunity on this one. There are opportunities for our various professionals to collaborate on cases through an interdisciplinary approach. Such collaboration will foster a well-intended, outcome-based referral system in which the patient receives a higher level of care. It's amazing to see what can be accomplished when people communicate and are incentivized to think in terms of "us" rather than "me." We're also talking about ancillary products and services. Pooling all that intellectual and technical capital can lead only to one thing — a higher standard of quality than has existed prior to a company called Genus taking the leading role as facilitator.

- **Technology.** The state of technology is incredible in some of these areas — a whole range of opportunities that technology brings to the table. You've got ultrasound and lasers and microscopes. Consumers are becoming so aware of the availability of this technology that many people are beginning to ask their own doctors if they are using some of this technology. Technology can also be used to educate and sell. Imaging technology in aesthetic medicine and dentistry is a huge opportunity. The challenge is to determine how much technology a given practice needs (or can afford). The tables are turned. Doctors once told technology companies what technology was needed. Today technology companies are taking their cases directly to the public. Doctors often are put in the position of buying everything "new" or appearing to lag behind. A corporate partner like Genus can help doctors better see beyond the smoke and mirrors in the technology race.

- **Cross-utilization of capabilities.** What we're talking about here is the interaction between the various aesthetic clinicians who can find better ways to extend their capabilities by working together. We might be talking about a multi-disciplinary approach for implant dentistry involving the general dentist, the prosthodontist and the oral surgeon. We might be talking about facial plastic surgery work that involves several types of practitioners working together. There are many cross-utilization capabilities out there than can bring better patient results and enhance businesses for everyone involved in the collaborative approach.

- **Same store growth.** I was able to see evidence of "same store growth" in the more traditional physician practice management model that we used at MedPartners. Same store growth is adding additional capacity to groups. This might come from increasing the utilization of a group's surgery centers, or increasing the utilization of the group's services. Often it's just a factor of facilitation, in which the management company is able to facilitate the growth and recruitment of incremental physicians or services. Sometimes it can involve creative scheduling to minimize duplication of space, equipment, and staffing. You can understand how doctors could be so focused on their day-to-day operations that they have not been looking at either growth or efficiency opportunities. So we talk about same store growth partly in terms of the company's ability to facilitate growth by adding new providers and also facilitation of relationships with existing providers. You can achieve some of this through economies of scale and bringing in increased revenue. During my MedPartners' experience, I saw where, even as we faced some declining per unit reimbursement that went along with the third-party, managed-care environment, we still were able to grow our same stores as much as 16 to 17 percent per year. And I think with Genus' wide-open volume-growing opportunities, Genus should be able to have percentages that go higher. With this comes higher margins, a major attraction to investors. By being a good "partner" to the doctors, Genus can help identify ways to reduce (or at least minimize) duplication for both higher profitability and professional gratification.

A Practice Development Company

Because of Genus' rather unique potential for growing and developing its affiliates, we have come to refer to Genus as a "practice development company" — a company aimed at enriching its affiliates.

We see Genus in that role because of its characteristics that differ from the more traditional PPMC model.

Genus is not like a traditional PPMC in that it is not seeking declining dollars from third-party payers, it is not dependent on information systems not yet developed, and it is not seeking to extract all of its margins from "cost savings."

Because of its freedom from these elements, Genus is free strategically to build an infrastructure that focuses on capturing marketshare and enhancing revenues for the practices of its affiliates. It's free to focus on "practice development" and building consumer, client and patient preference. Through this approach, Genus also will improve the quality of life for the doctors and aesthetic specialists who are its partners. That will lead to long-term and fulfilling professional marriages — in which everyone wins.

PART FOUR:

Dual Crises—Dual Motivators

11

A High School Football Game
to Remember: An Uncharted Entry
into the Healthcare Field

ACROSS THE street from the house in which I grew up in Binghamton, New York, there was a junior high school. And the junior high school had an athletic field.

For my two brothers and me, that athletic field became our own playground. Other kids in the neighborhood often would join us in playing ball on that field — join with my older brother, John (or "J. D." for John Donald); my younger brother, Rick, and me. We would play whatever ballgame was on our agenda that day, whether it was football, baseball or basketball.

We grew up in a neat but modest neighborhood. Families who lived there had the essentials of life — we weren't wanting for anything — but it was middle-income at best, far from affluence. The houses were close together, with very narrow passageways in between. The houses were close enough that if some kid was getting a spanking three houses down, you could hear him yelling.

In the environment in which I was reared, there wasn't much to do but to play sports. There wasn't much moving-around room in our small yards for us to play ball. But, then who needs much room in your own yard if you're only a few steps away from a big, convenient athletic field across the street?

There was many a day when John, Rick, and I would barely hit the front door from school before we were out the door again and on that athletic field.

Except for school and homework when we were young kids, playing sports was what we did with our time. In the summers when there was no school, playing some kind of ball on the athletic field was mostly what we did from the time we woke up until the time we went to bed. And we loved every minute of it!

When you're a kid, you don't think of the important role something is playing in your life. You just live your life. But, looking back, I know I felt this great love for athletics as far back as I can recall, beginning before I started to grade school. With every year that passed in my childhood, I was looking towards playing some serious sports in college, and — who knows? — maybe even eyeing the possibility of a stint in the pros.

What I had no way of knowing, of course, was that this junior high athletic field in my neighborhood was a key training ground in an athletic journey for me that would find a very premature end. That end would come in a fateful high school football game — a game that would place me unwittingly on a rather circuitous path to a career in the healthcare industry.

More than Just a Pastime

For many kids, sports are just fun pastimes that represent a small piece of their lives. That wasn't the case with me. It wasn't the case with my brothers. Sports were very much an integral part of our lives.

All three of us wanted to play contact sports, and we wanted to be good. We were impatient, too. I can remember, when we were real young, we were mischievously questioning how we could somehow forge our birth certificates so we could play Little League ball sooner than the rules allowed. I remember being 7 years old and wanting to play Little League real bad, but knowing that I had to wait until I was 9 to play.

Getting the job done on the ball field came easy for me. When I finally got old enough to play Little League (and it seemed that took forever!) I was an all-star player. When I was 11, I played on an all-star team that had all 12-year-olds except for me. When I played in the Babe Ruth League, I was usually the best player on the team, never less than the second best. I enjoyed playing everywhere, in every position, wherever I was needed. When I was real little, I was an outfielder. Then I was pitcher and shortstop. Probably my real talent was that I was a good hitter.

Baseball probably was my best sport. But I liked them all. And after I started playing school sports, I played a lot of baseball and basketball and football.

Since my birthday falls in November and I started school at age 5, I was usually younger than my fellow players. I found that challenging, and I think it probably was good for me. For instance, I was playing varsity football when I was 14 — playing offense and defense with kids who were 18, some of them closer to 19. It helped that I grew fast and I grew big; in high school I was tall and lean, 6' 1" and around 175 to 180 pounds.

One thing that tends to discourage some kids from playing contact sports is the fear of, and often the reality of, injury. I guess I loved sports so much I never gave much thought to that. Dad tells stories about some of my on-the-field encounters. I've heard him recall when I was a freshman playing football and I collided so hard with a kid on the opposing team that Dad said he was afraid neither one of us would get up. Well, we did manage to get up, and both of us went on playing. Dad chuckled when he remembered: "Bill did later admit to me that, after he got up, it was two or three plays before his head cleared enough to even know what was really going on."

The Two Brothers and Sports

Sports didn't take as big a hold on the future aspirations of either of my brothers as was the case with me. However, both John and Rick had their athletic strengths.

My younger brother, Rick, is 22 months my junior. But there's nothing "junior" about Rick in size. By the time he was in his mid-teens, Rick was equipped with towering height (6' 5") and the 200-pound-plus bulk and muscle tone to match. He was good athletically, especially in basketball. When Rick became a student at State University of New York at Oneonta, he was there on a basketball scholarship.

As for my brother, John, (2-1/2 years my senior), he liked sports, too. But John had to work at sports a bit more than Rick and I. He didn't have as much natural athletic ability as we did. John was very intellectually gifted, and ultimately when he went to Harvard his mission would be solely academic and not sports-related. However, as intellectually gifted as John was, when he was a youngster and then a teenager he had a well-rounded interest in so many things. John just seemed to have this intellectual curiosity about everything. He wanted to figure out whatever it was at hand that had caught his interest. And then he would work at learning about it. In that sense, sports was like everything else that John put his mind to. If he decided he wanted to do it, he just did it. One year when he was in high school, John decided he wanted to play football. He was big and strong enough; he had the size to do it. And he accomplished his goal. He ended up as a starting tackle.

Telling a Curveball from a Fastball

People are born with certain kinds of talents and capabilities. As the years went by, I realized that I probably was born with some God-given athletic abilities. Probably as important as anything was my keen eye-hand coordination. I'd always had that coordination. So it was just something I took for granted.

I won't ever forget a conversation my brother John and I had that related to this. The conversation took place one night at the dinner table, when we were teenagers. Like I mentioned, John was just so smart — and pretty intent on figuring out whatever interested him. That night, he was quizzing me on how I could tell one kind of pitch from another when I was batting. The conversation went something like this:

"Bill, how do you pick up on whether a pitch is a curveball or a fastball?" John asked me.

"It's the way the seams on the ball spin," I told John kind of matter-of-factly.

John wore glasses. He was blessed with that incredible brain of his, but he didn't have the good eye-hand coordination. As we sat there at the dinner table, John didn't have the foggiest understanding of what I was telling him about being able to "see" how a ball is spinning as it speeds toward you. Later on, Dad kind of chuckled as he recalled hearing that conversation, and said, "Poor John. With his eyesight, when someone threw him a ball it was a big deal if he could see a white blur coming toward him! And here was his younger brother just telling him matter-of-factly, 'Ahh, John, it's just the way the ball spins.'"

My older brother didn't give you many blank looks. But that evening, John did glance across the table at me with this blank look.

Parents Who Supported and Gave Some Room

Mom and Dad didn't push the three of us to do things. They just had some unspoken expectations for where they felt we should be headed, and they supported us toward those ends. They also had this willingness to support what we wanted to do, what mattered to us. And they were great role models.

They gave us an opportunity to learn to deal with responsibility as we grew up. I guess you could say that as long as we didn't screw up, we got some rope. I mean, I knew some kids that, after they went off to college, they just decomposed, because their parents had never given them any responsibility or freedom. Mom and Dad weren't like that. Too, although Mom and Dad were involved in what we did, including our sports activities, they didn't live their lives through us. They weren't in there hovering and being obstructive.

Mom is Irene Martinichio Dexheimer. She did a great job balancing the "two lives" of the homemaker and the working woman. When we were growing up, Mom was wife and mother and also a civil servant, a county employee — supervisor in the county's motor vehicle department and later in county social services. She would get up at 4:30 or 5 a.m., take care of what she needed to at home, work at the office all day, then come in and get everything in order at our household every night. She never let her job compromise her responsibilities as a wife and a mother. If John, Rick and I got in home at 8 o'clock at night from football practice, Mom was busy making sure we had clean uniforms for the next day. She just had that quiet drive and motivation and work ethic. She did whatever it took. I think she passed some of these traits along to John, Rick and me.

As for Dad, Robert "Bob" Dexheimer, he's a man with a lot of intellect, who has always been very knowledgeable in many areas. When we were growing up, Dad was self-employed, mostly in the area of sales — a manufacturer's rep for various companies. And later on for a period he had a car rental business. My dad has an independent streak. He always has been more comfortable doing something on his own rather than working for someone else. He is of the mindset that if you really believe in doing something, you need to do it. I think I'm a lot like him in that sense. I think Dad also planted some early seeds of the entrepreneurial spirit in me. For instance, the way Dad dealt with my brothers and me on cars was this: He would help us buy our first car. His expectation was that you would fix up the car, so you could sell it for more than he had paid for it. Then you could buy another one, and do the same thing. Dad paid $100 for my first car, and I sold it for $300. That's a pretty good return on investment.

One thing that Mom and Dad wanted, and expected, was that all three of us would attend college and earn at least one degree. It was unusual in the neighborhood where we were reared for all the kids in a given household to go to college. But with our parents, it was never a question of if we were going to college; it was just a question of where we were going.

In our academic and sports activities as well, the three of us received incredible support from home. Thinking back on it, I must have played in well over a thousand games of one kind or another. Dad rarely missed any games, for me or my brothers. He just saw to it that his schedule would accommodate that. Dad supported not only his three sons as individual athletes; he also was supportive of the school athletic programs. If the athletic programs had a need to raise money — to build weight rooms, for booster clubs or whatever — Dad was always involved in spearheading fund-raising efforts. Mom and Dad both were just there for us.

Sorting Through the Sports

I was aware that in terms of ability, natural talent, that my best sport was baseball. When I was in the ninth grade, I batted number three for the varsity high school team.

But, as a little time went by in high school, I began figuring out a couple of things about baseball.

For one thing, in New York the high school baseball season is a real short season. It gets warm slowly for Spring baseball.

And the second thing — something that mattered to a teenage boy — was that I came to realize baseball was not that much of a teenage spectator sport. Basically the stronger high school spectator sports were football and basketball. Most importantly, the girls didn't tend to come watch the baseball games. They came to the football games.

In terms of fun, I liked playing basketball. But, whereas brother Rick had natural ability there and had the 6' 5" height that was such an asset, for me talent-wise basketball probably ranked last.

By the time I was a senior in high school I was playing a lot of football.

The Football Game

It was the night of the first game of our high school football season during my senior year — in September 1973.

Life was good. It was good for me as a 16-year-old individual. And it was good for me as a team player.

I was captain and quarterback of Binghamton's varsity football team. I knew that several colleges had their eye on me for athletic scholarships. The colleges were courting me, and I was excited about the prospects. High school football had been rewarding. My year in freshman football had been such a good one and I was able to bypass junior varsity football and as a sophomore go straight to varsity as a starting player. Now, as I was starting my senior year, I was well aware that this senior-year football season was my chance to broaden my opportunities. I wanted to perform well for my team, and I wanted to perform well for those colleges that were scouting to make their picks for athletic scholarships. On that September evening as we opened our season in front of an enthusiastic crowd on our opponent's field in the little neighboring city of Endicott, I went into the game pumped up.

As a football team, we at Binghamton were in the spotlight, with good reason. We had an unusually strong varsity team that year, and we already had attracted a lot of press about our competitive edge. We were playing our opening game against an arch-rival, a perennial powerhouse, Union Endicott. We knew we were facing a challenge; we also knew that in this highly competitive setting we had a chance to show we had the right stuff. And we were ready.

I liked the challenge of playing Union Endicott. Only three years earlier, I had been quarterback of Binghamton's freshman team when we became one of the few teams ever to beat Union Endicott on their home field — in our last game of the season. Despite the win, I ran into a little trouble before the game was over. After scoring a touchdown, I got hit in the end zone, and I ended up with a broken leg out of the deal.

Little did I know that the simple leg fracture I sustained as a freshman would seem like child's play compared to what would come my way in that momentous senior year opener in September 1973.

Later on, after this September '73 fateful game, I would learn that I had been a "target" from the very start of the game. I would learn it had been a part of the game plan of the other team to take me out. Although I didn't have this information in hand while we were playing that night, it didn't take rocket science for me to figure that I was a focal point out on the field. I'd get hit on every play, whether I had the ball or not. On one hit, I took a pretty bad lick to my left leg. My leg felt somewhat numb, but I kept playing.

And then came the big hit, to the same leg.

I was running the option when it happened. I had my left leg planted, and I was turning when I got hit. Although my left foot stayed on the ground, my knee jutted out and bent . . . It was a catastrophic injury. To me, it felt like the leg in effect "blew up."

After the dust settled later on, I would learn that this was the damage that this injury dealt me: It tore my quadricep, the large muscle in front of the thigh. It tore my gastronemius, the largest muscle of the calf of the leg. It shredded my perineal nerve, the nerve in that tissue area that's the "boundary" between the pelvic outlet and the urinogenital ducts and rectum. It severed my media collateral ligament, the ligament that helps stabilize the knee — part of the key connection between the femur, the large bone extending from the hip to the knee, and the tibia, the large bone extending from the knee to the ankle. And it severed the anterior cruciate ligament, one of the ligaments in the knee joint that cross each other from the femur to the tibia, this one having to do with limiting extension and rotation.

I felt a pain that was intense. Then it kind of went numb. And then the pain returned, with renewed vengeance.

Those of us who follow sports have on occasion witnessed this kind of ambivalent unfolding of events when an athlete is injured on a playing field. I'm talking about this initial window of time following an athletic injury, when the extent of the injury is unknown and often is initially misread. In the first few minutes after an injury, what can appear to be a relatively minor injury can later prove to be quite severe. The opposite also can be true. What you see, or what you think you see, is not what you always get.

In the minutes immediately following my own injury that night, events moved forward with those in charge around me proceeding under the impression that I had suffered a much lesser injury than ultimately turned out to be the case.

A doctor who was at the game to take care of the players — the other team's doctor — came out on the field to look at me. He examined me and said, "I think you've got a pinched nerve."

They got me back to the sidelines. But I was not taken to the hospital immediately. I was sitting there on the bench, in a lot of pain. And my coach kept looking over there at me. I felt my coach was looking over to see if and when I was ready to go out on the field and play again.

It was my dad — sitting up in the stands — who got things moving and got an ambulance there for me. He and Mom, who was there with him, would later tell me the details of the emotional agony they went through as parents on what proved to be an extremely traumatic night.

A Father Takes Things into His Own Hands

Dad was watching through his binoculars at the time I took the hit on the field. He had seen me play in a lot of games and take numerous hits. He said he knew from the start that this one was different. The impact I sustained was overpowering, calamitous. I fell in a contorted heap. My facial expression and body movements spelled out a wrenching pain that Dad had never seen with me before.

After they brought me back to the bench on the sidelines, Dad continued to watch me through his binoculars. He said he could see the anguish written on my face. As minutes ticked by, I was showing no signs of improving, and in fact seemed to be getting worse. He became very concerned that they weren't getting an ambulance for me.

So Dad left his seat in the stands, made his way down to the sidelines, and started taking things into his own hands. He located a deputy — one of those special deputies who is charged with keeping order and handling emergencies during a game. The deputy had a two-way radio, which he could use to summon an ambulance. Dad told him I was hurt badly and needed to go to the hospital, and asked him to call an ambulance.

Well, obviously Dad was acting outside the lines of the accepted protocol. Ordinarily the team doctor would have been the one to set this in motion. The deputy wasn't taking direction from a concerned parent. He told Dad, "I can't do that."

My father usually keeps pretty good control of his temper. But Dad didn't view this as a "usual" situation. Dad told the deputy, rather directly as I understand it, that if the deputy did not use his radio to get an ambulance that he would take the radio away from the deputy and call the ambulance himself.

Apparently the deputy agreed with Dad that I needed an ambulance. At any rate, he summoned one.

"Pulling the Drumstick Off the Thigh of a Chicken. . ."

My memory of the rest of the night's events is a bit clouded, to say the least. I was first under the natural sedation that intense pain can bring, and, in later hours, under real sedation. But I was aware of the ambulance taking me first to a small hospital in Endicott — that proved too small and ill-equipped to deal with my injury — and then being transferred to a second larger hospital a few miles away.

When the first emergency room personnel were trying to assess my injury, Dad was still having to hang in there and be my advocate. It was taking a long time for them to get me undressed so they could see the extent of injury they were dealing with. They were having quite a bit of difficulty as they struggled to pull my uniform off, while at the same time having to be careful not to hurt or damage me further. Dad asked why they didn't just cut the uniform off. One of them told Dad, "Well, these athletic directors get real unhappy with us when we go to cutting these uniforms." Dad couldn't believe what he was hearing. He said, "Cut the uniform off!"

Reality about the severity of my injury began to show its face, as X rays confirmed my leg had sustained grave damage. My parents were stunned that this injury initially read as a non-emergency "pinched nerve" was about to send me into emergency surgery.

Dad later had his own graphic description of the shape my leg was in that night: "Just think of pulling a drumstick off the thigh of a chicken . . . well, that's about what had happened to Bill."

Trying to Save a Leg

I was in surgery all night long — about eight and a half hours. From the outset, Mom and Dad knew that my leg was in jeopardy. Somewhere along the way that night, they signed a consent form giving permission to amputate the leg if all else failed.

It was a terrible night for Mom and Dad in the waiting room. Up until that point, this was the most traumatic experience they had ever faced in their roles as parents.

For the first several hours in surgery, the orthopedic surgeon worked on my leg, mainly on repairing my knee. A plastic surgeon worked with him, as they made all the tiny, intricate connections.

The orthopedic surgeon who led the battle to save my leg had himself been an athlete in his younger years. My parents and I always have felt very fortunate that he was on call that Saturday night. He had both the ability and the commitment to go that extra mile to try to save my badly damaged leg rather than amputate.

Somewhere between 2 and 3 a.m., the orthopedic surgeon told Mom and Dad there were complications. He had finished his work, but he told them he was worried about my circulation — or lack of it. He said my leg was not getting warm. When they were closing me up from surgery, they saw that my leg was turning dark, becoming cyanotic, due to lack of oxygenated blood. The orthopedic surgeon called for help, in the form of a vascular surgeon. More surgery. I never left the operating room between surgeries. The vascular surgeon did a procedure to open up a blood vessel, to get the circulation going again.

In a course of a long, stressful night, my dad came very close to taking up cigarette-smoking again. Dad had not smoked for several years, not since we boys had come in from grade school announcing to him that "smoking is bad for you." John, Rick and I were in grade school during those years when cigarettes took their first licking after the initial "Smoking and Health Report" released by the U.S. Surgeon General in 1964. However, although we had made enough of an impression on Dad that he put his cigarettes down back then, he felt a real urge to return to his habit as he awaited news about me that night I was in surgery. He turned to Mom and said, "I want a cigarette!" I'm really glad she was able to talk him out of it.

Dad had actually come into this long rigorous night in the hospital waiting room as a very tired man. He had arrived back home the previous evening just in time to make it to the football stadium for the kickoff of my game. He had just driven back home from Cambridge, Massachusetts, where he had taken my brother, John, to resume his studies at Harvard University.

Later Dad would share with me some of the thoughts that went through his mind while the surgeons were working on me: "I sat there in the waiting room that night thinking, 'Here's this kid of ours lying in there in surgery. He's always been such a marvelous athlete. Now he's in there on the operating table, unaware of what's going on with him. He's out of it, under anesthesia. And his mother and I are sitting here wondering whether we're going to have to go in and explain to him in the morning that they had to take his leg off.'"

It was a dreaded message both Dad and Mom feared they would have to deliver. Fortunately, it was a message that never had to be spoken. Those surgeons did their job well. I would awaken in the morning with my leg still intact. There was permanent damage. The leg would never again be as strong. But I would be able to walk on my own two legs.

A Post-surgery Crisis

I had been out of surgery for about a week. And, all things considered, I was doing pretty good.

On this particular day, things were going along about as usual. Mom had just been over to visit and to help me with lunch. With all the apparatus they had attached to me, I welcomed her help.

Mom had only been gone a few minutes when all of a sudden I couldn't get my breath. I just couldn't get a deep breath. I didn't know what was wrong. So I told the nurse. And I mean there were people all over the place!

I had thrown a pulmonary embolus — a blood clot in my lung. If that night in surgery came close to being the time I lost my leg, the day I threw the blood clot came close to being the time I lost my life.

A "Foot Drop"

After you sustain an injury like I did, it sometimes takes settling down time after surgery before you know just how much return of strength and mobility you're going to get.

After I was released from the hospital and went through the healing process, it became clear that I was going to be left with a substantial "foot drop." I was not able to control the motion of my left foot at the ankle — I was unable to control the movement up and down and from side to side. The doctors said the reason was that I had a nerve that had been damaged beyond repair. What my New York doctors were recommending was that I undergo a procedure to stabilize my ankle. That procedure also would mean the ankle would be permanently stiff, that I would have a permanent limp.

Again, it was Dad who came to my rescue.

Dad would not accept what the upstate New York doctors were recommending without reaching for a better solution for me. He wanted a second opinion. And he knew exactly where he was going to procure that second opinion.

There was this accomplished neurosurgeon in Virginia that Dad had known since they were children growing up together. Dad had gone to grade school and high school with this neurosurgeon. Dad got in touch with him, and the neurosurgeon said he would take a look at me. Dad took me to Virginia. Dad's friend had his look. His assessment was encouraging but not conclusive: "I think we can do something. But we can't tell until we get in there."

So on to another surgery. My local doctors were giving Dad a hard time about this. They thought I had been through enough. They believed it was not good to subject me to a surgery which they felt would not improve my situation but instead would set me up for false hope only to be followed by a big letdown.

But Dad persevered.

This was 1974, and this Virginia neurosurgeon and his colleagues were using some microsurgical techniques that were still in their pioneer days. The nerve that was causing my problem was entangled in scar tissue. With the aid of microscopes, Dad's neurosurgeon friend was able to line up the problem nerve and remove scar tissue from around the nerve. This was the troublesome scar tissue that was impairing the blood supply and thus impairing my ability to move my ankle and control my foot.

Again, I was lucky. Again, I was exactly where I needed to be for surgical help. The surgery in Virginia was successful enough that I regained much of the ankle mobility I needed to control my foot. With the overall condition of my leg, the ankle would never be as strong and mobile as it was before the accident. But I would not have to undergo a procedure that would deal me a permanent stiffening of the ankle and a permanent limp. I could in fact control my foot enough that, unless someone knew I had been injured and was having to compensate a bit, I would appear perfectly normal.

When Mom and Dad saw me for the first time after surgery, they both began smiling the smile of seeing success unfold before their very eyes. Dad said, "Well, it worked!" The neurosurgeon, not wanting to get their hopes up, countered conservatively, "Well, it's really too early to tell." Mom said in her heart she knew she could see my foot move that day, whereas I had not been able to raise it at all prior to surgery. And the doctor's wait-and-see attitude didn't catch on with Dad either. Instead, Dad looked at my foot and said, "I've been looking at that thing for what seems a long time now. There has been no life and there has been no vitality. That foot is moving now. This was a success."

Mom and Dad were right on target.

A "Lost Ball"

I think it would be accurate to say that after I sustained the injury I was a little like "a lost ball in high weeds."

Before the accident, I had been a kid with the world by the tail on a downhill slide. There's no question I would have gotten a college athletic scholarship, and a good one. I was so focused in wanting a sports career that there's no telling where things could have led.

The injury put an end to all that. I could walk. And for that I was grateful. But any prospect of my ever participating in college or professional sports was over, for good. And for that I was devastated.

I went into that football game in September 1973 weighing 177 pounds. I came out of the hospital six weeks later weighing 140. I lost four inches in my waist. I had shrunk, deteriorated.

In the weeks and months prior to my being injured, I had been receiving phone calls and letters from colleges interested in me for scholarships. Well, my injury generated some press coverage. It got into the newspaper that the damage I had sustained was severe enough that it was career-ending where athletics were concerned. So, after I got home from the hospital, there were no more calls or letters from colleges wanting to talk to me about athletic scholarships. There wasn't just a gradual decline in these contacts; there was an abrupt and final halt. All the interest in me athletically stopped cold.

After my long stay in the hospital, I returned to high school and finished my senior year on schedule. Even though I continued to miss a lot of school because I had to be in rehabilitation so much, I still was able to graduate in the top tenth of my class. That wasn't a struggle for me, because I went into this period "ahead of the game" with my studies. While it's true I had directed my high school efforts more toward athletics than academics, I had done quite well academically considering the investment I made there. Mom has said I was a very good high school student in terms of grades; she also has said she seldom saw me doing homework. However, homework or no homework, I had managed to absorb what I needed. I was very aware that, while Mom and Dad didn't say a lot, they just expected that I would not participate in sports at the expense of my academics. All in all, that little "nest egg" I had with my high school grades came in handy after my injury, as I went on to earn my high school diploma without suffering academically.

Where I did suffer after the injury was in terms of direction. I had none. Looking back, I kind of "checked out" for two years — well, closer to three years. I tried this and that and didn't do well at much of anything and in fact had no goal for much of anything.

I really was confused. I was not quite 17 years old when I was injured. All my life, everything had been athletically based. Then all of a sudden I couldn't do that. It was hard for me to accept the fact that I couldn't play sports anymore, and I didn't know anything else I wanted to do. Back then I didn't even know what depression was. But, looking back on it, I probably was depressed and didn't know it. I felt like I was in a rut.

The injury had changed my whole direction. No more sports. No more football. I think after I got out of the hospital I had it in mind that I would go through rehabilitation and I would somehow be ready to play college baseball. But I gradually realized the leg was too weak, too fragile and vulnerable to risk it to collegiate competition of any kind.

As usual, Mom and Dad were in there trying to keep my spirits boosted. They targeted photography and golf as two constructive pastimes I could enjoy in the months after my injury. They had a darkroom for me in the basement, and they took me to a golf pro to get some golfing lessons. I don't think either of these activities hurt, but I wasn't all that receptive either. The best thing that came out of all that was that Dad got more interested in golf while watching me take lessons and went on to become an avid golfer.

When it came time to go to college, I went to college right on schedule. I went to Ithaca College in New York my freshman year. That was one of the schools I had been considering attending to play football. After I got to Ithaca and there was no football for me, I didn't have a game plan. My grades weren't good. Actually, my grades were terrible. I called home and told my parents I was wasting their money and my time. I said I wanted to come home, live at home awhile and be a day student at a college close by.

I enrolled at State University of New York in Binghamton. But about the biggest thing I did there was to enroll. I skipped a lot of classes. I was just marking time. I had gotten strong enough to play a little softball. So I spent time playing softball, including some softball tournaments, with a group of guys I was running around with at home. At night during the week, I hung out with these same guys and we'd drink beer. Actually, at night on the weekends we'd do the same thing. There was nothing really exciting for me. I wasn't challenged. And I wasn't going anywhere.

During this period when I was living at home, I also managed to get myself fired from a job. The employer who fired me was Dad. At the time, Dad had a car rental franchise. In the course of working for him, I think I dished out more shall I say "input" than he wanted about the way he was running his business. And he just fired me! In retrospect, it probably was a good thing he did.

Dad also was tiring of my lack of attention to my college studies. One day he said, "Bill, if you don't want to go to school, don't do your mom and me any favors. Actually, it's costing us money and you're not benefiting. Drop out if you want to, and decide what you want to do."

After getting fired by Dad, I got another job — teaching scuba diving and running a dive shop for some people. I did that for about a year and a half. That period turned out to be good for me. I enjoyed what I was doing, although I knew even then that I didn't want to do it for a sustained period of time. Still, it was a turning point for me. For the first time since my injury, I was getting my head together.

Although I still didn't have a clear game plan, at least I started being interested in developing some kind of game plan. I knew enough to know I was in the market for something different.

During the time I was working at the dive shop, I got to know a girl who was attending the University of Alabama. Her parents lived in New York, and she was visiting them. She talked about what it was like in Alabama and on the campus where she attended school. Warm southern weather, lovely campus. It all sounded good to me.

I formulated a plan of action, and implemented it. And it did involve doing something different from anything I had ever known. I was going to move to Tuscaloosa, Alabama, get a job there, and enroll at the University of Alabama. I packed my bags, and off I went to Alabama.

Mom had been a real constant to me during my mixed-up period. I had a feeling she had faith that sooner or later I would pull out of this prolonged slump and do something constructive. Years later she was amused as she reflected back on my sudden decision to pack up and move south to Alabama to go to college. She said: "At that point, even if it meant Bill was moving a considerable distance from home, I was happy to see him enroll in college to do something. I mean, as long as he got a degree, I didn't care if he got a degree in basket-weaving!"

A Career in the Healthcare Field

When I enrolled at the University of Alabama, it wasn't a basket-weaving curriculum that caught my eye. It was a major in healthcare management of all things. I say "of all things" because, prior to being exposed to the healthcare field as a patient, I had little knowledge of and absolutely no interest in anything that had to do with healthcare.

My mom later would say that, if she were to guess as to what might have happened with me career-wise had I not been injured, this would be it: "Oh, I think Bill would have played sports in college. Then I think he likely would have coached some football. He might have done some teaching — a subject such as history. There's no doubt that the injury changed the whole course of his career, the whole course of his life."

So what got me interested in majoring in healthcare management at the University of Alabama? It would be nice, I guess, if I could say my interest in healthcare and hospitals was triggered by something positive that occurred when I was a patient. That wasn't the case. During those long weeks I was in the hospital after my injury, I found my restless curiosity picking up on things I thought could be done better, more efficiently, in the daily hospital routine. I had a lot of questions about the way hospitals were run.

By the time I enrolled at the University of Alabama, it was January 1978. It had been four and a half years since I was injured. I was 21 years old, and I had made a complete passage through my ambivalent stage. It's strange. As unfocused and ill-directioned as I had been for so long, after I arrived on the campus at Alabama I began functioning practically on the other end of the spectrum. I was very focused and very directioned. I knew who I was and how I wanted to approach life.

I can clearly recall how I was thinking during that period. I was telling myself: "Now, I've got one asset left, and that's my brain. And I'm going to have to use my brain to position myself for the future. Because I can't play sports. And I'm not comfortable making $7 an hour." By then I had concluded that I needed a better way to make a living.

Coming to Alabama was like sweeping the cobwebs out in terms of being able to make a fresh start without having to carry around my past baggage.

When I got to Alabama, I knew only two people who lived there — this girl whose experience as a University of Alabama student had interested me in coming down in the first place, and her sister.

I was meeting new people who were getting to know me as I was in the present. No one knew I had been involved in high school athletics in a big way. I didn't get pulled into these conversations about how good I once had been in sports and how terrible it was I had been injured and what might have been. I wasn't driving or walking past ball fields where I used to play. In short, looking back to my past was not my focus. I was operating in the present, and looking ahead.

Suddenly it was very important to me to stand on my own two feet. I had lived through the experience of using my parents' money to go to college and making lousy grades and often cutting class. Since I had not performed well in college in the past, I thought it was time to do things more independently. Although Mom and Dad sent me a small amount of money after I got to Alabama, I handled the bulk of my expenses. I got a student loan. And I got a job, as a waiter in a restaurant in Tuscaloosa.

My performance during this period indeed was considerably improved over my past experiences with college. I was making good grades. And I really liked my job — enjoyed the variety of working and going to class.

Also, I was learning to rise to the occasion when obstacles came along. A good test came my way involving my restaurant job. One night, the restaurant where I was working burned down. I realized that night that, come tomorrow morning, most of my fellow workers in that now nonexistent restaurant would be out looking for jobs — mostly looking for jobs in restaurants. Tuscaloosa wasn't that big of a place, so there weren't that many restaurants that had jobs to offer. I knew I had to take action to compete well. So I made sure I was out of bed at the break of dawn the next morning. I hit the streets in time to be camping on some restaurant doorsteps before some of them even opened their doors for the business day. It worked. I got a job immediately as a waiter at what many considered the finest restaurant in town.

Out of that new restaurant job, I also got a bonus. I met a beautiful blonde Alabama girl, a college student, who was working there as a hostess. Her parents lived in Birmingham, Alabama, where her dad was a respected ophthalmologist. The girl, Lisa, would become my wife. An exciting health-related career would become my life's work.

If you measure the career in money, that's an easy measurement. I was earning a six-figure salary before I left my 20s; I was a millionaire before I left my 30s.

If you measure the career in terms of professional satisfaction and personal growth, I can't think of anything big enough to compare it with. So far, it has been a wonderful, phenomenal ride.

I enjoyed continuing to learn, earning my degree in healthcare management and then continuing on to earn a master's degree in business administration.

And I've thrived on my work. I was fascinated with the exposure I received in my job as an assistant hospital administrator. I found it exciting to be a hospital senior vice president and CEO of a primary-care physician network — a physician network that became an incubator for ideas I transferred to MedPartners. I'm proud I was one of the founders and the first chief operating officer of MedPartners, which forged new ground to become the biggest company in the nation in the growing physician practice management industry. And now I feel I'm entering the most exciting period of my career to date as president and CEO of my own new company, Genus Aesthetic Medical & Dental Group.

I date it all back to a night in September 1973. To a 16-year-old fired up to win a football game. A 16-year-old who that night met a crisis. It was a crisis he felt had cost him everything. Instead, it was a crisis that became a step toward his winning more than he bargained for.

12

John: A Brother . . . and Forever an Inspiration

BY THE time my older brother John was in the second and third grades, his teachers were telling Mom and Dad he was so smart they felt they, the teachers, should sit in the classroom while John taught the classes.

When we were in public school in New York, we were required to take state exams. On one state physics exam, John scored a solid 100. A perfect score!

The public schools we attended in New York were good. In the classrooms, we had considerable academic competition with our peers. And Binghamton was a good-sized place when we were growing up — about 300 to 400 in the graduating classes. Still, even with high standards set by the schools, large classes, and a competitive environment, when John graduated at Binghamton he had the highest scholastic average of anyone who had attended that high school.

John had a knack for electronics and computers. He could read a schematic electronic diagram when he was as young as 12. Although we were growing up a few years before computers became so popular, I can remember when John was around 15 that he sometimes would stay up all night writing code, writing computer programs.

My parents said John's gift of exceptional intelligence was evident from the time he was a toddler. His teachers were amazed at his abilities from the time he first began functioning in a classroom. And, with every day that passed in his life, John's knowledge and his abilities seemed to multiply. For some people in that situation, superior intelligence can almost become a prison; it can separate them from socialization and from mainstream living. I've known some highly intelligent people who outside their realm could barely function. But that was never the case with John. He wasn't just one-dimensional, he wasn't just book smart. Fortunately for John, he had common sense and was broad-based. He was diverse in his intellectual pursuits, enthralled with his hobbies, and warm and comfortable in his demeanor and interaction with other people. John was sensitive, compassionate, enthusiastic about life. He had it all.

For John, his intelligence was his key to open the world. He was interested in everything. He reacted to the world as though it was his oyster — lapping up everything he could absorb. It seemed that brain of his virtually consumed the hardcore academics — the math, biology, chemistry and physics in which he was so gifted. But he didn't expend all his efforts there. He also participated in sports. He took subjects like arc welding. He learned to play chess. He loved playing cards — although it was tough on those playing against him, because his ability to compute mathematically was just unbelievable.

He would express an interest in some subject that was new to him, and then be very open in his delight once he mastered knowledge about the subject. When that new knowledge began sinking in, he'd grin and say, "That's neat! That's really neat!"

From a very young age, John became a devoted library patron. When he felt an interest in something he didn't know about, he'd go to the library and check out every book he could find on the subject. He would sit and read, and read, and read — rapidly. That's how he got started playing chess; he went to the library and checked out books on chess. Before he was old enough to cross the street by himself, Mom seemed to be escorting him to the library constantly.

To Mom and Dad's credit, they supported John in his desire not to just focus on hardcore academics, but to be well-rounded. They resisted pressure to double-promote him, to push him ahead of his peers. When he was a high school senior, the school officials wanted to graduate him a semester early. However, Dad told them, "No, we're not in a hurry to push John out the door." So John spent another half year in school, finishing on schedule with his classmates. By the time he began this "extra last semester," he had completed the college-prep curriculum that he had to have in order to go forward with his plans to enter Harvard University. So, with his required courses behind him, during that last semester John spent in high school he had a ball taking courses in whatever caught his fancy. That's when he took arc welding. He also took auto shop, drafting and public speaking. He loved it all!

"Let's Hire That Kid!"

Mom and Dad did a great job walking that tightrope between challenging John's intellect on the one hand and making sure he was exposed to a big slice of normal living on the other.

They looked for opportunities to expose him, to fuel his abilities and his interests.

Dad always had his eye out for opportunities to introduce John to new options. When John was 15, Dad had a memorable experience while on an outing he had arranged for John.

Dad had a friend who was a very bright electrical engineer. This man had a company that was involved in progressive research and development in areas such as automation. Dad thought John would find this very interesting. He made arrangements with his electrical engineer friend to bring John over so he could experience these people doing their work.

By the end of the visit, it was obvious that the engineers at this company apparently were looking even harder at 15-year-old John than he was looking at them.

Dad recounted what happened like this: "John and my engineer friend began talking. I was aware that John had read some engineering books, but then, he read all kinds of books. And I don't think I had given much thought to it. But here he was, at age 15, discussing intricate aspects of engineering on a peer level with my engineering friend. And this guy was a graduate electrical engineer who was one of the brightest people I've ever known. As I stood there listening to the two of them talk, that's when it dawned on me that John not only had read these books; he actually understood the engineering details in the books."

Before Dad and John left the company that day, this engineer friend of Dad's was trying to hire John. Well, he couldn't. John was too young. He had to wait until he was 16. Dad's friend hired John as soon as he could, and John worked at the electrical engineering company after school.

80 Years of Living in 33 Years

After a time, John's high achievements no longer surprised us. We were proud good things were happening for him.

He earned a scholarship to Harvard and graduated magna cum laude in physics and chemistry.

For a short time after college graduation, John worked as an actuary with an insurance company. There was a series of tests he had to pass in his work. He passed these tests faster than anyone had ever been known to pass them. Then he went to work for General Electric and was a star there for several years. He was selected to go through a training program for General Electric's highly talented people. At GE John was into highly automated manufacturing and design, writing some of the software they were working with. He was involved in designing robots that design other robots — artificial intelligence.

He did so well during his several years at General Electric he received an offer to go with a smaller high-tech company that was highly dependent on John's ability to develop product. John accepted this opportunity. By this time, John had married — a bright, lovely girl named Marabeth. And they had a daughter, Julie. They were making their home in a nice area of New Jersey not far outside of Manhattan. There was this big wide world of opportunity continuing to open up for John.

Then, boom! It was all over. John was stricken with acute lymphoblastic leukemia. He battled bravely for months. He lost the battle. John died in March 1988. He was 33.

All that incredible intelligence. That passion he had for life. I've thought many times that John was so brilliant and took in every day so fully that it was as though he packed 80 years of knowledge and 80 years of living into 33 years.

John left his mark on every member of our family and on many others as well. His Harvard diploma hangs in my office. What he stood for hangs tight in my soul.

Too Tired for Racquetball

It was after John and I became adults that we were the closest. After we were established in our respective careers, married and settled, it seemed our relationship grew stronger. We had a deepening mutual respect for one another.

In our youth, John and I had been so opposite. I had skills John didn't have — I was so focused on excelling in athletics. John had skills I didn't have. I made good grades. But intellectually I never put myself in the same league with John, never felt I could play at the same level. John never did anything to make me feel that way; it was that he was so smart it was eerie. Actually, John and I were going in such different directions as kids I think we often just did not understand each other that well. We probably had more arguments than we should have had.

By contrast, in our adult years, we enjoyed our time together, both on the telephone and in person. We enjoyed talking about our work. We enjoyed talking about our families. I had become a dad before John. Lisa and I had a son, Paul, who was 4 years old when John and Marabeth's only child, Julie, was born. Then, a few months after Julie's birth, Lisa and I also had a daughter, Drennan.

John was excited about his future with this small high-tech company he was working with up in the Northeast. And my career in the healthcare industry in Alabama was everything I had hoped it would be, and more. I was enjoying my work as a senior vice president for American Medical International (AMI), developing and heading a primary-care doctor network for AMI's large hospital system in Birmingham.

As part of both of our careers, John and I did some traveling. In the

Spring of 1987, one of John's trips brought him to Alabama for a brief stay. He was working about 30 miles from where I lived.

We decided we would play racquetball one evening while he was on this trip.

But this usually energetic older brother of mine was just wiped out. He was feeling inexplicably very tired for some reason. We cancelled plans for the racquetball. John said he just didn't have the stamina.

We all get tired at times. But John's fatigue would prove to be an early symptom of something much more serious than any of us could ever have imagined.

"I Want Billy to Go with Me"

Sometimes we feel a bonding with siblings that even we don't totally understand. If we asked our parents, they probably could tell us stories about the beginnings of this bonding that took root when we were very young.

That was the case with John and me.

Although we would go through our grade school and high school years often marching to very different drummers, John and I were close in age and experienced deep bonding that was firmly in place years before we became school-age.

Mom and Dad have told stories about how John carried out his "older brother" role to the hilt with both Rick and me. Dad called John the "consummate big brother" who was extremely protective of both of his younger brothers. My parents said John would cut them as dirty a look as he felt he could get away with when they took steps to reprimand or punish either Rick or me.

John also enjoyed having Rick and me around. For example, Mom and Dad tell a rather amusing story of John embarking on a "great adventure" quite early in life and deciding he wanted a little brotherly company from me.

This occurred when John was about 3 1/2 years old and I wasn't quite a year old yet. (Rick wasn't yet born.)

On this particular day, it seems that Mom and Dad had done

something that displeased their firstborn son. John's solution was that he would just pack his suitcase and leave home.

Now, considering the circumstances, John's adventuresome plan was not quite as daring as it appeared on the surface. John's plan was to leave home and go to our grandmother's house. She didn't live far away; she lived just down the street from our house.

Typical of the way Mom and Dad handled things, they gave John a little rope. They let him pack up his little suitcase with whatever was important to him. And then, suitcase in hand, John walked out the front door, with his sights set on running away to greener pastures at Grandma's.

Well, John was a very smart little kid. And, once he got outside, he obviously was savvy enough to realize that, although Mom and Dad were allowing him to leave, he could venture only as far as their "rules" permitted. Even though our grandmother didn't live much distance from our house, "the rules" nevertheless presented young John with a tough obstacle. Mom and Dad had this rule that under no circumstances could John ever cross the street without an adult. In order to get to her house, he wouldn't get too many steps down the sidewalk before he had to cross a street.

So, perplexed as to what to do next, young John "hung out" there on the sidewalk for a few minutes. He was thinking things out. All along, from the time he had left, Mom and Dad had been peeking out the window watching him closely, to make sure he was okay.

It started to sprinkle rain. John's adventure was becoming a bit uncomfortable. And he hadn't figured out what to do about the crossing-the-street thing.

Besides, he had decided he had forgotten something, or somebody.

He re-entered our house, coming in the back way. Once inside, he sprawled out on the indoor stairway.

Mom was amused. But she kept a straight face and was very business-like about things. Shortly after she and Dad heard John come in the back door, Mom "happened" to run into John lying there on the steps. She said to him casually, "Oh. You're back. I thought you were leaving home."

"I want Billy to go with me," John told her.

Since I wasn't even old enough to be walking yet, that would have been a little much. Mom explained, "No, Billy can't go out there with you."

So John decided he would rethink things, and that he would eat dinner before he charted his next move. When he had finished dinner, he was viewing his situation with a full tummy, the knowledge that the don't-cross-the-street rules were still intact, and Mom's pronouncement that he could not take brother Billy along to keep him company.

The way things were going at our house started suiting John a little better, and he decided to abort his mission. So much for John's leaving-home plan. (Mom and Dad strike again!)

The Diagnosis

After John was in Alabama in early 1987 and was too exhausted to play racquetball with me, he kept having to deal with chronic fatigue.

The tired feeling was intensifying. After a few weeks went by, John knew he had to see about this. This was very different for him. John typically was a workaholic — worked six or seven days a week. And what he was feeling now wasn't simple fatigue. He was feeling generally rotten.

So one day he left work in time to see a doctor on his way home. The doctor hospitalized him immediately. It didn't take long to make the diagnosis of acute lymphoblastic leukemia.

The contrast between robust John and this ominous diagnosis was something hard for all of the family to comprehend. Dad would later say: "John got sick like lightning striking out of the sky. Really, it was as though lightning suddenly struck this big, healthy kid who had never been sick!"

To me it was ironic that John, of all people, would be stricken with a form of cancer. I know that many cancers occur without being traced to a causative agent or habit or exposure. But we also know that many cancers can be traced at least in part to bad lifestyle habits, to things we ourselves do to our bodies. For John Dexheimer to have cancer ran counter to any predictors and probabilities. Here was a guy who would never drink a beer, never smoke a cigarette, never do anything that could be suspect as being destructive to his body, to his brain — nothing that was known to possibly damage or destroy a brain cell.

A Bone Marrow Transplant

I began reading every article I could find on acute lymphoblastic leukemia. From what I was reading, I thought John had a high chance of a good remission, even a cure.

It was not to be.

John's initial treatment was at Memorial Sloan-Kettering Cancer Center in New York. They put him through their research protocols. Then they said there was nothing else they could do. He went to a specialist at another New York hospital and went through an experimental protocol there.

In my opinion, John never really got a first good remission.

John was told that his only hope for survival was a bone marrow transplant.

All of us in the family were realistic. We knew that we were fighting for John's life. We all worked together in this. And fate and circumstances sorted out our respective family roles as to how each of us could help.

Because I was the one in the healthcare field, it logically fell to me to research where John should go for a bone marrow transplant. I went to the literature; and I went to some physician friends, including some cancer specialists. I asked for their opinions as to the best place, the second best place, the third best place. Their answers were all the same. Seattle. And Seattle. And Seattle. The renowned Fred Hutchinson Cancer Research Center in Seattle, Washington. So we pulled some strings, we got people to pull strings for us, and we got John admitted to the bone marrow transplant program there.

It was the laboratory assessment, of course, which decided who in the family was the best match to donate the bone marrow for John's transplant. I was not a good match. Younger brother, Rick, on the other hand, was an excellent match — in fact, the only closer match would have had to come from an identical twin. So Rick was the donor for the bone marrow. He also was a designated donor for blood, to provide platelets that John would need.

Dad's blood also was a match to supply platelets.

Mom traveled to Seattle and remained there to support John and his wife Marabeth. Mom was in Seattle continuously from early January until early March 1988. This gave Marabeth a chance to alternate her time between John and their 2-1/2-old-daughter Julie.

All of us would have done anything to maximize John's chances. We would have quit our jobs. We would have sold our houses. We were willing to do what was needed without question. I look back on it, and I realize that in a situation like that you see what a family is capable of under adverse conditions. We all felt so committed to helping John that it came as a shock to us when we saw firsthand that all families are not like that. In the bone marrow transplant program in Seattle, there were families like ours that pulled together. There were other situations in which family members argued constantly, complaining about what they were asked to do, sometimes even openly questioning how they would be compensated for their time and assistance.

Our younger brother Rick really gave his all. At the time John went to Seattle to undergo the marrow transplant, Rick and his wife, Linda, had just moved to Buffalo, New York, where Rick had taken a new job. Since Rick was the bone marrow donor and also a platelet donor, he had to leave his new job and his new home repeatedly and spend a lot of time in Seattle. He never complained, and in fact was proud he was able to do this for his brother.

Genuinely Optimistic

I guess the role I played through the whole process, through John's sickness, was that I was kind of the coordinator.

I would try to keep my parents pumped up. I would try to keep my sister-in-law, Marabeth, pumped up. I'd try to be the one who came up with the clinical information for the family, because I had access to a lot of doctors. I would pose questions to doctors I knew, and they would make phone calls for us and get more information. Also, articles that I was reading helped fill me in on the probability of this or that.

In a sense I felt like the air-traffic controller, trying to keep all the pieces going. I felt I had to be the unemotional one — basically maintaining objectivity and reality but also being the cheerleader. Based upon clinical information I had either read or obtained from other people, I was communicating optimism.

It wasn't a stretch for me to keep the family pumped up, because I genuinely was optimistic. I really thought John was going to make it.

I wasn't by myself in my optimism. Dad later looked back and reflected on his own optimism this way: "So many times out there in Seattle, John bounced back from oblivion. He had that incredible will to live. I really thought John somehow was going to pull a rabbit out of the hat and beat this thing."

One Complication after Another

I have no doubt that John was in exactly the place he should have been — at the superb Fred Hutchinson Cancer Research Center in Seattle. That place is great to patients and their families. Miracles are wrought there.

John had some miracles come his way. Actually, John himself at times seemed like a miracle. But he encountered so many problems that there just weren't quite enough miracles to save him.

My brother was pretty well beaten up by the leukemia by the time he got to Seattle. And once this last-ditch-effort treatment via bone marrow transplant starts, it's rigorous. On the front end, to be prepared for the transplant, John had to undergo extensive radiation treatments to wipe out his entire immune system. Then they transplanted the marrow and hoped the transplanted marrow would bring the counts up.

The bone marrow transplant itself was successful for John. It worked. But what happened was that John just experienced every possible complication you could get. He kept bouncing back, but finally the chain ran out.

His complications were like sequences in a nightmare. He developed graft-versus-host disease. He got pneumonia. The neurologist thought at one point the tumor cells had crossed the blood-brain barrier, that the cancer cells were in his spinal fluid. He was actually in a coma. He was on a ventilator. There was even talk of "pulling the plug" on him.

But, even after all that, John started to come back. I won't ever forget telephoning Seattle one day during a period when things were real touch-and-go with John, when he was on the ventilator. Even with my optimism, I wasn't expecting an encouraging report that day. I spoke with his nurse and I asked her, "How's John doing today?" She said, "Well, he's doing great!" I was taken aback. I said, "What?" She said while she was changing out the ventilator apparatus, John woke up and began communicating.

John's blood counts started coming up. The transplant obviously was working. He was able to come off the ventilator. They even started him on physical therapy. I talked to him on the phone, and mentally he was sharp. John was so determined that, when they prescribed the physical therapy once a day, he requested to take it twice a day — so he could get better faster.

The people taking care of him in Seattle couldn't believe what had happened with John — that he had come back time after time after being on the brink of death, that he had survived some of the things he had survived. The staff really did think John was a miracle patient.

After John was able to come off the ventilator and started taking the physical therapy, I really thought he was going to make a total comeback.

Then came the final complication. This wasn't even a complication that had to do with the leukemia itself. It had to do with the treatment for the leukemia. This complication was a result of John's having undergone such powerful radiation and chemotherapy treatments, beginning when he had been treated in New York. Those treatments had caused a fibrous mass to grow in his pericardium, the sac or membrane that encloses the heart. This mass wasn't malignant; it was more like scar tissue than anything. However, it was restricting the ability of John's heart to function properly.

The doctors taking care of John decided they had no choice but to perform surgery to remove this mass. Like Dad said, John's doctors at that point were in a "Catch-22" situation: If they left the mass alone, it was likely to kill John. If they performed surgery on him to get the mass out, the surgery was at risk to kill John.

On the operating table during this surgery, John suffered a cardiac arrest.

They were able to "get him back" in the operating room, to resuscitate him.

However, within hours after the surgery, it was all over. John died the next morning following surgery. He was so beaten up from all he had gone through; the surgery proved to be the final blow.

I would not have been shocked to hear John had died during many critical points when he was in Seattle. However, I was shocked that he died when he did. Except for that one complication, things had been going so well before he went into surgery.

John's Attitude Through It All

It was almost as though John took his entire mental capacity — which was huge — and focused it on beating this disease. And I never once heard him say or even hint that he felt sorry for himself.

John's attitude was not to ask, "Why did this happen to me?"

Instead, John's attitude — spoken, unspoken, and put into practice — was this: "I've got to deal with the hand that has been dealt to me. And I'm going to try to beat this thing."

If you were to chart it out, for about nine months there in John's battle against leukemia, it seemed that if a complication could happen, if something bad could come along to block John's path, that's what happened. But through it all, John never turned inward. He continued to focus positively on other people. When I would phone him in Seattle, I would of course say, "Well, John, how are you doing?" He would respond, "How are you doing, Bill?"

One of the nurses who took care of John in Seattle told my parents how remarkable she thought John was. She couldn't believe how it was with John, how upbeat and positive he was no matter how tough things became for him. One day this nurse asked my dad, "Was John always this way, even before he got sick?" Dad told her like it was: "John has not been changed by this. He always has been this way."

To the very end, John had his own ways of letting everyone around him know that he appreciated what they were doing to help him.

For instance, one of the nurses taking care of John in Seattle commented that Dad's platelets seemed to give John a "boosting" effect. John just nodded, smiled as he obviously thought about Dad donating these platelets for him, and told his nurse, "My dad wills it to be that way."

The Impact I've Felt from John's Death

I was 31 years old when John died. John's death at age 33 has had a deep impact on the way I view things, both personally and professionally.

It gave me a deep understanding that everyone is mortal, that time is very important and that you should not waste time.

After John died, I had a clearer picture than maybe otherwise I would have ever had that you should get all you can out of today. I now believe strongly that you shouldn't postpone something you want to do. Don't postpone something unnecessarily to a future point in time, to your retirement, to tomorrow. Because there might not be a tomorrow.

In a personal sense, John's death made me understand a little bit more how important it is to have a cohesive family — and how much you should appreciate a cohesive family if you have one.

His death also brought into my personal life a whole new sense of responsibility with this new role I suddenly had as the oldest son in the family. I think in a sense it's an unspoken thing in a family that the oldest has a family leadership role. John had always lived this role well. Then, all of a sudden, he was gone. And these oldest-son responsibilities had become my responsibilities. While John was sick, I had played the coordinator role. And right after he died, I realized I should continue to fill this role. Suddenly I felt responsibility for everyone in the family. I felt I needed to go into the game and do well as a quarterback. This was sinking in with me right after John's death, when Lisa and I took Mom and Dad to Gulf Shores for rest. I really wanted to help my parents. For

Rick and me as John's brothers this was rough enough. But I knew it was a living hell for Mom and Dad. It's strange how in times of tragedy and grief you often recall something someone has said in the past which, in the light of current circumstances, takes on a stronger meaning. After John died, I remembered something Dad had said for some reason years before. He had made the comment: "I think one of the worst things I can imagine for a parent is to have one of your children predecease you."

As for the impact John's death had on me professionally, the impact there was more subtle. But it nevertheless was there, and it still is. I didn't change course professionally after John died; I was already pretty much on track with where I wanted to go professionally before John got sick. But I missed talking with him. We had shared a lot of career thoughts. John was a sounding board for me. I know that his death did spur me to move as fast as possible professionally— that feeling I mentioned concerning the urgency of time. I felt this boost, that I didn't need to wait around to do things. I know that his standards for excellence have inspired me. I'd be lying if I didn't admit it has pleased me from time to time when Mom has commented, "J. D. would have been proud of you." (Mom often refers to John as J. D., for his full given name of John Donald.)

I've been a bit nostalgic from time to time, wondering what might have been between John and me if he had lived. For instance, I wonder if maybe John and I could have gotten together at some point on something professionally, using his talents and my talents. I somehow think that along the way there could have been some mutually beneficial venture involving the two of us. I'd like to think that a little bit of John is going into what I'm doing now.

The Impact of "The Hutch"

Mom spent two months in Seattle when John was being treated at the Fred Hutchinson Cancer Research Center. She said very sincerely: "I've never in my entire life been in any place like Fred Hutchinson. The care they give to the patients, and the caring they give to the families, is extraordinary."

Dad spent many days at Fred Hutchinson not only in his role as John's father but also in his role as a platelet donor for John. On repeated occasions, Dad underwent a "pheresis" procedure there, whereby the staff would take blood from him and remove the platelets John needed and then transfuse the remaining blood back into Dad. Thus, in a sense, my dad was seeing Fred Hutchinson from the view of both a family member and someone who on some days was a "patient." In the opinion of my father, the high quality of care and caring he saw there was unparalleled. In fact, he loves the place so much he usually calls it by the affectionate nickname "The Hutch."

In my phone conversations with the staff at Fred Hutchinson, and when I had a firsthand look when I visited John there in the hospital, I had a chance to see why my family was so impressed with what I call "the service standard" at Fred Hutchinson Cancer Research Center.

In short, I feel there is no way you could ever point your finger at anyone at Fred Hutchinson who came in contact with John or other members of my family who was not giving 150 percent in that environment.

I have such positive thoughts about our family's experience there that I now hold the Fred Hutchinson Cancer Research Center in my mind as a model when I stress "the service standard" in my new company, Genus Aesthetic Medical & Dental Group.

The population that will be served by Genus providers and the population served by Fred Hutchinson are very different. Fred Hutchinson was dealing with patients and their families in intensive care, life-and-death situations. By contrast, Genus providers will be dealing with patients who come for elective cosmetic procedures that are not life-threatening.

However, I think there are some elements of "the service standard" at Fred Hutchinson which can be transferred to many health-related arenas — including Genus:

• I feel that one of the factors that accounted for Fred Hutchinson's incredible service standard was that this was a place in which there truly was a team approach, in which people genuinely worked together to help those they served. What we were seeing at Fred Hutchinson was one-to-one and sometimes two-to-one care, in which patients like John had one or two critical care nurses with them 24 hours a day. These nurses were viewed as crucial members of the team that cared for the patients. We were seeing professionals make rounds on the patients every day as a team, planning and implementing the care of each patient as a cohesive unit. Those making the rounds included not just the doctors who were caring for the patients, but the nurses and other crucial non-physician personnel as well. And we saw a sincere and successful reaching out to the families of patients to incorporate them as members of the team. At Fred Hutchinson I saw a situation in which it wasn't just lip service given to the team approach; I saw the team approach consistently function and generate results in a productive way that impressed me as being exemplary. I strongly believe this model of the true team approach can be tailored to transfer to other arenas.

• I feel that Fred Hutchinson's approach was based on both compassion and communication. The staff members at Fred Hutchinson told patients and their families what they needed to know, and they made sure they understood. The staff members at Fred Hutchinson also cared about the patients and their families. They didn't just pretend to care; they really cared. And they showed that they cared.

• The whole process for each patient and the patient's family members was managed at Fred Hutchinson like an overall unit, with each piece of the puzzle fitting together. I call this "the experience." I believe this efficient and caring management of "the experience" can be transferred to non-life-threatening situations. In managing "the experience" at Fred Hutchinson, the staff members were managing not only the care for critically ill patients but also the accommodations and caring for patients' families. Most of these families were many miles from their homes; all of them were under unrelenting stress. In managing "the experience" for families, Fred Hutchinson staff arranged accommodations such as housing, and they arranged transportation between the place of lodging and the hospital. The staff members added the extras as well — such as arranging for basketball tickets so that families could take much-needed breaks. Everyone at Fred Hutchinson — and I mean everyone — was involved in managing this experience for a bone marrow transplant patient and his or her family. Even the shuttle-bus drivers obviously had been carefully recruited and trained. The drivers demonstrated to families that sincere element of compassion. They, too, were part of the team.

The Legacy of John

In the short period of time that he lived, John influenced a lot of people. He was always a teacher. John helped people to use their minds. He helped them to build character. John just always wanted to help people to be better.

In August 1987, seven months before he died, John put on paper some of his beliefs. He was very open in expressing his feelings in this particular communication. Although John was hopeful he would recover from leukemia, he also was aware that the disease might claim his life. He was writing his feelings to someone very precious to him. This was a letter to his only child, daughter Julie, written by John a month before Julie turned 2 years old.

I know this letter will always serve as an inspiration to Julie. It serves as an inspiration to me as well. I hope it will help those of you reading this to better understand why the legacy of John is such an inspiration:

Dearest Julie,

I am writing you this letter while I am battling a terrible disease. My chances are good for spending a long time with you, but there is also the possibility that I won't be there. I want to ensure that you know some things just in case I can't be there to tell you and teach you.

First of all, you are a very lucky girl. Your mother is one of the strongest, most loving, and smartest women you will ever meet. I was very lucky to marry her. She loves you very much. Don't ever doubt that fact. She will always do what is best for you. And truly, I love you more than you can imagine.

Secondly, when you have children you will understand the love you can feel.

I honestly feel that my life did not begin until the day you were born. The day you first smiled at me was the greatest moment I can remember. My biggest thrill is spending time with you.

You are an exceptional girl. You are smart, very beautiful, and have a personality that wins over everyone. You will be able to do anything you want with your life. You have all the tools, and your mother will make sure you have the opportunities. I want you to take full advantage. I want you to try as hard as you can to reach your full potential. Set high goals. You will reach them.

I have big dreams for you. You will grow up in a world where there are less obstacles to a woman than the world in which your mother grew up. You should be able to accomplish anything you want.

I hope you will enjoy academic pursuits. I expect you to do well in school and to be at the top of your class. I hope you will develop an appreciation for the basics — mathematics, reading and writing — for they are the key to all learning. Especially reading and writing. Reading is the best way to acquire new knowledge. And writing is the essential skill in learning to communicate your thoughts and ideas.

I hope you will learn to recognize character. Character is that quality you will see in your mother. Choose your friends well. Look for character and the same values your mother has taught you. Don't try to be the most popular person in your school. It is much more important to be true to yourself and your own values. A teacher once told me to always behave as if my father and mother were watching me. Well, your father will always be watching you.

I hope you will learn the value of family. Your family will never let you down. No matter what you do, they will always love you.

I hope you will have a good friend. A good friend is a blessing.

Remember though that the most important things in the world are not material, but relationships with other people. Everything that you do will involve other people. Always treat them fairly and with respect. Try to see the other person's position through their eyes. Everyone has value and behaves in about the same manner you would behave if you were in the same circumstances.

Your love for your family is most important. You can always rely on your family. I hope you will remain in contact with my parents. You are very, very special to them.

I have only a few concerns about not being here for you:

First, financially. I think that there will be adequate insurance to provide for you and your mother for many years. It is my hope that your mother would not have to work if she did not want. It may be important for her to work, especially when you are in school. And you will have to understand.

Second, I want you to remain in contact with your grandparents, my mom and dad. They love you very much and can see a lot of me in you.

Third, I want your mother to remarry. You need and deserve a father. Your mother will pick the right man. She is very wise. Give him all the love and respect you would have given me.

Lastly, Julie, I want you to know that even though I am 33 years old you have made my life complete. You have made me very happy and I consider myself a very lucky person. I know that you will be provided for, loved, and have the best mother you could possibly have. As you can tell, I love her very much.

Remember that I will always be with you in spirit. I will be watching over you. You are a part of me that I will never let go of. I know that you will make me proud of you. I will always love you.

Your Da-da

PART FIVE:

Lessons Learned

13

Running into the "Brick Wall": A Lesson in Managing a Medical Practice

HE ROSE to the rank of full colonel in the United States Army. He did two tours of duty in Vietnam, where he was charged with responsibilities that would test one's fortitude. He served in Germany, where he tackled difficult problems with common sense. He worked in the Pentagon, where he mastered the meanings of budgets in an environment where mammoth volume and intense pressure were the name of the game.

Strange as it might seem — and lucky for me — it was from this man that I received my strongest lessons in the ideal approaches to managing a medical practice.

The man's name was Frank B. Wall, Jr. But I imagine very few people in his lifetime called him by his given name. From his early years, he was known by a nickname that stuck — "Brick" Wall.

After he retired from the military as a full "bird" colonel, Brick Wall elected to work in the civilian sector. The last job he held was as the office manager, or clinic administrator, of a physicians' practice. It was a position he held for 12 years and one which endeared him to the doctors for whom he worked and the employees whom he supervised.

It was in 1983 when Brick became the office manager of a medical clinic, in a rural setting in Columbiana, Alabama. Columbiana is the county seat of rapidly growing Shelby County, which borders on Alabama's most populated county of Jefferson, where Birmingham is located.

In taking the job, Brick became office manager of a bustling practice where three busy doctors conduct a general family-care practice. One of those physicians, Dr. Harry Phillips, became my personal friend and mentor. Brick Wall also became my personal friend and mentor.

Brick became office manager about two and a half years before these physicians sold their practice to American Medical International (AMI) and thus became associated with AMI's Brookwood Medical Center in the Birmingham area.

A couple of months after AMI Brookwood purchased this particular practice, I was hired by Brookwood to expand its primary-care center network, to head up what became known as AMI Brookwood Primary-Care Centers. In my new job as a senior vice president for development, I started developing, acquiring and managing new primary-care centers. I also took the responsibility for primary-care centers Brookwood already owned, including the one in Columbiana where Brick was the office manager.

Brick Wall became my first, and to date my most significant, "laboratory" to observe the importance of the role of an office manager in a management company or management division environment.

He demonstrated to me the great values a management company can derive by recognizing and making maximum use of the talents of a capable office manager.

He became to me a real-life example of the great value the right person in this office manager slot can provide to both parties — the physicians and the management company.

In terms of structure, Brick was a clinic office manager who was interacting with a hospital system — working for a clinic-management division set up to deal with hospital-owned clinic practices. However, in many ways his situation closely resembled the interaction a clinic office manager would have in today's world of physician practice management companies, or PPMCs. Brick's experience in this position mirrored the environment that exists for an office manager working for a physician organization that has a management-services agreement with a traditional PPM company like MedPartners or with a PPM "niche" company like Genus Aesthetic Medical & Dental Group. Many of the issues Brick dealt with in the 1980s and early 1990s at the primary-care clinic in Columbiana, Alabama, have direct similarity to the issues an office manager deals with today in a doctor-group/management-company partnership anywhere in the United States.

During the two and a half years Brick had been the Columbiana clinic's office manager before I appeared as the "new corporate guy," he already had been making a major positive impact on the clinic's operations. For example, he had just made some very lasting contributions that had taken place over a period of months immediately prior to my coming on board. These contributions had to do with Brick's guidance and managerial leadership during the period when the physician owners were negotiating with AMI Brookwood to put together the deal to purchase their practice. I've heard Dr. Harry Phillips say that if it had not been for Brick's superb organization skills there never would have been a deal. He said Brick had the organizational ability needed to keep the negotiations moving forward at an orderly pace, never letting them break down or fall victim to bureaucracy or emotion.

By the time I met Brick, he was technically an employee of AMI Brookwood Primary-Care Centers. When I took over as head of the AMI Brookwood Primary-Care Centers, I was in my late 20s. Brick was three decades older than I. Our age difference never factored into our relationship as we both treated one another with respect.

I watched Brick Wall function as what I would term the ideal "balancer." He became my model for the skills an office manager should have in the type environment in which he was working. The amount of savvy, toughness and timing I saw Brick exhibit in balancing everything was nothing short of incredible.

In his role as the ideal balancer, Brick showed me that it is possible to balance the interests of the doctors and the interests of a management company or a hospital clinic-management division without compromising either party's interests. Brick remained loyal and true to the needs of the doctors who took care of patients at the clinic he managed. At the same time, he never ever compromised the company's interests or investment for the interests of himself or the interests of the doctors. He maintained this great balance of being the very effective person in the middle — between corporate, the employees, and the practicing physicians.

It was Brick who consistently functioned as the buffer for the illogical and irrational — the buffer for the often senseless stuff that was rolled out by hospital people who never set foot in a physician practice except as a patient. He made sure that regardless of what kind of controversy might be in progress, the clinic's operations continued to go forward without missing a beat. Even in the most trying situations, Brick kept his eye on the ball, focusing on doing the best job he could do in the clinic and never compromising the clinic's day-to-day operations.

It was no accident that the three-man group in Columbiana did so well. The doctors were a key. So was Brick.

I've seen office managers in physician practices come from diverse backgrounds and strengths. There's a wide range of backgrounds that can produce top-flight office managers.

Brick Wall did indeed come from a background worthy of note. I think these next few sections will give you some insight into what he was all about.

His Military Background

Brick was well prepared before he joined the Army, including military school training. He was further prepared after he went in, including earning a master's degree in business administration while he was in the military.

During the 26 years he was a military man, he took on some tough assignments.

In Germany, Brick took over a commissary that was losing thousands of dollars a month, mostly as a result of small quantities of commissary items being stolen on an ongoing basis. This was in the early days of his career, in the 1950s, not long after the end of World War II. Brick found ways to stop the pilferage and also to reach out to some of the Germans — many of whom literally were starving to death. One thing he did was to devise a system for saving all the scraps of food at the commissary, to make sure that instead of being thrown away the scraps were used to make huge quantities of soup. Many hungry people who needed the food very badly were the recipients of this soup. Through Brick's management approach that was both constructive and humanitarian, the pilferage at the commissary gradually came to a virtual halt.

During one of his tours in Vietnam, Brick was placed in charge of the proper handling of the body bags — the identification and tagging of the dead soldiers. There were some 60 people under his supervision in this gut-wrenching task. The emotional stress was off the map. Some of the soldiers he was supervising became extreme disciplinary problems; many were retreating into a fuzzy existence made possible by their chronic smoking of marijuana. The military area in which Brick held this supervisory responsibility was averaging two or three courts martial a month. Brick was committed to doing an efficient job of identifying and tagging the dead. He strongly felt that, no matter how gruesome this job might be, it was a mission that must be carried out with the highest efficiency. He felt that handling this job thoroughly was necessary in order for the U.S. Army to meet its responsibility to the dead soldiers, the soldiers' families, and also to the Army itself. In supervising the reluctant, stressed, and often unruly military men under his command, Brick communicated to them the significance of the difficult duty they faced; he communicated that he expected them to perform that duty well; he communicated that those who shunned their duty would be punished. Brick had a way about him — a firm way of communicating what he meant and of meaning what he said, a demeanor that garnered respect even under adverse circumstances. Gradually the men who worked for him became more orderly. Their performance and behavior improved, and the job was handled at the level of Brick's expectations.

Brick's last stop in his quarter of a century career with the military was at the Pentagon. He was there the last 10 years of his military career. He worked in the budget department — where they rounded off budget items to the nearest million dollars.

Talents That Transferred

When the three-man doctor group in Columbiana, Alabama learned that retired Army Colonel Brick Wall was interested in talking to them as a candidate to fill the post as their office manager, the response from the doctors was not 100 percent approval.

After all, what they thought they needed Brick to do was a far cry from what he had done in the military.

But I think there's a moral here. Talents can transfer. People who know how to manage can manage in all types of environments and situations. And I'm sure these doctors congratulated themselves many times that they didn't miss the opportunity to hire Brick Wall.

"You Can Run over Me, or You Can Talk to Me!"

One day, a confrontation occurred at the clinic in Columbiana — a confrontation involving Brick Wall. I think this story speaks for itself in how Brick maintained order at the clinic, and how he earned respect from employees.

This particular incident came about as a result of the clinic's occupational health relationship with a company that was located in the area. The doctors at the clinic provided this company's employee healthcare work, handled the Workman's Compensation, performed physicals, and treated work-related accidents. This unionized company had been having labor problems and was having to hire temporary employees to fill in during this period. Under the agreement, the physicians were doing the physicals on the workers applying for the temporary jobs.

The situation stirred the anger of some of the union leaders in the area — to the point that one of these union leaders walked into the clinic with whiskey on his breath, cursing at the personnel working in the clinic front office. He shouted at the staff about how the doctors were doing physicals on these "scabs." The man had his say, disrupted the operation, and stormed out of the office and got into his vehicle to leave.

Brick was not within hearing distance when this was going on; however, word spread fast. The employees who worked in the clinic respected and loved Brick Wall. They knew he respected them, cared for them, was fair to them, and was their advocate. Employees at the clinic scurried around and located Brick quickly. They were able to tell him what the union guy had done before the fellow even had time to drive out of the clinic's parking lot.

It did not set well with Brick that anyone would create a disturbance at his clinic. It particularly did not set well with him for someone to insult and threaten employees who were under his supervision.

Brick walked out into the parking lot. As the union guy sat at his steering wheel trying to back his vehicle out of its parking place so he could drive away, Brick defied him and stood directly behind him to block his path. At first, the man didn't stop. He just kept backing up. He obviously did not want to listen to Brick.

"You can run over me, or you can talk to me!" Brick told the man.

The man stopped backing up. He listened.

"If you ever show up at this office with whiskey on your breath, if you ever show up here cursing one of the girls in the office, I'll break you into a thousand pieces," Brick told him evenly.

The man offered no resistance to Brick's order.

"How Much Vaccine Do You Want?"

One of the most valuable assets an office manager can have is the ability to develop and maintain relationships that benefit the doctors and patients he or she serves.

Brick Wall was a master in cultivating and maintaining those relationships. It came naturally for him, because he genuinely enjoyed people and it was his nature to go out of his way for them.

No matter how busy he was, Brick would listen to people. If a person wished, Brick would offer advice. And Brick gave excellent advice.

During those years he was an office manager, Brick enjoyed getting to know men and women with whom the clinic did business. He knew the people at the local drug store. He knew the United Parcel Service worker who delivered most of the clinic's packages. He knew the key people at the pharmaceutical houses and the other health-related companies.

These people knew they were more than passing faces to Brick. Some of them leaned on Brick for advice. Brick did favors for them. Some of them considered Brick their personal friend.

And when Brick needed a favor, they were there for him.

There was one occasion in particular that stands out for how a Brick Wall relationship paid off. During one of the years that Brick was office manager, there was a crucial shortage of influenza vaccine. Doctors were having a virtually impossible task of obtaining the vaccine they needed to immunize their patients — even their most at-risk patients.

Dr. Harry Phillips relayed to Brick that he and his partners badly needed some vaccine for their patients.

One of the individuals with whom Brick had a long-established relationship worked at a company that was a supplier for this vaccine. Brick made his phone call. His friend on the other end of the line didn't give Brick the standard "we-can't-do-anything-to-help" answer. Instead, the friend said, "Well, Brick, how much vaccine do you want?"

As things turned out, Brick was able to procure not only enough flu vaccine to supply the needs of the three doctors for whom he worked. He also was able to procure enough vaccine to share with some other doctors in the AMI Brookwood Primary-Care Centers network.

I think it's significant that Brick Wall's ability to develop and maintain relationships had created more leverage in this situation than existed with a multi-billion-dollar national healthcare company like AMI. Here was a situation in which AMI-affiliated physicians badly needed this influenza vaccine. Despite its expansive buying power, AMI did not have the leverage with the pharmaceutical company to procure the vaccine. However, an office manager in a rural Alabama medical practice did possess such leverage. In my opinion, Brick Wall possessed that leverage because of the consistent, sincere, reciprocal manner he interacted with people on a day-to-day basis.

The Special Traits of Brick as a "Balancer"

I don't feel and never have felt that the ideal role of an office manager is to be a "yes" person.

I particularly do not look with favor on a passive office manager role from where I sit — as president and CEO of a practice development company that enters into partnership agreements with physicians.

In my opinion, an office manager needs to be a strong individual, a knowledgeable and competent person who can provide information and valuable background, make recommendations, and implement decisions.

The office manager also needs to be an individual who has a mature head and has sound judgement about when to take issue with something, when to acquiesce, when to compromise, and when to dig in and hold his or her ground.

Above all, an office manager needs to be someone who is respected by both the doctors and the management company so he or she indeed can function, as Brick did, as the "balancer" between the two.

These are some of the traits I observed that made Brick Wall effective as a balancer:

Brick had strong character. He was fair and honest. His integrity was impeccable. The 15 to 20 employees who worked for him at the clinic loved Brick. They knew Brick was their advocate, that he always would be fair, and yet he also was as demanding of them as he was of himself. As for the doctors for whom he worked, they loved him like a brother.

Brick was a meticulous record-keeper. He kept accurate, complete files on communications and transactions — on everything. If he thought enough time had elapsed between communications, he wrote letters to prompt the next step. And he had a detailed file on what was said in the last phone call or meeting or letter. Accurate documentation in his mind left no room for speculation on who was to follow up or perform on a particular issue.

Brick was a great communicator. He had the ability to communicate his thoughts, both verbally and in written form. He was a master of the English language.

Brick was a provider of valuable, reliable information about the clinic, and this enabled him to be the clinic's advocate. He was able to provide the organization with crucial information that helped others understand his business. One thing that always struck me about Brick was how thorough he was; he knew the Columbiana clinic inside and out. And he was more than up to the task of using that information to put his clinic in a favorable position. A good example came when budgets were developed annually. If Brick believed a proposed budget needed to be modified for reasonableness, he was outspoken. He did not quietly stand by if he felt a budget was about to place what Dr. Harry Phillips described as "handcuffs" on the clinic, or present unrealistic expectations for performance. If Brick saw a need for something that was outside the proposed budget, he would present a compelling case to justify his request in providing information to support the clinic's financial needs.

Brick did not succumb to intimidation. I don't think Brick Wall was ever intimidated by anybody.

Brick kept a cool head. As strong a personality as he was, as tough as he was, Brick impressed me with being able to speak his mind and take his actions while remaining unemotional. If Brick had something to say, he wasn't shy about saying it and you would have no doubt about what he meant when he was finished. He was up front and straight to the point and consistent. When he saw something that was ridiculous, when he saw a policy or a memorandum that absolutely made no sense, he would raise his hand and say, "Wait a minute. You know, this makes no sense. Let's discuss this." At the same time, when tensions reached a high level, Brick had this sixth sense about when to speak his mind and when to hold off for a while until things cooled off. I personally saw Brick navigate through some difficult situations with AMI. I saw tense situations in which Brick did not get emotional and did not waste energy reacting, but instead used common sense and strategy to help resolve whatever problem was at hand. I'll have to say that, had I been in Brick's shoes, there indeed were some illogical bureaucratic situations at AMI in those days which I think would have sent my blood pressure rising to the point where I would have been at risk for a stroke. However, Brick just kept his head as he methodically filtered the "BS" out of these situations.

Strong Character to the End

Brick remained active with the clinic in Columbiana until he was stricken with the malignant brain tumor that in the summer of 1995 claimed his life.

Throughout the last months of his life, as he confronted this devastating and debilitating terminal illness, Brick continued to show the same strong character he had shown in times of good health. He was truly a soldier, strong and fearless to the absolute end.

And, almost to the very end, Brick used whatever abilities he still retained to communicate. When his condition worsened to the point that his voice would fade with fatigue when he tried to talk, he continued to communicate to his loved ones — through the written words of Brick Wall. Many of his final letters I will never part with.

14

"Talking to the Birds": A Physician Who Taught Me What It's All About

IT WAS a Saturday afternoon in 1989. I visited Dr. Harry Phillips at his primary-care office in Columbiana, Alabama. At the time, I was deep in the process of trying to organize a big medical mall project fraught with issues, oppositions, complex economics and unknowns. Dr. Phillips was giving me some advice from the doctor side.

A friend of mine, Daryl Brown, accompanied me on my visit to see Dr. Phillips that day. Daryl and I had become close friends when we were fellow graduate students at Birmingham-based Samford University, where both of us had earned our master's degrees in business administration. He is one of the most intelligent people I have ever met, and we share a mutual respect for our viewpoints on issues and strategies. Daryl has done well — is now president and chief operating officer of the outpatient division for HealthSouth Corporation.

On this visit to the small town of Columbiana to see Dr. Harry Phillips, Daryl and I were the typical "gung-ho" young healthcare executives who had all kinds of new knowledge about strategic planning, internal rates of return, marketshare, etc. As we sat in the conference room in the clinic where Dr. Phillips and his two partners practiced medicine, we were discussing rather detailed financial planning for this proposed medical mall.

Daryl and I were armed with our Hewlett-Packard calculators. We were using all the "modern-day" approaches.

By contrast, easygoing Dr. Harry Phillips stood at the blackboard in his conference room and methodically went about his business of using his refined methods of "country arithmetic." Without a microprocessor, Harry's common-sense longhand was turning us into students.

Along the way, Harry was tossing in a lot of wisdom that neither Daryl nor I had lived long enough to acquire. This was wisdom that unassuming Harry seemed to take for granted, as though ideas and insights just came to him out of the blue. As Daryl and I were driving back from Harry's office toward neighboring Birmingham that day, Daryl turned to me and said, "You know, Harry was standing there at the board doing this, and doing that, and always he came up with the right answer!" It wasn't only Harry's arithmetic that impressed Daryl. It also was his knowledge. Daryl and I discussed that as we drove along. Daryl said, "Bill, Dr. Harry Phillips may have forgotten more than we'll ever know. The guy is savvy."

By that time, I had known Harry for three years. I already held the same opinion that Daryl was expressing, that Harry was uniquely bright and insightful. In the years that have passed since that day in 1989, I've come to believe more and more in the wisdom of Harry Phillips — and have found myself increasingly guided by Harry's wisdom. I could sit and talk to Harry forever. He's a man who always seems to be thinking 20 years ahead of most people. As a doctor, Harry is about as close to the "Marcus Welby" model as I think you could get. As a human being, he has no peer.

Over the years, Harry Phillips has become to me a close friend, a model for a great person, and a great teacher.

From time to time I've found myself wondering if Harry realizes how bright he is. He's such a modest and straightforward man — never looking for personal accolades, just being what he is. In fact, during this observation I've enjoyed for more than a decade, Harry has prefaced many of his thoughts by saying in his low-key way: "Bill, I was talking to the birds today. And the birds said . . ." And then he would tell me whatever it was he had to say.

Well, suffice it to say that, through Harry and his so-called "talking to the birds," I have learned lessons that have exponentially increased my insight.

Through Harry, I've learned about doctors. By listening to and observing Harry, I've come to know and to understand many of the challenges that doctors face and many insights into healthcare. I credit my getting to know Dr. Harry Phillips with being a key reason as to why I understand doctors.

Through Harry, I've been able to explore, sort through, expand upon and validate some of my own feelings, opinions and values. And through my long conversations with him, I've been able to mold a number of my own views into a clearer picture. For example, I've gained much insight through our conversations about two of my favorite subjects — third-party payment and excessive corporate bureaucracy.

Through Harry, I've matured. For example, I've learned valuable lessons on how to keep a better handle on my temper — which all my life has tended to be a bit quick on the draw. And, through learning about some of the good deeds that Harry Phillips does for other people, I've learned real lessons about the true meaning of caring and compassion. I've learned that when you feel a strong urge to reach out and do something compassionate for somebody else, you should do more than think about it; you should do it.

Harry has influenced my skills in developing vision and strategy. Dr. Harry Phillips is a natural visionary, and I think he is probably the best strategic organizer I have ever met in terms of seeing the compelling reasons to do this or that.

And, last but far from least, through a common experience with Harry, I have learned that some of your greatest lessons can come not from your successes but from your failures. Harry joined me in talking through, analyzing and semi-implementing what I consider to be the biggest failure I have ever experienced in the medical-business world. This project that failed was that same "ahead of its time" medical mall project that Daryl Brown and I were discussing with Harry back in 1989. Partly through hindsight analysis with Harry in which we analyzed what was right and what was wrong with that project, I learned lessons that helped me in my work at MedPartners and continue to help Genus. From the good ideas and the failed implementation that I shared with Harry, I took with me from that project lessons I know will stay with me through the rest of my career.

Learning from Ill-fated Medical Mall Project

When I asked Dr. Harry Phillips to give me "doctor-type" advice on an innovative medical mall project back in 1989, I had several reasons for wanting his counsel.

I knew that Harry was well-respected among his peers. He has a unique ability to build relationships, to get things done through other people. I knew that Harry commanded a kind of "quiet power" among some of his colleagues. They listened to Harry, even voted the way he suggested on certain key issues in medical and political circles. This medical mall project I was putting together would involve both primary-care and specialty doctors. I knew that on the primary-care side, Harry was the quiet leader who represented the needs of the primary-care doctors.

But even the wisdom and guidance of Harry Phillips couldn't save us on this project. For that matter, all my carefully-done research, hard work and enthusiasm couldn't save me with this project either.

This medical mall project was not meant to be at the time we launched it. The project I was trying to implement was a first-of-its-kind medical mall in the Birmingham area. I was doing this at the time I was a senior vice president for development in charge of the primary-care centers for AMI Brookwood Medical Center. My key backing for financing the project was AMI, or American Medical International.

It appeared the medical mall had every chance to work. There was $2 million in the bank, cash, for this $11 million project. We had enough physicians lined up who were interested that we could have had the mall 100 percent leased.

But this was a real estate-driven plan. And on two counts, the timing killed us.

First of all, as we were doing the deal, a savings & loan crisis reared its ugly and powerful head. We were finding it virtually impossible to finance real estate. I couldn't have been involved in a real estate deal at a worse time than in the middle of an S&L crisis.

The second problem had to do with my key funding source, AMI. As we got deep into the project, AMI was going through a leveraged buyout. And, because of the leveraged buyout situation, AMI temporarily became a credit-unworthy company. This occurred when I needed AMI's credit the most. I found myself confronted with a short-term AMI credit problem in which, in the eyes of the banks, AMI was unable to stand behind a 20,000 square foot lease.

As the key funding source for the project, AMI had the first rights of refusal on the project's diagnostic centers, surgery centers, all these ancillaries. And, although AMI's credit was in the tank, AMI still retained its rights with the project, because its rights were not contingent on its credit. It was a mess. In my wildest dreams I would never have considered as a possibility that a multi-billion-dollar company would for unforeseen reasons have its credit frozen for a period of time, and that this period of time would just happen to be critical to a project I was facilitating.

In this environment, the banks wouldn't finance that kind of project without personal guaranties. And at that time very few people with whom I was dealing on potential leases for the medical mall understood healthcare development off-campus of a hospital. I was not going to be able to get personal guaranties from leading physicians in the area — not on a project with a concept that was such an unknown in the Birmingham area.

In addition to the AMI temporary credit problem, the S&L crisis, and the issue of putting physicians at personal financial risk, I faced a fourth problem with this project which I've discussed earlier in the book — in Chapter 8. That problem had to do with the advice I was getting on the specialty end of this project. Whereas the primary-care advice I received from Dr. Harry Phillips was superb, some of the specialty advice I received presented a real obstacle to me. The specialty physician advising me was a doctor who believed strongly in the need for consensus. This meant that he believed we should share inside information about this project with many other doctors in the Birmingham area, including our opponents. The results of that flawed strategy posed some real problems for me.

Talking of lessons to be learned! After the deal crashed and never happened, I spent hours re-hashing it with Harry Phillips. I learned these four key lessons from this failed project:

- **The first lesson** I learned had to do with the necessity for having contingency plans. I would never again place myself in the position of putting all my eggs in one basket, as I did with depending on AMI as the key funding source with no Plan B. I would not be involved in a deal of that magnitude again depending on just one funding source. And I wouldn't do that kind of deal again without a contingency plan. If I were involved in the medical mall project today, the financing would not crash. I could do the deal, and I could put it together rather quickly, because if one approach didn't work I'd be prepared to go to a second approach. In 1989 and 1990 with the medical mall project, I was dealing with a multi-variable equation in which every variable had to work. If one variable did not work, the deal was dead. With the medical mall project, I had no Plan B, no contingency plan, no plan of action for "if, then" — "if this falls through, then we do this." Since the failed medical mall project, I have thought out in advance my course of action concerning contingency plans. For example, I had a specific lineup of contingency plans when I was raising money for the capitalization of Genus Aesthetic Medical & Dental Group.

- **Secondly,** as I stated in Chapter 8, from the failed medical mall project I learned the dangers of trying to strive for doctor "consensus." The advice I was getting on the doctor-specialty side resulted in our spreading the word about our strategy. This meant that we revealed to too many people, and in some cases to the wrong people, exactly what we were planning to do. As a result, we allowed some people who would have been affected competitively by our project to have time to develop their opposition and shoot at us from every angle. We robbed from ourselves a tool that is very valuable when trying something innovative and controversial — the surprise element. From this I learned the value of keeping things close to the vest.

- **Thirdly,** I learned that just because you have an idea that does not succeed at a particular time, this does not mean the idea is not sound. As many of us are well aware, the medical mall concept caught on in the 1990s and a number of successful medical malls have been developed. One of the medical mall development leaders nationally has been healthcare icon Abe Gosman, whom I greatly respect and who is on our Genus board of directors. A few years ago, as Abe was making headlines with his medical mall development and some news writers were reporting this as a new concept, I couldn't resist the impulse to tease Abe a bit. I mailed him a clipping of a Birmingham newspaper article written when we were planning our medical mall project and reminded him we had this idea a while back. A lasting lesson I learned from my medical mall experience is that if you go through an experience with an idea that does not bear fruit, do a "postmortem analysis" in which you separately analyze the quality of the idea and the reasons it did not bear fruit. That can help you with evaluation of future ideas and also with implementation. With the help of Dr. Harry Phillips, I came to understand that the reasons the now-validated medical mall concept did not bear fruit for us had nothing to do with the idea not being sound. Instead, our attempt to go forward with a medical mall failed because of timing — because the medical mall concept still was a bit ahead of its time in 1989-90 — and also because of the problems I detailed in previous paragraphs — problems with the way our financing was structured and with doctor consensus. As I look back on our medical mall experience, I find myself feeling proud that our project no doubt contributed some innovative ideas relevant to patient convenience and access that helped fuel the medical mall movement nationwide.

- **And fourth,** from that wise physician, Dr. Harry Phillips, I received great ideas during the failed medical mall project that now, almost a decade later, I have made a core part of Genus. In 1989 when we were conceptualizing the medical mall, the basic plan called for a mall that would consolidate doctors' offices and other outpatient facilities to meet the needs of physicians — to meet the needs of medical doctors in the primary-care areas and in various specialties. One of the prevailing concepts of the medical mall project was to create a structure in which physicians could share facilities and also enjoy collaboration. It was Harry who envisioned that maybe we shouldn't stop with creating this structure for medical doctors. He suggested that in a second stage of this medical mall we should consider setting aside part of the mall area for dental specialists. Harry said: "Bill, we could put in a second building in this mall that could be used for various dental specialties. There really is considerable collaboration among the dental specialties. It would be a good concept to bring together in one location various dental specialties and have a dental specialty center." Some of the concepts that Harry espoused have gone into my thoughts as we've put together the Genus Aesthetic Medical & Dental Group.

Checking Me Out

I first met Dr. Harry Phillips shortly after I was hired by AMI Brookwood as the senior VP in charge of the Brookwood Primary-Care Centers in the Birmingham area. A few months before I came on board in early 1986, Brookwood had purchased the clinic where Harry and his two partners practiced medicine in neighboring Shelby County.

I would come to know that Harry is a man of few words. He doesn't talk a lot. But when he talks, you'd better listen. Because he's going to be right on target. And you won't find a lot of "BS" in Harry.

Well, the first four or five times I was around Harry, he really didn't talk much. He just kind of sat back and let one of his partners and me talk. Harry was taking it all in, sorting through it.

I was the "new kid on the block" so to speak. Harry and his partners already had one new relationship — with AMI Brookwood. And now there was yet another new player involved in a new relationship. I was that player. And I would have an important role in their lives, because I was the one heading up the Brookwood clinic management division that would interact with their clinic.

So, in those first few meetings Harry was studying me, just checking me out.

Seeing "Doctoring" Through the Eyes of a Friend

I have never had aspirations to be a doctor. From the time I decided I wanted a career in the healthcare field, it was the business and administrative side of healthcare where I wanted to work and not the patient-care side. However, since it became apparent to me early on that I wanted to make a major contribution in helping doctors develop and manage their practices, I really wanted to learn what I could about doctors and their views and their needs.

By the time I came to know Dr. Harry Phillips, I already had worked closely with doctors for five years as an assistant hospital administrator. And already I had met and worked with a number of doctors I liked and respected.

But it was through Harry that I developed such a close friendship with a doctor that I really came to understand doctors to a degree that I think otherwise could never have been possible. As that understanding matured, I found myself feeling a kind of easy rapport with both physicians and dentists. I wasn't just listening to them; I was genuinely understanding what they were telling me. Because I had come to understand through Harry.

In Harry's case, he grew up in Alabama's rural Elmore County in a family where no one before him had ever become a doctor. So it was Harry and not someone else who planted in his mind the desire to go into medicine. Once the thought of becoming a doctor entered Harry's mind when he was around 12 years of age, he never wanted to be anything else.

In 1962, Harry started practicing medicine in the small town of Columbiana, the county seat of Shelby County, Alabama. In this environment, Harry simultaneously functioned in worlds that on one hand were very rural and on the other hand very urban. He saw many patients who had never known any lifestyle but the quiet country life. Yet in his professional interactions he often found himself dealing with the "urban boys" next door in Birmingham. As part of that urban exposure, he and his partners in late 1985 sold their clinic to the large, modern AMI Brookwood Medical Center, which was built in the mid-1970s on a strategic mountainside site in a fashionable suburb of Birmingham. I watched Harry function well in his split rural/urban environments, understanding both worlds and making them work for the benefit of those who held priority in his eyes — his patients.

Learning about Caring for Patients

Through Harry I came to understand the deep caring that a doctor can feel for his patients. I've heard Harry say, "Bill, if there's one thing that I hope you've learned from our conversations, it's this: It's important to a patient that he or she have a doctor who really cares."

I have seen in Harry that regardless of what happens, no matter what comes down the pike, his patients really are his motivation. His patients are his focus, his concern, his goal. As I'm writing this, Harry is 66 years old. He has been practicing in Shelby County for well over three decades. And as long as his health is good, I can't imagine Harry taking down his shingle in the foreseeable future.

I've seen Harry's face light up and his eyes twinkle when someone asked him, "Are you glad you became a doctor?" He didn't hesitate. He said, "Oh, yehhh! Good gracious! Oh, yehhh!"

He's been in one place practicing so long that he's now seeing the third generation in some families. I've heard him describe how his patients inspire him, how they bring him gratification and joy. "I feel that I get a lot more from my patients than they'd ever get from me — for the simple reason that I get the satisfaction of knowing them," he says. "What I love about practicing medicine is that you do have an ability to do something where you can be needed. And you have an opportunity to do something where you can be satisfied with what comes out at the end. For me, the end of the day is a good day 90 percent of the time."

An Insight into What Drives Doctors

In listening to Harry, I've learned about the pride and ego that motivate doctors to work, and work, and work.

He knows that doctors through the years often have been accused of being egotistical and obsessive. Harry doesn't deny that doctors are sometimes egotistical. But, in his quiet sense of humor approach that gets relevant points across so well, he explains how some of this works.

He grins slightly, lowers his voice even lower than usual, and speaks as someone who has lived what he's saying as he quietly lays out his own concise version of one thing that makes doctors tick: "Well, doctors are different from lots of folks in the sense that in order to get where we are, even to go through all that training, we've sort of had to go through some 'strainers' that a lot of people couldn't or wouldn't go through. Some of that gets translated into ego."

These "strainers" to which Harry refers in his low-key way actually represent huge demands placed on individuals who become doctors. I mean, if we just think about the "strainers" that young men and women have to go through even to be selected to go to medical school! Then the demands that are placed on them mentally and physically to withstand the rigors of medical school and postgraduate training. And that's just the beginning. Think of the typical doctor's schedule for one week's work on the calendar. These are the kinds of "strainers" to which Harry refers. Having given considerable thought to these strainers has helped me to have a deeper appreciation and a deeper respect for doctors — both physicians and dentists.

Harry also talks about that drive doctors have — the same kind of drive for which many of them are criticized. "Well, if a doctor weren't a little obsessive-compulsive, which is supposed to be a disease, he couldn't get through medical school!" Harry says with a laugh. "So you've got to have this disease to even get to where you are."

A Good Businessman and a Great Strategic Thinker

As I've noted previously in this book, in Chapter 8, I disagree with some who feel that doctors don't tend to be good businessmen. I think many doctors are very good businessmen.

As I've also noted previously, where I believe many doctors fall short in a business sense — and where they often need some professional guidance — is that they are not good at strategic planning. However, I think there are a few doctors who have natural ability as strategic planners and many more doctors who can be taught to be good strategic planners.

Dr. Harry Phillips has been a real model to me on both these counts: Harry has natural business savvy. Actually, Harry is the best physician/ businessman I've ever been in contact with. Also, Harry is one of the best strategic thinkers and planners I've ever seen.

In terms of being a good businessman and strategist, I have seen several indicators of this with Harry and his partners in the way they have practiced medicine.

For one thing, they were able to look ahead and see the value of converting their medical practice to one that's totally outpatient — a medical practice that does not include taking care of patients in the hospital setting. Beginning some five years ago, whenever Harry and his partners had patients who needed to be hospitalized, they started referring their patients to appropriate hospital-based doctors. If the patient needed breast surgery, they referred the patient to a surgeon. If the patient had an illness that needed to be treated medically in the hospital, they referred the patient to an internist. Then, when the patients were discharged, the patients returned to Harry and his partners to continue their ongoing primary care. I found it admirable that Harry and his partners were savvy enough, and brave enough, to take this step — during a period when very few of their primary-care peers were doing this. As they made this major change in their practice, Harry and his partners refrained from being paranoid. They did not allow themselves to be encumbered by a fear that if they referred their patients to hospital-based doctors for inpatient care that these doctors would "steal" their patients on a long-term basis. Instead, they trusted in their own abilities to maintain their patient base rather than viewing their fellow physicians as competitors. In making their decision, what Harry and his partners

did was to take a look at current trends, from their view as doctors and from their view as businessmen. They looked at the amount of time it was taking them to travel back and forth between the hospital and the clinic, and they decided that they could make better use of their time by being totally outpatient-based. Also, they studied tightening third-party regulations for inpatient care reimbursement (especially for Medicare) — one result being that hospitalized patients were tending to be sicker than in the past and usually were needing specialists' care. The decision to convert to a totally outpatient practice has worked for Harry and his partners. Other doctors are not stealing their patients. Harry and his partners have a smoother operation at their clinic. And it's all because they were able to assess their environment realistically, and they were willing to take steps that made sense from both a business and a patient-care standpoint.

Harry Phillips and his partners in Columbiana were also ahead of many of their peers in participating in clinical drug research trials with pharmaceutical companies. As far back as 1980, they began clinical trials that involved various types of drugs. They did studies with their patients that related mainly to new antibiotics and new drugs to control high blood pressure, and were involved in a few studies on drugs to control arthritis. Many of these studies were part of very structured patient-based protocols the pharmaceutical companies were conducting as a last step before marketing the drugs. In addition to arranging for some of their patients to participate in these structured protocols, Harry and his partners have been able to arrange a number of what are called "compassionate studies." In this latter group, Harry and his partners have been able to gain access to not-yet-marketed drugs for some of their severely ill patients even when the patients' situations didn't qualify for structured studies. In exchange, Harry and his partners have kept records on their experiences with the drug studies which assisted the pharmaceutical companies with their information base. The clinical drug studies have proved to be a winning situation for all parties involved. Obviously, the pharmaceutical companies have benefited with information about the drugs. The patients at the clinic who have received these drugs have benefited. For example, Harry tells one story of how they gained access to a new antibiotic that added more than two years of quality life for a very sick young woman suffering from an incurable lung disease. Harry and his partners have benefited from this clinical drug research, because they've been able to stay on the cutting edge of medicine. The dedicated staff who work with them at their clinic have benefited. These clinic employees have had the satisfaction of taking part in progressive studies to help many patients who badly needed these not-yet-marketed drugs. Also, Harry and his partners have seen to it that the clinic employees who have helped with these studies have been rewarded financially. The pharmaceutical companies pay the doctors for this work. And over the years, Harry and his colleagues have shared these financial rewards with the employees who helped them. Harry feels strongly about that: "If you've got a team effort, if people contribute to what you do, you ought to split up the money."

Tips in Helping the Doctors Manage Their Business

Out of the wisdom of Harry Phillips has come much insight I use in the priorities for addressing the business needs of doctors. These ideas first were planted when I was dealing with hospital-owned physician practices, in my AMI-Brookwood days. Those "Harry-concepts" grew and matured and helped guide me in my MedPartners days. And now they're very much with me in my new Genus company.

These are a few of the Harry-inspired guides:

• **Keeping the patient in mind.** Our role as a management company is to facilitate business-related matters for doctors. However, I know I must think also of patient care — in this context: It's always in my mind that our business support must be an enabler and not an obstacle for the doctors in their primary mission of practicing quality patient care. Dating back to my Brookwood days in the mid-1980s, I remember Dr. Harry Phillips telling me, "Bill, we have to create and maintain a patient-care environment that's very patient-friendly and that's very competent. The patients must feel very comfortable, and they must not feel intimidated."

• **Allowing room for flexibility in implementing policies from one doctors' office to another.** Harry feels strongly that "there are no two practices exactly alike." Consequently, he thinks management companies should be flexible enough to take into account the varying needs of different doctor-practices. Harry says: "When you start managing physicians' practices, a model might fit 80 percent of the time. But 20 percent of the time it doesn't take into account the differences in various practices. A management company needs to involve the (clinic) manager and the physicians, to make sure everyone is singing off the same sheet of music."

• **Being careful not to allow a corporate culture to evolve into a cumbersome and inefficient corporate bureaucracy.** I've noted earlier in the book that I believe it's crucial to any company to develop a strong "corporate culture" — a sense of the company's values, the company's mission, the company's style of doing business. However, it's also true that a company has to be very careful that "corporate culture" does not become isolated, too introspective, too bureaucratic. The company has to be careful to take steps that ensure its culture continues to relate strongly to the practical day-to-day needs of the people it serves. Over the decades, Harry has seen the problems doctors can face if bureaucracy gets in their way of practicing good medicine. He has warned me to be on the lookout for symptoms of intrusive bureaucracy in companies with which I'm involved. Harry would tell me: "Bill, bureaucracies feed on themselves." I will be on the lookout for such symptoms at Genus. Harry said one sign that a corporate culture is becoming too bureaucratic is that the people at the corporate level have theories that are too much out of step with what's actually going on in a doctor's office: "You can easily see the development of a bureaucracy that's not responsive to the pain that the man (the doctor) out on the line is going through." He points out that it's imperative that people at the corporate level listen to doctors and their clinic managers about needs in the clinic: "You can have very bright people in a management company who have very good theories. But most of these people have never been on the firing line that the doctors are on. And in order to have value, theories must be integrated down into the practice." Harry points to procrastination as another sign that a management company is becoming too bureaucratic — not making decisions in a timely way. Harry says that when a corporate culture becomes inefficient, this can happen: "If procrastination is the thief of time, an inefficient corporate culture can make Al Capone look like a choir boy!"

Why Make It So Complex?

By the time I met Harry Phillips, I already had some views that were fairly well in place.

Although Harry and I had differing views in some areas, it was amazing to me what a match many of our ideas really were.

With the 24 years of age difference, Harry has a generation on me. There's no doubt that he has contributed many ideas to my vision and has validated other ideas I was beginning to develop.

Harry and I think in a similar manner about simplicity and using common sense. Harry believes — and I agree — that many people try to make things too complex. The way Harry puts it is this: "Most problems that can be solved can be solved with some simple kind of doings."

He talks about how effective President Ronald Reagan was in using this non-complex approach. Harry gives the example of Reagan insisting that his staff and advisers be able to develop proposals that were direct, simple, concise and to the point.

I know that Harry Phillips' belief in keeping things simple and using common sense has had some impact on how I view the entire concept of vision.

I've been flattered from time to time when someone would say to me, "Wow, Bill! You have great vision!" But frankly I think vision is just common sense.

My concept of vision is not that it's some extraterrestrial type of thinking. It's not that you're looking in a crystal ball and making profound proclamations based upon some abstract impressions. Instead, it's that you're thinking in a logical sequence. I think vision is just boiling things down to basics — understanding environmental factors and the current situation and trends, and then using some forecasting skills to predict what may be out there in some future time. Does a guy really have great vision if he purchases key real estate ten years before the interstate is built and causes the value of that real estate to skyrocket? In my way of thinking, what this guy did was to understand population growth and migration patterns and physical characteristics of land. And then he had the foresight to move ahead of the times, to use common sense.

I feel we have accomplished this by coming up with the basic concepts for Genus. With Genus, we've moved away from management company concepts that depend on third-party and managed-care to reimburse the doctors for services. We've made this move because managed care has been eroding the per unit income. To connect with another source of reimbursement, we have moved toward a market that's consistent with current-day trends. We've moved toward a more affluent baby-boomer patient population that's willing and able to pay directly for aesthetic medical and dental services. The primary trend that accounts for this population's willingness to pay for these aesthetic services is today's emphasis on youth preservation and self-improvement. I don't think that's complex. I think that's common sense.

And Harry Phillips has been an inspiration for me in advocating the use of common sense.

Hold That Temper!

Harry also has been an inspiration for me in learning how to get a better handle on my quick temper.

In my younger days, I was very quick to react. I would get all worked up. If someone said or did something that angered me, I would get red-faced and was prone to get verbally aggressive. I was real quick to fire back.

When I came to know Harry in my early 30s, I still had some of these tendencies — a sort of volatility. Something would happen that made no sense at all to me, I would be mad, and sometimes I would phone Harry or go visit him and talk with him about the situation.

I would tell Harry how I felt and how I planned to react. And he would counsel me on how to deal with the situation by saying something like, "Bill, don't do that. I wouldn't do that. Let some time go by. Wait three days, and take a look at it in three days."

Harry had an edge on me in that he was further along with the aging and maturity process. I think as you get a bit older, you're not as reactive and are more prone to sit back and think things out before you react. Also, Harry had an edge because of that wisdom, serenity, and easygoing manner of his. I learned a lot from these conversations. When I encounter a difficult situation that could become adversarial, I think back to those conversations.

A Third-party Concept

Over the years Harry and I have spent hours discussing our views on a wide range of subjects.

One of the subjects that has surfaced repeatedly has been third-party payment — how insurance is and is not meeting the needs of patients and healthcare providers — mostly how it is not meeting those needs.

Harry is a positive person. When he criticizes something, he's forthright enough to say why he feels there's a problem. And he's always thinking. Usually if you probe deep enough with him, you can learn some of his ideas for making things better.

He has some definite ideas as to how insurance coverage should be changed.

His biggest idea about changing insurance is that "the power should be placed in the hands of the people. It's their money that's being spent and they should control how it's spent."

What Harry is saying is simply that insurance purchasing should be changed so that individuals negotiate their own insurance contracts, rather than having their employers negotiate the contracts for them. In Harry's way of thinking, if individuals were empowered to negotiate their own contracts, two big pluses would have a strong chance of emerging: One plus, he says, would be that individuals would be more motivated to become educated about insurance — how to select coverage, how to negotiate for coverage, how to persevere to make sure the coverage actually is provided by the insurer when it's needed. "As things stand now, the average person has no reason whatsoever to educate himself, because someone else is going to control his destiny anyway," says Harry. The second plus, says Harry, is that insurance companies likely would become more accountable, because they would deal with a highly motivated insurance purchaser who not only is the one purchasing the insurance but also the one who's using it.

Along this same line with third-party accountability, Harry believes the time will come when there will be much more standardization of insurance contracts — maybe as few as five to 10 standard insurance contract models. Further, he thinks that insurance will be regulated to the point "that the person buying the coverage will be guaranteed the coverage that he signed up for. And the coverage will be understandable, so that the individual will understand what he bought, what he signed up for."

In this scenario, the individual doing the negotiating would make choices according to what kind of coverage he wants and what kind he can afford.

This is in keeping with a "Harry theory" to which I've heard him refer many times over the years — concerning "choice" about healthcare. He says America is and will continue to be set up for different levels of healthcare just like it's set up for different levels of everything else. "Medicine is never going to become homogeneous in our society, 'cause the people won't put up with it," Harry says. "This is a nation in which you have one group of people who have money who are willing and able to pay for more than somebody else. This is the same concept in operation that exists in this country when we drive different types of cars and we live in different types of houses."

The Caring and Compassionate Hand of Harry

Whether it's spending some time with someone to show he cares, or spending a little money to bring some joy or to ease some pain, Harry Phillips is there for people.

Compassion is not a part of Harry Phillips' life; it is his life.

Making an effort to reach out to people with compassion is not something that Harry talks about. He just does it. In fact, Harry becomes obviously uncomfortable when other people talk about his extraordinary compassion.

He and his doctor-partners get a big kick out of showing how much they care for the employees that work at the clinic where they practice medicine. Over the years, when many employers have long since abandoned the concept of giving Christmas bonuses, Harry and his partners still play Santa Claus at their office. Harry loves it. If someone mentions it, he just says quietly, "Yeah, everybody had a big Christmas."

Harry's there for people in the sad times, too. His longtime office manager, Brick Wall, the subject of Chapter 13 in this book, was so close to Harry that he knew of many of the "anonymous" things Harry did for people. In fact, as Harry's friend and also his office manager, Brick helped Harry implement some of his good deeds. Brick had a tremendous respect for Harry, and Brick told me some of the things Harry did for people. One thing Brick told me that really stuck in my mind was this: "Bill, you wouldn't believe the people that Harry Phillips has helped bury. In cases where their families couldn't afford to bury their loved ones, Harry has helped. He never looked for gratitude for it. In fact, in some cases the families he helped didn't know he was one who did it."

Harry's reaching out has made a big impression on me. From him I have learned a lot about helping other people. I believe as Harry does that you should reinvest in people, that if you do that you'll be able to see the returns. I'm not talking about monetary returns. I'm saying that in some way you'll be able to see evidence that you have made a worthwhile investment.

A Visit to Westchester County

The time was late 1987. Something happened that will always remind me of how much Harry Phillips cares. And by accident I stumbled across the fact that these arrangements were being made. Nobody made a big deal of it.

My secretary at AMI Brookwood Medical Center received a telephone call. It was from Brick Wall. He was phoning her to get information for Dr. Harry Phillips — information about my brother John, who was hospitalized in New York.

It seems that Harry and his wife were taking a trip to New York City. Harry knew that my brother John was waging a battle against leukemia. It was a battle John would lose only a few months later.

At this particular time when Harry and Sue Phillips were traveling to New York, John had just completed all the treatments that Memorial Sloan-Kettering Cancer Center could offer him. He had been rehospitalized to try a different experimental treatment, in a hospital in Westchester County, north of New York City.

Dr. Harry Phillips had never met John. But, having listened to me talk about John, I'm sure he felt as though he knew him. And Harry knew how concerned I was about my brother.

So Brick Wall called my secretary and found out where the hospital was located. Brick didn't call me and say, "Hey, Harry's going to see your brother." And Harry didn't say anything to me about his planned visit.

After Harry and Sue got to New York City, they boarded a train and traveled to Westchester County. They went to the hospital, introduced themselves to John, and spent a few minutes with him.

That visit meant a lot to John. It meant a lot to me. Actually, it had a huge impact on me.

The visit was typical Harry Phillips.

I'm glad I know Harry. I'm glad for every bit of Harry that has rubbed off on me.

I'm glad that Harry "talks to the birds." And I thank him for sharing with me some of his valuable wisdom.

Index

About the Author

BILL DEXHEIMER has been working with physicians for 17 years. His experiences have contributed immensely to views about the healthcare industry and have molded projections for the future. In the 1980s he developed a primary-care physician network for a large hospital system. In 1993 he co-founded MedPartners, which grew into the nation's largest physician practice management (PPM) company. In 1997 he founded Genus Aesthetic Medical & Dental Group Inc., a company that partners with plastic surgeons, cosmetic dentists, and other aesthetic professionals. He resides in Birmingham, Alabama, with his wife, Lisa, and their son and daughter, Paul and Drennan.